BUSINESS STUDIES
for you

David Needham ● Robert Dransfield

STANLEY
THORNES

DEDICATION

*For Ruth and Laura: Enjoy your Business Studies lessons
and best of luck in your exams*

Contents

CONTENTS

UNIT 8

Acknowledgements

The development of *Business Studies For You* has not been an easy project. It has involved the help of many people from different organisations. We would however particularly like to thank Sarah Wilman and Louise Watson from Stanley Thornes and Sandra Ingham from European Passenger Services.

Our aim has been to develop a usable book with a lively and interesting style and presentation which students from all backgrounds and abilities can enjoy. We have also endeavoured to provide thorough and detailed coverage of all syllabus areas with the objective of helping students to 'pass with flying colours'.

We would like to thank the following organisations and individuals for their help in the preparation of this book:

Abbey National PLC, Ark Geophysics Ltd, Katherine Beane, Biro BIC Ltd, The Body Shop PLC, British Airways PLC, British Gas, British Nuclear Fuels PLC, British Telecommunications PLC, Cheltenham Borough Council, Coca-Cola, Co-operative Union Ltd, Ben Cribb, Department for Education and Employment, European Parliament, European Passenger Services, Eurostar, *The European*, Ford Motor Co., Franchise Development Service, Geest PLC, Jean Hooper, Huntley, Boorne and Stevens, *The Independent*, Levi Strauss Co., Marks & Spencer PLC, the Metro Centre, Nestlé Rowntree, Nissan, Bryan Oakes, Sainsbury's, Laura Schuster, Shell Education Service, SmithKline Beecham PLC, Transport and General Workers Union, Unilever, Virgin Group, Wolters Kluwer (UK), Sue Woollatt, Yorkshire Water

David Needham
Robert Dransfield

Photo Credits

The Advertising Archive Ltd (p. 116), Denis Doran (p. 302), Environmental Picture Library (p. 287) Greenpeace Comunications Ltd (p. 291), PA News (pp. 262, 292), Pictor International (p. 50), PowerStock Photo Library (pp. 24, 56, 134), Shell International Ltd (p. 88)

A message from Frankie and Cleo...

Welcome to Business Studies For You!

We hope that reading and working through this book will give you a firm foundation for your business studies course.

The text provides you with a detailed coverage of everything you will need for a good exam pass, as well as a colourful and interesting insight into all the latest developments in business.

More than that, we hope it encourages you to ask questions and to challenge existing ideas.

Enjoy your time with us!

Best wishes.

Frankie

1 Learning About Business

Why learn about business?

Learning about business is both interesting and useful. It is also challenging and requires imagination.

In learning about business you will need to be creative and to have a questioning mind. Business decisions are open-ended. There may be more than one way of going about things. Therefore you will need to ask lots of questions and to weigh up alternative ideas and proposals.

Frankie and Cleo

In this book we would like you to follow the model of Cleo and Frankie. They are keen to set up their own business making shortbread in their town. However, first they want to find out as much as possible about business and business activities. Throughout this book they ask questions in order to find out information that will help them to make better decisions. Having found out information, they try to make sense of it in order to draw balanced conclusions and make sound judgements.

'We are both looking forward to learning about business!'

Ron Rust

In contrast, the model we *don't* want you to follow is that of Ron Rust. Ron is a bit of a 'know-it-all' who has worked for a number of years as a scrap metal dealer. His business hardly ever makes a profit and he is always getting into scrapes. However, he thinks that because he has 'experience' of business everyone should listen to his opinions.

When you come across Ron in the text, examine the things that he says, and try to explain why he is getting it wrong. What is he saying that doesn't quite make sense?

'You win some, you lose some!'

Tasks

Throughout the book there are tasks for you to carry out. The tasks should only take 5 to 10 minutes and should be copied up into your notebook or file. Some will be more difficult than others. The tasks headed with a yellow band will take you longer and require more thought. Tasks with a blue band are easier.

TASK

TASK

Coursework

Coursework activities are activities for you to carry out in your own private research time. For these, you will need to find out information for yourself. This information will increase the breadth of your knowledge of business.

Case Studies

Case Studies appear in nearly all the chapters. These provide examples of business activities and problems, usually taken from the real world. At the end of each Case Study, there are a number of questions for you to answer in your notebook or folder.

Match It!

At the end of nearly all the chapters you will find 'Match It!' activities. The aim of these is to help you to build up a business dictionary.

Each 'Match It!' consists of two columns. The left-hand column shows a list of business terms, and the right-hand column shows a list of definitions. However, the definitions are in the wrong order. Your job is to list the terms in your notebook or folder and write the correct definitions alongside them. As you do so, you build up your own glossary of business terms.

The world of business

All businesses set out to achieve a particular result. Different businesses set out to achieve different results.

- ◆ For example, Benetton sets out to sell fashion clothes to the public while at the same time making a profit for its owners.
- ◆ The charity Oxfam sets out to raise funds, and to provide famine relief and other help to people throughout the world.
- ◆ Newcastle United Football Club sets out to play attractive, winning football that will attract spectators through the turnstiles and into the club shops so as to make a profit and to raise pride in the city of Newcastle.

TASK

*S*et out a table like the one below showing five organisations and the results which you feel that they set out to achieve.

Organisation	Desired result
Newcastle United	Play attractive, winning football, achieve high gate figures, sell club souvenirs, make a profit, raise pride in the City of Newcastle, etc
Midland Bank	?
My school/college	?

What do businesses do?

Business involves adding value to **inputs** so as to create more valuable **outputs**. For example, if you buy ingredients worth £1, you may be able to make a cake which you can sell for £3. The value you have added to the ingredients is therefore £2.

The difference between the price paid for the inputs needed to create the cake and its selling price is the **value added**. Business activity is concerned with adding value in making things.

Value of cake ingredients	Value added	Value of cake
£1	£2	£3

'But supposing you burn the cake! What happens to the value added then?'

◆ Benetton buy clothes from suppliers. They transport these clothes to their stores where they are displayed and sold by their staff. All these activities involve adding value.

◆ Oxfam receives donations from the public and channels them to its projects overseas. This requires a lot of organisation. Oxfam adds value to the donations by making sure that they are used in the best way possible. If Oxfam carried out any of its activities in a disorganised way, it would fail to add value to the donations.

Being organised

Businesses need to be organised. As we shall see later (Chapters 10-23), there are a number of ways of organising. However, whether you are talking about a large organisation employing tens of thousands of people or a small corner store, you will find that a disorganised business will never be successful for long.

There are a number of characteristics of organisations:

1 Organisations have a **name** – e.g. Marks and Spencer, WH Smith, etc.

2 Organisations set out to achieve particular **end results** – e.g. to be the biggest company in their field in the country, to make high profits, etc.

3 Organisations have **rules and regulations** which govern the way they operate – e.g. a school's code of discipline, or a business's procedures for dealing with customer complaints, etc.

4 Organisations have **posts and offices** – e.g. managing director, supervisor, etc.

5 Organisations have a **public image**. All organisations will try to create an image which reflects the way the business runs. For example, a hospital will want to create an image of being a caring organisation.

COURSEWORK ACTIVITIES

Choose a particular organisation that you are familiar with. This may be a small business near you, an organisation that you work for on a part-time basis or an organisation to which you belong, e.g. a sports club, school, etc.

Produce a short illustrated report setting out:

* The name of the organisation
* The end results that it is working towards
* The rules and regulations of the organisation
* The posts and offices in the organisation
* The public image of the organisation

Compare the organisation you have chosen with those looked at by other members of your class.

Business ideas

All business organisations start out from an original idea. Many new business ideas have come 'out of the blue' to inventive people. An example of this is the Sony Walkman. Other ideas have resulted from careful work over a period of time. Examples are the development of the ballpoint pen, the photocopier and the dishwasher.

There are many ways of coming up with a bright idea. They include:

'Your idea will only be worthwhile if someone has already tried it out in your area before and made a success of it!'

Do you agree with Ron?

◆ Spotting a gap in the market

◆ Improving on an existing product or service

◆ Listening to people and finding out what they want or need

◆ Using a special skill or talent that you have

◆ Developing a hobby

◆ Combining two or more existing products or services

◆ Setting out to solve a particular problem

Frankie and Cleo have been developing a recipe for shortbread which is very popular with their friends. It doesn't take long to make and the ingredients are not expensive. They could make the shortbread in a bakery oven in part of an industrial unit which has been rented out by Frankie's Uncle Abe. Do you think that this is a good idea or not?

TASK

Working in a group with two or three other students, brainstorm 10 ideas for setting up a small business in your area. You need to make sure that your ideas meet the criteria listed below.

1   Think of at least one idea for each of the sources of ideas listed on page 4 – i.e. at least one idea that involves solving problems for people, one idea that involves developing a hobby, etc.

2   Each idea must be capable of being developed for less than £1,000.

3   Each idea must be practical given the skills of the group you are working with.

Choose the best idea and decide how you would go about setting up your business and making your idea work. For example, what resources would you need? Who would be involved? How much would it cost to buy the resources you need, and how much could you sell your product or service for?

Present your idea to the rest of your class. Be prepared to answer questions.

Can you help Frankie and Cleo to match the following terms and definitions?

Value added	Improvements to the original inputs in the production process
Input	A business opportunity that results from a lack of competition
Organisation	A body that sets out to achieve chosen results
Charity	A material or resource to which an organisation adds value
Gap in the market	A starting point from which to develop a business
Business idea	A not-for-profit organisation

1 2 Business Activity Within Markets

What is 'business activity'?

Businesses operate within markets in which buying and selling takes place.

Within the market, business organisations make and sell goods. The act of preparing a good or service for sale is called production. All of the people involved in producing goods and services receive rewards, usually in the form of money.

With this money, they buy goods and services for themselves and their families. Anyone who uses a good or service is a **consumer**. We are all consumers.

Consumers at a modern shopping mall

Satisfying consumers' wants and needs

Everybody has **wants** and **needs**. We need food, drink, clothing, shelter and other essentials to stay alive. Other things are not quite so essential, but we still want them so that life can be enjoyable. Different people have different wants depending on their personalities and experiences. Business activity is concerned with satisfying consumers' wants and needs.

Demand for goods and services

The demand for a good or service is a want backed up by the money to purchase it. If a good is in 'great demand', there will be a lot of people wanting to buy it at the current price.

Business organisations want to know how much the demand will be for their products at different prices. They will then be able to decide what to make, and how much to make in order to meet demand.

Price per kg	Quantity demanded
45p	1,000 kg
35p	3,000 kg
25p	4,500 kg
15p	6,500 kg

Above: Demand for apples at different prices per kilo

Below: The same data displayed in graph form

Plotting demand

The demand for a product can be plotted on a table of figures. This shows how many items would be demanded at given prices. It is also useful to plot the demand for a product on a graph. When you look at the graph, it becomes obvious that larger quantities of any good will be bought at lower prices, and lower quantities at higher prices.

For example, the table on the right shows the demand for apples at different prices per kilo. The graph shows the same figures transferred onto a demand curve.

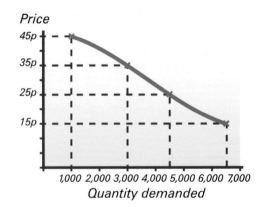

Price

45p
35p
25p
15p

1,000 2,000 3,000 4,000 5,000 6,000 7,000

Quantity demanded

The demand curve is constructed by showing prices on the vertical axis and quantities demanded along the horizontal axis. You can see that:

◆ Higher prices lead to lower quantities being bought.

◆ Lower prices lead to higher quantities being bought.

Supply

The supply of any good is the quantity that producers and sellers supply at different prices. Suppliers will supply more to a market if the price is higher than if it is lower. In other words:

◆ Higher prices lead to higher quantities being supplied to the market.

◆ Lower prices lead to lower quantities being supplied to the market.

This rule applies both for individual producers – e.g. a single farmer growing tomatoes – and for the whole market, i.e. all the tomato growers in a particular area.

Plotting supply involves plotting the quantities that would be supplied at different prices. For example, if there are three bakers in a town, we add their individual supplies of bread together to arrive at market supply as follows:

'Are there any goods that suppliers would produce more of at lower prices, and fewer at higher prices?'

What do you think?

| Price per loaf | Supply | | | |
	Jolly Bakers	Better Bakers	Healthy Bakers	Market supply
15p	100	150	200	450
20p	200	300	400	900
25p	400	600	800	1,800

A supply curve can then be drawn on a graph *(right)* showing the quantities that would be supplied at different prices. A typical supply curve slopes upwards from bottom left to top right.

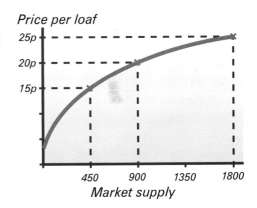

A typical supply curve

The market price

All markets are made up of buyers and sellers. We can show the relationship between buyers and sellers by placing the demand curve and supply curve for a product on the same diagram.

The point at which the two curves cut shows the **market price**. This is the only point at which the wishes of buyers and sellers match at a given moment in time.

For example, the graph on the right illustrates the demand and supply for chocolate spread.

You can see that, at a price of 60p for a 250g jar, 100,000 tonnes of chocolate spread would be bought each week. At this price consumers are happy to buy 100,000 tonnes and sellers are happy to supply this quantity.

This is called the **equilibrium point** because there is nothing forcing a change from it.

We can see why this point is an equilibrium point by considering non-equilibrium ones.

For example, at 80p a jar, consumers would purchase only 75,000 tonnes while suppliers would make 125,000 tonnes available to the market. At this price, sellers would be left with unsold stocks and would quickly reduce supply to the equilibrium point.

If the price were below the equilibrium – at say 40p – demand would be for 150,000 tonnes with producers only willing to supply 50,000 tonnes. In this situation chocolate spread would be snapped up as soon as it was put on the shelves, and stocks would run out. Prices would soon be raised towards the equilibrium point.

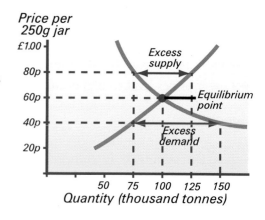

The market for chocolate spread (250g jars)

TASK

Frankie and Cleo have been finding out how much demand there would be for their shortbread at different prices. Can you plot their demand curve on a piece of graph paper?

'Please could you answer our questions? First try a piece of our shortbread. How many pieces would you buy per week if the price was 20p?'

Later:

'At a price of 20p we would be able to sell 1,500 pieces per week...'

'...And at 30p we could sell 850 squares.'

'But at 40p we would only be able to sell 200 squares.'

'Let's plot our figures on a demand curve..'

The demand for chocolate biscuits

Midwich village shop sells – amongst other things – one very popular brand of chocolate biscuits. The shop is able to buy stocks of these biscuits in bulk at 15p per packet. The shopkeeper has found out from five local families how many packets they would buy per month at different prices.

Price per packet	Amount bought by families					Total
	Jones	*Patel*	*Cray*	*O'Rourke*	*Sylvio*	
10p	15	15	20	20	15	85
15p	12	12	20	15	11	70
20p	8	8	15	10	9	50
25p	7	7	12	9	5	40
30p	6	6	9	7	2	30
35p	5	4	6	5	-	20
40p	-	2	3	-	-	5
45p	-	-	-	-	-	-

  TASK

1 What is the relationship between price and quantity demanded in the table?

2 How would you explain this relationship?

3 Why might it be more sensible for the shop to charge a price of 25p for its biscuits, rather than 15p or 40p?

Choose a product which you use regularly, e.g. a brand of toothpaste, chewing gum, or a particular chocolate bar.

Set out a list of possible prices for the product. Interview five of your friends to find out how much they would buy at each of the prices you have chosen. Construct a demand curve using the information you have researched.

The importance of the market place

The market brings together buyers and sellers. Buyers show what they prefer by 'voting' with their money for certain goods and services.

Every day millions of buying and selling decisions are made. When you go shopping, you may make a decision to buy a particular kind of breakfast cereal. Your decision has a great impact if thousands of other consumers make the same choice as you.

If we all decide to buy a particular type of cereal, then cereal manufacturers will benefit by switching resources (such as labour, machinery and materials) into making that cereal.

The diagram below shows how important the market is in bringing together consumers and producers.

The market place: bringing together producers and consumers

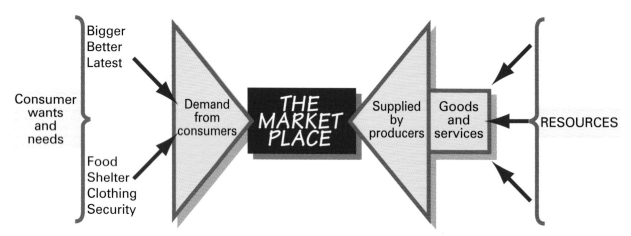

Consumer wants and needs

Bigger Better Latest

Food Shelter Clothing Security

Demand from consumers

THE MARKET PLACE

Supplied by producers

Goods and services

RESOURCES

Meeting customer requirements

Not all consumers are customers. For example, a mother may buy the type of cereal her children prefer. The children are the **consumers**, but the mother is the **customer** because she makes the decision to buy that particular product from that particular shop.

Customers are the lifeblood of any company. Without enough customers a business will close. To keep their customers, companies need to be sure that they are producing goods that meet the customers' needs at the right quality, time and price.

The demand curve for a product does not always stay in the same place. Tastes and fashion change, incomes rise and fall, population changes and the prices of other goods change. Suppliers need to be aware of these changes in the market and react to them.

'Hum! I meet customer requirements by selling them the things that I can do best. If I make a good product then it is guaranteed to sell. The producer is king — and that's me! It works every time!'

MATCH IT!

Can you help Frankie and Cleo to match the following terms and definitions?

Producer	The sum total of individual demands
Wants	A way of illustrating quantities brought to market at different prices
Supply	The quantity that producers will provide at different prices
Needs	A situation where many products are required at low prices
Market demand	People's requirements for luxuries and other non-essential items
Supply curve	The place where consumers' and producers' needs come together
Equilibrium point	The end-user of a product
High demand	Basic requirements such as food, shelter and clothing
Market place	Someone engaged in providing goods and services for consumers
Consumer	The intersection of the demand and supply curves

3 Types of Business Activity

Business activity is concerned with adding value by converting inputs into outputs.

The way in which value is added will vary from one type of industry to another and between businesses within the same industry.

Business activity is often broken down into three types:

◆ Extractive (primary industry)

◆ Manufacturing and construction (secondary industry)

◆ Services (tertiary industry)

Extractive industries
These are concerned with using natural resources. They include farming, mining and oil drilling. Farmers grow and harvest crops and farm livestock, while miners take out fuel and minerals from the ground.

Farming: a primary industry

Left: Car production – a manufacturing industry

Below: Banking – a service industry

Primary industries sometimes produce raw materials like iron ore (for making steel) and oil (for making petrol, plastics, fibres, etc.). They also produce final products like fish and oranges.

Manufacturing and construction industries
These are concerned with making and assembling products. Manufacturers use raw materials and parts from other industries. A **semi-manufactured good** is one that is only partly made. Most products go through several stages of production. Examples of manufactured products are furniture, cars, chocolate and oil rigs.

Service industries
Service/tertiary industries are particularly important in Britain today. **Services** give something of value to people, but are not physical goods. You can physically touch or see a sandwich, a car, or a television set. You cannot touch or hold life insurance, a haircut, or the protection offered by the police. These are all services. Other examples are banks and public transport.

'What is the point of making things yourself, when other people make them better !'

FIND THEM! Frankie and Cleo are trying to sort the following activities under the headings of Primary, Secondary and Tertiary Industry. Can you help them?

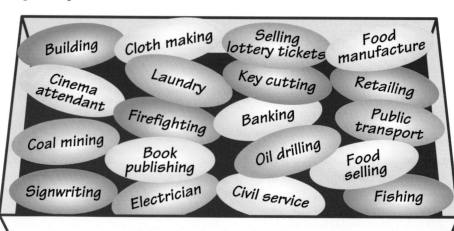

Building　Cloth making　Selling lottery tickets　Food manufacture

Cinema attendant　Laundry　Key cutting　Retailing

Firefighting　Banking　Public transport

Coal mining　Book publishing　Oil drilling　Food selling

Signwriting　Electrician　Civil service　Fishing

The illustration below shows some of the activities of Eurostar. What sector of the economy do they show Eurostar to be operating in? How do the illustrations show that Eurostar adds value in the process of production?

Services are sometimes classified as **direct** (to people, e.g. the police, hairdressing) or **commercial** (to businesses, e.g. insurance, banking). However, the difference is not always clear-cut. Some commercial services like banking are used by individuals as well as by other businesses.

The changing face of business activity

Many experts talk about **three waves** of industrial development.

In the first wave, countries are dominated by agriculture and farming. This was the case in Britain until the Industrial Revolution of the late eighteenth and early nineteenth century.

In the second wave, countries are dominated by manufacturing, when industries such as coal, steel, car manufacture and shipbuilding become important.

In the third wave, services become the most important sector of the economy, with many people working in insurance, banking, office administration, leisure and similar industries. This is sometimes called **de-industrialisation**.

The evidence suggests we are now in the third wave. In 1959 the service sector in the USA produced a greater value of goods than manufacturing. Today, services produce more than 70% of the value of all goods in the USA, Britain and France, and just over 60% in Germany and Japan.

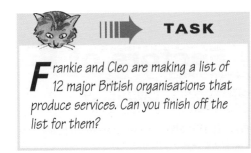

TASK

Frankie and Cleo are making a list of 12 major British organisations that produce services. Can you finish off the list for them?

Marks and Spencer – Retailing
National Westminster Bank – Banking
Central Television – Television Broadcasting

MATCH IT!

Can you help Frankie and Cleo to match the following terms and definitions?

Extraction	The process of adding value
Secondary industry	Manufacturing and construction
Third wave society	Good that is only partially made or finished
First wave society	Harvesting or exploitation of natural resources
Semi-manufactured	A society in which service industries predominate
Business activity	Reduction in importance of manufacturing
Tertiary industry	A society focused on agriculture
De-industrialisation	The production of services

4 Factors of Production

What is production?

Imagine that you are visiting a modern food processing plant. What do you see?

The first and most obvious sight would be large areas of land and building. Inside, you would find machinery, equipment and employees. In order for the machines to work, they need energy, raw materials and semi-finished products. Enter a production area and you will find people blending and mixing food. Other workers will be loading and unloading supplies and finished goods. Others will be tending equipment.

The **factors of production** are the ingredients that make a business work: land, labour, capital and enterprise.

◆ In the case of our food processing plant, the **land** includes the site on which the factory is built.

◆ The **labour** is the factory employees.

◆ The **capital** is the buildings and equipment which are used to make the products.

◆ Finally, **enterprise** is the art of bringing together the other factors of production to make a successful business.

CHAPTER 4

We use the French word **entrepreneur** to describe someone who brings together factors of production in order to achieve business objectives. The entrepreneurs in a food processing plant would include the people who set up the plant in the first place.

Definitions

Over the years the four factors of production have come to mean more than the examples used above.

◆ **Land** is now used to refer to *all* natural resources, e.g. farm land, water, coal, etc.

◆ **Labour** is used to refer to *all* the physical and mental contributions of an employee. So it is more than just the physical effort of digging coal, or making car parts. It also includes the mental effort of an accountant or the services provided by a bank clerk.

◆ **Capital** includes all those items that go into producing other things, e.g. a machine manufactures products, tools contribute to this process, and so on.

Machines, tools and buildings are all examples of physical capital. In order to purchase these items you would need money capital.

◆ **Enterprise** is the factor that brings the other factors together to produce goods in order to make profits.

COURSEWORK ACTIVITIES

Talk to the owner of a small local business. Find out how the business uses its land and capital, the type of labour employed, and the enterprise skills needed to ensure that the venture is successful.

 TASK

Frankie and Cleo are visiting a bottling plant owned by George, a local business person. They are trying to identify the factors of production employed there. Can you identify:

• 4 items of capital
• 2 items of labour
• 1 entrepreneur
• 1 item of land?

CASE STUDY

Rewards to factors of production

Richard Branson is a good example of an entrepreneur. He is able to make things happen by bringing together factors of production in exciting combinations to produce products as different as airline flights, contraceptives, and cola drinks.

However, in order to run his business successfully, he needs to reward the factors of production that work for his business organisation – Virgin.

Richard Branson rewards:

- **Labour** with **wages**
- **Land** with **rent**
- **Capital** with **interest**
- **Enterprise** with **profits**

Wages

Attractive salaries and wages have to be paid to the employees who work for the organisation.

Rent

Virgin needs to pay rents to any landlords that have rented out land or other natural resources to the company.

Interest

Like most other major businesses, the Virgin organisation will borrow money capital from banks and other lending institutions. Interest must be paid at regular intervals for these loans.

Profits

Finally, profits are the reward for enterprise. The profits of Virgin will be shared among the company's owners. These are the shareholders, and will include Richard Branson himself. Many of his managers and employees may also be shareholders.

'The only factor of production in my scrap metal business is "enterprise" – and that's me. I don't need other factors of production because that is a drain on my pocket. In this business everything is down to the entrepreneur.'

Has Ron missed the point?

TASK

1   Why is Richard Branson often described as an entrepreneur?

2   What are the rewards of being an entrepreneur?

 **MATCH IT!**

Can you help Frankie and Cleo to match the following terms and definitions?

Rent	Part-owner of an organisation
Entrepreneur	Money paid to the owners of land or buildings which are used by a business
Interest	A risk-taker who brings together other factors of production to make a successful business
Rewards to factors	Physical and mental effort expended in production
Capital	Return to providers of capital
Shareholder	Money and machinery used in the production of goods and services
Factors of production	Returns to those who contribute factors of production
Labour	The ingredients that contribute to the production process

5 Business Objectives

The nature of objectives

A business organisation sets out to achieve certain goals. In doing so, it must balance the needs of its customers and the people involved in the organisation. It is like making sure that your snooker balls go into the right pockets.

'Who decides on the goals?'

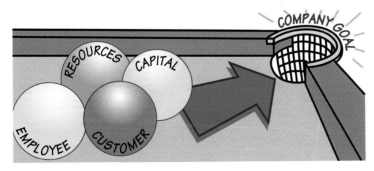

The goals of a business are the future state of affairs that it is working towards.

'Me! I decide what I want and how I am going to get it!'

Stakeholders

Organisations usually involve a number of interested parties. Take a school, for example. If you look at the diagram below, you can see that there are a number of people with a stake in the running of a school.

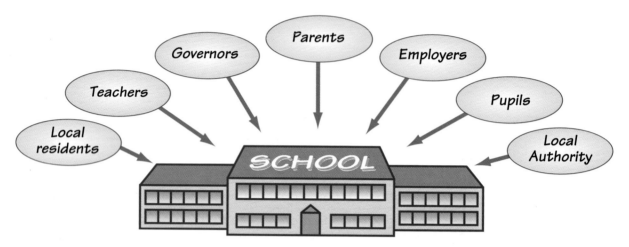

Stakeholders in a school

Clearly these stakeholders will have different views about how the school should be run. They may agree on some of the goals of the school, but disagree on others. In the end, the goals that are chosen depend on who has most power to make decisions.

The same applies to any organisation. There are a number of stakeholders with different views about what the goals should be. Those with most power will determine the main goals.

Objectives

An **objective** is something that a person or organisation sets out to achieve. Objectives need to be:

◆ Measurable

◆ Time-limited

◆ Attainable

◆ Relevant

The mission statement

Today most large and many small organisations set out their objectives in a **mission statement**. The mission statement provides the basis for producing more detailed objectives for the people within the organisation.

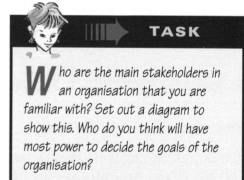

TASK

*W*ho are the main stakeholders in an organisation that you are familiar with? Set out a diagram to show this. Who do you think will have most power to decide the goals of the organisation?

'The mission statements on the opposite page look interesting. Which do you think is the best?'

TASK

Study the four different mission statements below. Which is the most:

- *Customer orientated?*
- *Production orientated?*
- *Service orientated?*

Give reasons for your answer.

European Passenger Services (EPS) aims to:

- Offer high-quality European journeys
- Be first choice in our markets
- Anticipate the needs of our customers
- Operate safely, reliably and profitably
- Be efficient and flexible
- Look always for improvement
- Respect and use the talents of our employees
- Take pride in our company
- Be fair and professional in all our dealings

"My company sets out to be the best company in the scrap metal business. We will work hardest to make the biggest profits. I will give a square deal to all employees who are loyal to the company."

"We all want a company that our people are proud of and committed to, where all employees have an opportunity to contribute, learn, grow and advance based on merit, not politics or background. We want our people to feel respected, treated fairly, listened to and involved. Above all, we want satisfaction from accomplishments and friendships, balanced personal and professional lives, and to have fun in our endeavours..."

"Ford Motor Company is a worldwide leader in automotive and automotive-related products and services as well as in new industries such as aerospace, communications and financial services. Our mission is to improve continually our products and services to meet our customers' needs, allowing us to prosper as a business and to provide a reasonable return for our shareholders, the owners of our business."

Types of business objective

In the long run most firms need to make a profit. People will only invest their money in a business if they are satisfied with the returns from it. But although profit is a major business objective, it is not the only one.

Some individuals set up in business because of the freedom it gives them to make decisions for themselves. Other motivations for running a business might include:

◆ **Maximisation of sales:** In some large companies, the salaries earned by managers may depend on the size of the business. Thus, their objective may be to make the business grow as large as possible.

◆ **Building a reputation:** For other people the image and name of a company may be very important. The company may spend a lot of money on public relations so that it will be well thought of.

◆ **Survival:** In some businesses, the objective may just be survival. For instance, an old-established company may have the objective of staying under the control of the original family owners.

◆ **Pleasure or interest:** Some small businesses are run for pleasure rather than profit. Their owners keep them going mainly because they enjoy it.

MATCH IT!

Can you help Frankie and Cleo to match the following terms and definitions?

Mission	The ability to make decisions and influence company policy
Objective	Someone with an interest in the success of an organisation
Stakeholder	Making sure that the organisation keeps running in its existing form
Profit maximisation	Making sure that the biggest possible return is made from company business
Maximisation of sales	A vision or overall goal for the organisation
Survival	A more detailed, measurable target for an organisation to work towards
Power	Ensuring that the maximum quantity possible of goods is bought in the market place

6 Types of Economic System

The wider business environment

A business organisation works within a wider system. Every day, people involved in business make decisions. These decisions are influenced by what is going on in the wider economic environment.

A good way of looking at the wider environment is to do a PEST analysis.

This is an analysis of changes which are taking place around organisations all the time involving:

◆ Political (P) changes

◆ Economic (E) changes

◆ Social (S) changes

◆ Technological (T) changes

Political changes are made by those with power to bring in new laws and regulations. For example, the UK government has the power to make anti-pollution laws either stricter or softer. Britain is also part of the European Union (EU). The EU has the power to pass laws and regulations affecting all 15 member countries.

Economic changes are concerned with the wider economy of the country. For example, the UK may be experiencing a boom period or a slump, unemployment, rising or falling prices and so on.

Social changes are those which affect attitudes and values in society as a whole. They can also be changes in the make-up of society, such as an increase in the number of old people.

Technological changes are changes in the way we make things, and in the tools and equipment we use. Today we live in an age of rapid technological change.

'What is a PEST?'

'A PEST is something which interferes with your business!'

Above: EU laws are passed at the European Parliament in Brussels

Below: An environment of change

Political changes → The organisation ← Economic changes

Social changes → The organisation ← Technological changes

Resources

In any society **resources** are scarce compared to our needs for them. There are two main types of resource:

◆ **Physical or natural** resources such as soil, climate, water, minerals, forests and fisheries

◆ **Human** resources – i.e. people and their various skills

Opportunity cost

Businesses use up resources which are scarce. Imagine society had all the land, labour, raw materials and other resources it needed. Then we could produce all the goods we wanted without making sacrifices. In reality, resources are scarce. When we use resources to produce an item, we are taking away these resources from producing something else. This is a major problem for all societies.

The real cost of using resources for one purpose is the loss of the next-best use to which they could have been put. The **opportunity cost** of any activity is the next-best alternative which is given up.

Economic systems

Because resources are limited, it is necessary for society to decide how its available resources will be used. Important questions to consider are:

◆ **What** will be produced?

◆ **How** will it be produced?

◆ **For whom** will it be produced?

TASK

Can you classify the following factors under four headings: political changes, economic changes, social changes, and technological changes? (Remember that it may not always be possible to define a change under one single heading).

- A rise in unemployment
- A rise in taxes
- The growth of the European Union
- New ways of making food
- Growing numbers of working women
- People living longer
- A general rise in prices
- The Chancellor's Budget speech
- Use of factory robots
- Pollution laws
- Rising interest rates
- People becoming less conformist
- Laws protecting employees at work

TASK

Look at the following newspaper headlines and sort them out according to whether they raise a 'what', a 'how' or a 'for whom' issue:

Pensioners to get higher benefits

Wages increase for key workers

Textiles in decline while leisure centres boom

Teachers to lose out in a new pay deal

NEW TECHNOLOGY BOOSTS OUTPUT

Call for revival of craft skills

UK to produce more machine tools

Systems for making economic decisions

In the distant past, decisions about what to produce, how to produce it, and for whom, were made by custom and tradition. For example, the way that crops were grown and shared out was decided by folk tradition. In most parts of the world, traditional economies have given way to three major systems:

◆ The **centrally planned system**

◆ The **free market** system

◆ The **mixed system**

Central planning

In a centrally planned system, many decisions are made by a central planning organisation. Smaller groups such as factories and other business units submit their plans to a local committee. The local plans are then fed back for approval at the centre. The central organisation may decide what resources to make available to each local area. In turn, resources are allocated to each factory, farm or other productive unit.

Up until the end of the 1980s, most Eastern European countries had centrally planned systems. Today, however, many of them have moved towards a free market system.

TASK

Cleo's favourite type of cat food is "Vegichunks" which cost 40p a tin. Her next favourite is "Superveg" which also costs 40p a tin.

Every week Frankie has £2.80 available for cat food. She buys Cleo 7 tins of "Vegichunks".

What is the opportunity cost?

'When I buy something there is no opportunity cost! I always buy the best so there is no alternative that I sacrifice.'

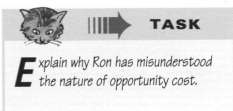

TASK

Explain why Ron has misunderstood the nature of opportunity cost.

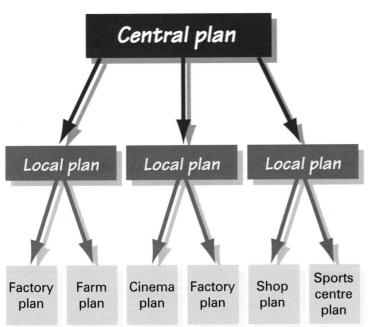

A centrally planned economic system

CASE STUDY

The end of the line for the Trabant

In 1990 the new Germany was created. Former East Germany had been a centrally planned economy. West Germany had been a mixed economy in which prices had been free from government interference.

Before reunification, a car known as the Trabant was almost the only model available in East Germany. More than three million Trabants had been sold since production began in the late 1950s. The same model of car was sold from 1964 to 1991. Because people could only buy one make of car there was no competition. The planners saw no need to change the design because they could sell every car that they produced.

The Trabant was functional (i.e. it served the purpose of getting a driver from place A to place B), cheap to run and easy to repair. It was said it could be repaired with a hammer, a ball of string and chewing gum. However, it was an environmental disaster. It was noisy and gave off a lot of exhaust fumes. It was made largely from a cheap fibre-glass material called Duroplast, which is

Trabant cars pouring out of East Germany at the time of reunification

everlasting. The car could only be destroyed by burning, which gave off poisonous fumes.

Before the joining together of East and West Germany there was a long waiting list for the Trabant. After reunification, nobody wanted to buy a Trabant. The Trabant was obsolete in a modern market. It was no longer possible to continue producing a car which cost 11,000 DM (£3,700 in 1991) and could only be sold for 9,000 DM. In May 1991 the company was forced to close down and 9,000 employees lost their jobs.

  TASK

1   Why do you think that so little change was made to the Trabant over the years?

2   What would be the benefits to (a) producers and (b) consumers of sticking to the standard model?

3   Why would free market forces introduce change?

4   How could the Trabant survive in a free market?

5   What problems do you think would have been caused by the disappearance of the Trabant?

6   Explain in detail why you think that the disappearance of the Trabant was a good or a bad thing for (a) people living in former East Germany, and (b) the world economy.

COURSEWORK ACTIVITIES

Find a newspaper article about changes taking place in Poland, Russia, the Czech Republic or another East European economy.

Cut out the article and study it. Write a commentary next to the article highlighting some important changes that the article describes.

The free market

In a **free market** the decisions about what to produce, how, and for whom, are made by consumers and producers. The government does not intervene. The laws of supply and demand control the market place (see Chapter 2).

In a free market, producers are forced to pay attention to the wishes of consumers in order to survive. Of course producers often try to manipulate consumers into buying their goods by aggressive marketing and advertising campaigns. These techniques can be very persuasive.

The mixed economy

The mixed economy combines elements of both the free market and a centrally planned system. Some decisions are made solely by individual businesses and consumers. Other decisions are made by the government.

The UK is an example of a **mixed economy**: Some parts of industry are owned and run by the government, but large sections of the business world remain in private hands.

TASK

1   What factors decide whether consumers have more power to keep prices low, or producers have the power to push prices up?

2   List five advantages that (a) the free market has over central planning; and (b) central planning has over the free market.

TASK

1   In recent years the demand for videos has increased. How have producers responded?

2   In recent years the demand for black and white television sets has fallen. How have producers responded?

3   Every year the fashion industry spends a lot of money on advertising clothes. How do consumers react?

 **MATCH IT!**   Can you help Frankie and Cleo to match the following terms and definitions?

Terms	Definitions
Resource	A situation in which what is produced is determined without government interference
PEST analysis	The next-best alternative which is sacrificed
Economic system	A system of government control of economic activity
Price system	A means of support e.g. oil, coal, human labour
Free market	An examination of the external environmental factors influencing organisations
Mixed economy	The determination of output by demand and supply interactions
Central planning	The means by which resources are allocated in any society
Opportunity cost	A combination of central planning and the free market

1 7 Interdependence

What is interdependence?

Interdependence is a basic fact of business life. The dictionary definition of 'dependent' is:

'Depending on a person or thing for aid, support.'

In business, interdependence is when a number of people, groups or organisations depend on each other in some way or another for their survival and prosperity.

'What does the word "interdependent" mean?'

Types of interdependence

In business, there are many types of interdependence between individuals, organisations and countries.

Interdependence between people

In a business organisation many people work together. Managers depend on employees doing their jobs well. At the same time, employees depend on managers managing well.

'I've got no time for interdependence. My motto is "Look after Number One!" I don't depend on anyone else. I'm a self-made man!'

Often this interdependence is far more than just sharing tasks – it is a joint responsibility, sometimes involving life-or-death issues.

Good examples of this kind of interdependence can be found in a hospital operating theatre or on the flight deck of a Jumbo Jet.

TASK

Could Ron survive on his own? What are the disadvantages of having an attitude like Ron's?

Interdependence between organisations

Any business organisation will turn inputs into outputs by using a number of processes. All of these processes create interdependence both within the firm and between the firm and its wider environment.

For example, in baking bread the **inputs** will include flour, yeast, water, electricity/gas, human skill, an oven, baking trays and so on.

The **processes** will include measuring, sifting, mixing, kneading, heating and cooling.

One of the **outputs of the bakery** will be the finished bread. Other outputs will include the wages of the employees, the satisfaction of consumers, taxes paid to the government and so on.

The bakery itself can also be seen as part of a larger productive system. This is the economy of the country as a whole, which uses the inputs of individual organisations to produce outputs of its own.

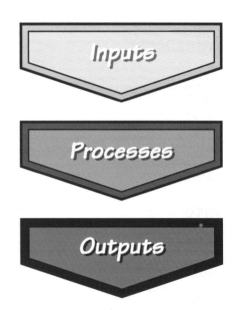

Production creates interdependence

CHAPTER 7

Inputs, processes and outputs at Huntley, Boorne and Stevens

An example of interdependence

Huntley, Boorne and Stevens make a range of tin boxes of different shapes and sizes. These boxes are used for packaging biscuits, sweets, tea and many other products.

The company also has an aerosol line which is highly automated. As well as specialist management, the firm employs a wide range of staff including:

- Salespeople
- Design artists
- Engineering designers
- Printers
- Factory-floor workers
- Engineers
- Buyers
- Office workers
- Cleaners
- Lorry drivers
- Canteen workers
- Secretarial staff

If we go on to study the **inputs** of the business, we can see that they come from various parts of the UK and the world. If we look at the **processes** involved in production, we can see a wide range of specialist, yet interdependent, tasks. If we look at the **outputs** of the firm, we notice that many outlets are supplied and eventually products will be distributed all over the world.

The process of manufacture and distribution is held together by a transport network. In addition, the firm will have to use a wide range of specialist business services. These include banks, insurance services, import/export agencies, translation services and postal and telecommunications facilities. Business takes place in a wide environment. Changes in Bristol and Belgium can be as important to the organisation as changes in its immediate neighbourhood.

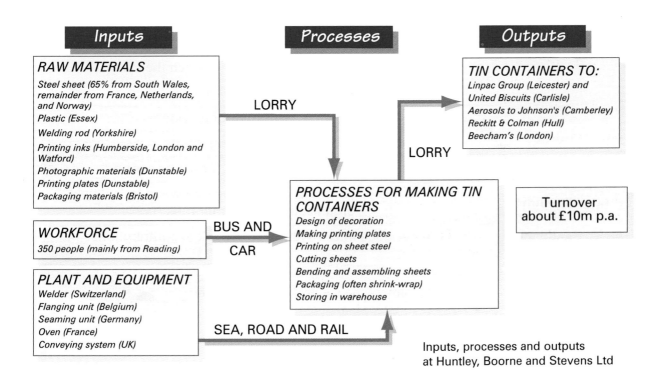

Inputs

RAW MATERIALS
Steel sheet (65% from South Wales, remainder from France, Netherlands, and Norway)
Plastic (Essex)
Welding rod (Yorkshire)
Printing inks (Humberside, London and Watford)
Photographic materials (Dunstable)
Printing plates (Dunstable)
Packaging materials (Bristol)

WORKFORCE
350 people (mainly from Reading)

PLANT AND EQUIPMENT
Welder (Switzerland)
Flanging unit (Belgium)
Seaming unit (Germany)
Oven (France)
Conveying system (UK)

Processes

LORRY

BUS AND CAR

SEA, ROAD AND RAIL

PROCESSES FOR MAKING TIN CONTAINERS
Design of decoration
Making printing plates
Printing on sheet steel
Cutting sheets
Bending and assembling sheets
Packaging (often shrink-wrap)
Storing in warehouse

Outputs

LORRY

TIN CONTAINERS TO:
Linpac Group (Leicester) and United Biscuits (Carlisle)
Aerosols to Johnson's (Camberley)
Reckitt & Colman (Hull)
Beecham's (London)

Turnover about £10m p.a.

Inputs, processes and outputs at Huntley, Boorne and Stevens Ltd

Interdependence between countries

Today we are particularly aware of the impact of the world market on business life in the UK. When the world market prospers, countries prosper, companies in those markets prosper, and individuals benefit.

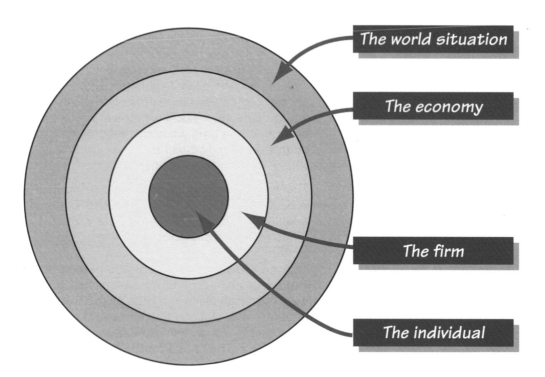

- The world situation
- The economy
- The firm
- The individual

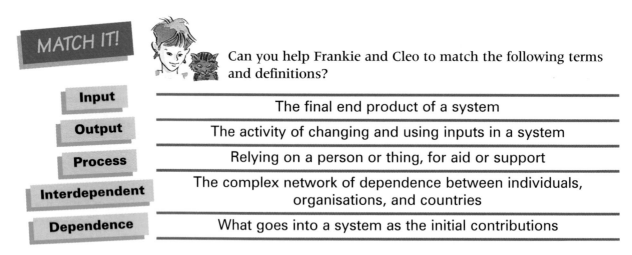

MATCH IT!

Can you help Frankie and Cleo to match the following terms and definitions?

Input	The final end product of a system
Output	The activity of changing and using inputs in a system
Process	Relying on a person or thing, for aid or support
Interdependent	The complex network of dependence between individuals, organisations, and countries
Dependence	What goes into a system as the initial contributions

8 Locating a Business

Choosing a location

One of the most important decisions affecting the success of a business organisation is its location.

◆ Local businesses need to decide on the best location within a particular town or area.

◆ National businesses need to decide on the best spot in a country.

◆ International companies often search all over the world for the right location.

Costs are an important factor to bear in mind when choosing a location. However, cost is not necessarily the only factor. For example, some shops selling luxury goods will probably want branches in city centres where property costs are at their highest. Therefore, the best site will be the one where the business gains the most commercial advantage.

Gateshead's Metro Centre on Tyneside is well placed to attract car-borne shoppers and those who wish to use public transport

Distance to markets

Availability of raw materials

Availability of labour

Regional factors

Safety

Communications

Transport costs

Utilities

BUSINESS LOCATION

Availability of land

Government incentives

Factors affecting business location

1 Distance to market

Many businesses need to be located close to their market, i.e. their customers. Think of the florist at a railway station, or the local newsagent.

Service industries such as entertainment and banking also have to locate near their markets to be available for their customers. Many manufacturing industries locate close to their markets, particularly if they produce bulky or fragile items which are expensive to transport.

Centres of population tend to attract **bulk-increasing** industries. These are industries where the output is more expensive to transport than the raw materials. They need to be close to their market in order to minimise transport costs. For example, London is ringed by bulk-increasing consumer goods industries.

Bulk-increasing industries are better placed near their market.

Left: Location factors for a newsagent

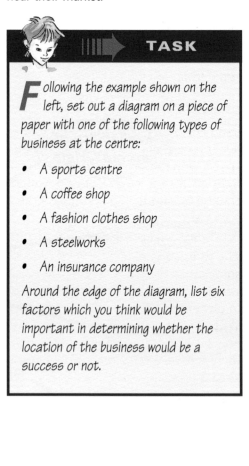

TASK

Following the example shown on the left, set out a diagram on a piece of paper with one of the following types of business at the centre:

- A sports centre
- A coffee shop
- A fashion clothes shop
- A steelworks
- An insurance company

Around the edge of the diagram, list six factors which you think would be important in determining whether the location of the business would be a success or not.

2 Availability of raw materials

Some businesses use a lot of heavy and bulky raw materials in the construction of their products. However, these products may be a lot smaller and lighter than the ingredients which have gone into them. For example, finished steel is a lot lighter than the ore, limestone and other materials which have gone into making it.

If the raw materials are bulky and expensive to transport, it makes sense to locate near to them. These industries are known as **bulk-decreasing industries**, as their output is much cheaper to transport than their input.

3 Transport costs

Different industries have different transport needs. Two major influences are the pull of the market and of raw materials. These depend on whether the industry is bulk-increasing or bulk-decreasing. However, many industries markets are spread out and raw materials come from several suppliers.

4 Availability of land

Land costs vary a lot from area to area. Some firms dealing with large quantities of goods require a lot of space. Others may need to check that a site has the right geology to support heavy weights, or the right climate for producing certain goods.

5 Availability of labour

The right sorts of labour and skills are easier to find in some areas than others. If a firm moves to an area which does not have the right sort of labour, it will have to pay employees to 'relocate', or train people in the skills it needs. This costs money. In some areas there may be a tradition of work in a particular industry and there will be a large pool of workers with the right skills already available.

Footloose industries are ones which do not have to be located anywhere in particular. These industries will be attracted to areas where labour is cheap.

6 Safety

Some industries have to locate their premises well away from heavily populated areas – for example, nuclear power stations, munitions factories and some chemical plants.

Bulk-decreasing industries are better placed near their source of raw materials.

'A scrap metal business needs to be set up close to the market for scrap metal!'

Do you agree with Ron?

7 Utilities

A business must consider five standard utilities:

◆ Gas

◆ Electricity

◆ Water

◆ Disposal of waste

◆ Drainage

Aluminium smelting, for example, uses vast quantities of cheap hydro-electric power. Industries such as food preparation and paper production use large quantities of water. Food-processing creates waste, and the cost of disposing of this waste is a key locational factor.

8 Communication

Access to motorways, ports and airports has become an increasingly important locational factor in recent years. These services and other vital communication links make up what is called the **infrastructure** of a region. A good infrastructure can attract businesses to move to an area. Many towns have expanded partly as a result of good communications. For example, the M4 corridor between London and South Wales has been very successful in attracting industry to Wales.

9 Regional factors

Locating in an area which contains similar businesses, suppliers and markets may be a considerable advantage. The quality of local schools, housing, leisure and recreational facilities can also help to maintain the quality of staff and keep them happy and motivated.

10 Government incentives

Unemployment rates vary considerably between regions. The government tries to reduce these differences by rewarding firms which set up in areas of hardship. However, such government incentives can make problems worse in neighbouring areas. In some cases the new industries created have not been very labour-intensive.

In the 1990s many local councils tried to attract new firms into their area by advertising in national newspapers. Some firms researched the facilities that new businesses were looking for and then built factory units to meet their needs.

COURSEWORK ACTIVITIES

Find out which of the ten factors discussed in this chapter have been most important in leading to the location of five firms in your area.

Locating a tin box factory

Firms in a particular industry need to look at many different factors when deciding where to locate their plant or factory. Important ones are:

1 The cost of transporting the finished product to the market

2 The cost of transporting raw materials to the plant or factory

3 The cost of labour travelling to work

The firm will locate its plant where these costs, taken together, are minimised.

In this activity, a tin box manufacturer is deciding whether to locate nearer to its labour supply, its markets or its raw materials. The purpose of the exercise is to let you compare the transport costs involved and make a recommendation. You should calculate the transport costs of producing tin boxes at each of the four possible places, A, B, C and D shown in the diagram on the right and choose the one with the lowest cost.

To make the task easier, it has been assumed that a market exists for the tin boxes only at B, C and D, but workers would have to commute from B if the factory was to be located at A. A labour force is therefore only available at B, C and D. We will also assume that production costs within the factory are constant wherever the factory is located.

For each thousand boxes produced:

1 It costs 10p per mile to transport the required labour from B to A.

2 Transporting oil (raw material) from the refinery at A costs £12 per mile by road and 20p per mile by canal.

3 The cost of transporting tin boxes is £6 per mile by road and 20p per mile by canal.

4 Transporting metal (raw material) from the metal works at D costs £9 per mile by road and 30p by canal.

Work out the transportation costs of locating the factory at either A, B, C or D and display the results in a table *(see right)*. Some parts of the table will be blank. For example, there will be no costs for transporting metal to D.

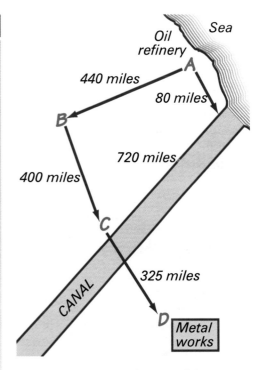

A, B, C and D are the four possible locations for the tin box factory.

Location	A	B	C	D
Labour transport costs				
Oil transport costs				
Metal transport costs				
Market costs				
TOTAL				

A table for working out the costs of locations A, B, C, and D

 **TASK**

1 Which is the location with the lowest cost?

2 Which is the location with the next-lowest cost? Would the business necessarily locate at the site with the lowest cost?

MATCH IT!

Can you help Frankie and Cleo to match the following terms and definitions?

Regional advantages	The network of communications and other services which create a foundation for business activity
Infrastructure	The five standard services of gas, electricity, water, waste disposal and drainage
Utilities	The costs involved in moving products and people around in business activity
Bulk-decreasing industries	Industries which locate near to their market because their output is bigger, bulkier, or heavier than their inputs
Bulk-increasing industries	Industries which are not influenced by any particular locational factors and set up where labour costs are low
Footloose industries	Industries which locate close to their raw materials because their inputs are reduced in size and weight in the process of production
Transport costs	The benefits of setting up in a particular locality

9 The Influence of Government

'How and why does the government get involved in business activity in this country?'

This chapter looks at how government affects business in a general way. It explains:

◆ **Why the government gets involved in business activity**

◆ **How the government gets involved**

◆ **The effects on business activity**

'Involvement is the wrong word. Interference – that's what I call it!'

Left: The 15 member states of the European Union

Levels of government

Today there are three levels of government which affect us all:

1 European Union government

The UK is one of 15 countries belonging to the European Union. The EU is responsible for policy-making on economic and social issues, and member states co-operate closely on a wide range of other issues. The European Commission and European Parliament are bodies representing all 15 member states. EU laws override national laws in important areas and the European Court makes sure that these laws are enforced. National governments signed over responsibility for making these decisions to European bodies when they joined the Union and when they signed the Maastricht Treaty in November 1993.

2 Central government

Central government runs the country. Citizens choose Members of Parliament. MPs belong to political parties which have leaders. Central government passes new laws in Parliament. Civil servants run the day-to-day activities of the state, such as collecting taxes.

3 Local government

Local government looks after only a small part of the country, e.g. a county like Lincolnshire or a heavily built-up area such as Manchester. Citizens vote for councillors to represent them at local-government level.

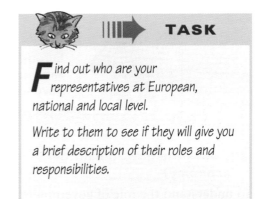

TASK

*F*ind out who are your representatives at European, national and local level.

Write to them to see if they will give you a brief description of their roles and responsibilities.

Organising refuse collection is a responsibility of local government

CASE STUDY

What sort of Europe should we have?

Different people have different ideas about how strong the links between EU countries should be. Here are some of the options:

Union à la carte

Europe should be seen as a lunch. Pick the courses (or policies) that you fancy and avoid the others.

The hard core

Europe should be like a peach with a hard core. Some countries – the core countries – should join together closely with rapid integration of policies. The others can catch up when they can.

Concentric circles

This view sees Europe as an onion. The 'good' (i.e. committed) Europeans are in the middle, followed by succeeding layers of 'less good' Europeans, with possible new members on the outside.

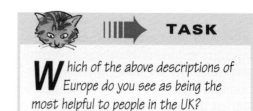

The multi-track, multi-speed approach

Europe is a giant motorway system. Everyone must obey the same traffic rules (free trade, open markets, fair competition), but beyond that, anything goes.

Why does the government get involved in the economy?

To understand the role of government, take a walk in a group along a road outside your school or college. List ways in which the government influences everyday life. For example, who has paid for the roads, street lighting and maintenance of the pavements and parks? Why are drivers wearing seatbelts, and why are lorries only allowed to use certain roads?

◆ Some goods and services are provided by the government because it is felt that all citizens benefit from them, either directly or indirectly. For example, most people in the UK believe that children should have some form of healthcare and education.

◆ Some goods and services from which everyone benefits can only be provided adequately if they are funded and organised at national level. The armed forces are one example.

TASK

*W*hich of the above descriptions of Europe do you see as being the most helpful to people in the UK?

◆ Some people believe that the government should try to reduce inequality in society. They believe the government should tax some people at a higher rate than others and give more benefit to those who are worse off. Others see inequality as a useful way of encouraging people to try to better themselves.

◆ The government can also try to make the economic system run more smoothly. For example, it passes laws to protect consumers and takes measures against pollution and other antisocial practices.

A very important role played by the government is to set the rules within which business activity takes place. These rules are constantly changing, so some people lose out and others benefit. It is important to think about the following questions:

1 *Who makes the rules? For whom?*

2 *Why do the rules change?*

3 *How do they change?*

4 *Who loses, and who benefits when they change?*

How the government becomes involved in the economy

There are many areas of government involvement in the economy. These include:

◆ Employment policy

◆ Industrial policy

◆ Regional policy

◆ Inflation policy

◆ Industrial relations policy

◆ Education and training policy

◆ Taxation policy

◆ International policy

The effect of government activity

The effects of government legislation vary from one sector of the economy to the next, but inevitably the government has an important influence on how businesses behave. Today, businesses need to be familiar with local, national, and European-wide issues and rules.

  TASK

Use the four questions listed on the left to analyse the following recent changes in the law:

a) Compulsory publication of school league tables, showing the exam results that pupils achieve at GCSE and A Level

b) Cutbacks in the government road-building programme

c) Reduction of income tax in the 1995 budget

d) Compulsory provision of all-seater stadiums at major football grounds

'I support the saying: "The best government is no government". Whenever the government interferes, it makes things worse! People should be left to spend their own money in the way they think best, so there should be no taxes, and no government laws. In fact there should be no government!'

Do you agree with Ron?

MATCH IT!

Can you help Frankie and Cleo to match the following terms and definitions?

European Union	The nucleus of countries that see themselves as committed Europeans
Hard core Europeans	The agreement between 15 European countries covering economic, social and political co-operation
Local government	The body responsible for governing within a country
Multi-track Europe	Those bodies which are responsible for governing a local area of a country
Central government	Process allowing EU member countries to move at their own pace towards greater integration

10 Starting a Business

Have you got what it takes?

Setting up and running a business is something that only energetic, enthusiastic people should tackle – people who like hard work, who enjoy challenges, who can adapt to change, and who are not put off by failure. Perhaps you are one of those people!

Starting up on your own is a big step. It is always vital to carry out a lot of research and think things through carefully before rushing into it.

People start their own business for a variety of reasons. Some have a bright idea that they think will make them rich. Others find themselves unemployed and start their own business to survive. Some can only be themselves when they are their own boss. Others want to give something to their community and can see no other way of doing it except by setting up on their own.

'This is an important chapter for me. I am keen to start up my own business making biscuits. I find it really useful to find out about other small businesses and how they have been set up.'

Business ideas

Of course, an important starting point for a business is the business idea. Most people at some time or another have said things like: *'If only someone sold x here they could make a fortune…'* Or: *'I have a great idea for a new product.'*

There are many ways of coming up with a bright idea. The table below shows a few examples. Try to add two suggestions of your own for each example given.

Source of idea	Example
Developing a hobby	Making wooden toys
Using your skills	Plastering/painting
A chance idea	A musical toothbrush
Spotting a gap in the market	A home hairdresser
Improving a product or service	A better restaurant
Combining two existing ideas	Coffee shop/bookshop
Solving problems for people	Financial adviser
Listening to people	Teenagers want a mobile disco

Above: Big businesses can start with bright ideas…

Sally makes a start

Frankie's friend Sally has set up her own sandwich-making business.

Frankie has been asking Sally what was involved in setting up the sandwich business.

Sally says:

'The sandwich business is booming. Supermarkets are increasing their range and many large cities have phone-in sandwich delivery services.'

But how do you start up a sandwich business?

'Well, there's a daft idea if ever I heard one. No one is going to buy sandwiches – they'll just make their own! My bright idea was buying and selling scrap metal! There will always be a demand for scrap metal!'

Is Ron right?

Sally decided to set up a small sandwich delivery business to earn money and have some fun. First, she carried out research in the area where she planned to deliver...

Checking out the competition

'I thought busy people in the area where I lived needed better-quality lunches. I looked around the local lunchtime places and asked people what was on offer. The choice was very limited, so I thought there would be no difficulty improving on that.'

Bread research

'I wanted to make unusual sandwiches, and I needed a variety of good-quality breads. I visited the local supermarket and bought their range of breads. I tested them for taste and texture. Bread has to be the right shape and size, and go well with the fillings.'

Refining the recipe

'I couldn't find a pitta bread that was the right shape or size. So I have invented my own using dried yeast, strong white flour with wheatgerm, water and a little olive oil. The bread is rolled out in stone-ground flour from a country flour mill. This gives a nutty flavour.'

Fillings

'I chose fillings using flavours from around the world, such as the Greek sandwich with feta cheese and olives. There is also a vegetarian choice, with avocado, tomato and alfalfa sprouts. All the fillings were tested on friends before I made my menu choice.'

CHAPTER 10

CASE STUDY (CONTD.)

Costing it out

Banks may lend money to help small businesses to get started. Some banks have special offers such as free printing of menus and business cards.

For her small business, Sally had to buy special catering equipment. She also needed a basket with a tablecloth, napkins, plates and containers for the delivery round.

The selling price of each sandwich was costed according to the bread used, the price of the filling and the packaging. Then this sum was doubled to cover labour and other expenses.

'Everyone I know eats white bread. She stands no chance with all that fancy stuff! Her only hope is to stick to the standard favourites such as white bread sandwiches with cheese and pickle. If I were her, I would sell pork pies. That's what I call a good idea!'

Do you agree with Ron or Sally?

Starting off

Sally couldn't afford promotion or advertising. So she just set off with a basket full of sandwiches, fruit, cakes, crisps and drinks. Her efforts were rewarded the next day when a satisfied customer remarked: 'Thank you for making such decent sandwiches.'

What changes had to be made?

'The weather affects what people choose. If it's sunny, they prefer salads, but the weather can suddenly change and the salads I have made remain unsold. Shop assistants don't like eating raw onions as it can make their breath smell – and that's no good for customers.'

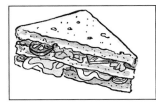

Customer tastes

'People turned out to be very adventurous in the choice of sandwiches. Club sandwiches and avocado, bacon, lettuce and tomato are the two bestsellers. I've stopped making plain ham and beef sandwiches.'

The future

'I'd really like to open a shop or get a helper, since the delivery takes up so much time. But that all costs money, so we will have to wait and see.'

|||||⟶ **TASK**

The Case Study on pages 40–41 highlights some important areas that need to be thought about in setting up a small business. These are:

- Coming up with an idea
- Finding out if there is a market
- Looking at the competition
- Product research

- Costing it out
- Pricing
- Promotion and advertising
- Looking to the future.

Task 1

Working in small groups, study a small local business. Find out what was done under each of the above headings when it was set up.

Prepare a group presentation for the rest of the class. The presentation should be 20 minutes long. Use visual aids - diagrams and charts, examples of products, illustrations, etc.

Task 2

Identify an opportunity for setting up a small business of your own to provide a product or service to be sold in your local area. Carry out some research using each of the headings outlined above. Look at possible competitors, different ways of providing the product or service, etc. Produce your findings in the form of a 1,000-word report supported by charts and diagrams.

 **MATCH IT!** Can you help Frankie and Cleo to match the following terms and definitions?

Product research	A novel idea for a product or service
Costing	An opportunity that has not already been filled by an existing business
Bright idea	Studying appropriate ways of making goods or developing services to meet consumer needs
Pricing	Studying the various costs of producing a good or service
Gap in the market	Deciding how much and how to charge for goods or services

11 Business Growth

From tiny acorns...

Most of the giant businesses that we know in the world today had very humble origins. Many products started off as homemade efforts. Coca-Cola was originally brewed up on a kitchen stove, and many mechanical goods were first hammered together in a garden shed.

Many business ideas started off as the brainchild of one person. The creator then brought a partner into the business, and eventually went on to bring in other part-owners by forming a company.

The size of the business

Business owners must choose the scale of production which suits the business best. Many businesses thrive as they become larger. The benefits they gain from growth are called **economies of scale.**

Internal economies of scale

The most obvious benefit of growth is the ability to produce units of output more cheaply. For example, the cost of serving a customer with a pint of beer will be a lot lower in a busy pub than in a pub with very few customers.

'It's all very well setting up a small business. But at what stage should we try and grow bigger? What are the dangers of growth?'

'In my business small is beautiful!'

Below: The economies of scale that come into play as a result of growth

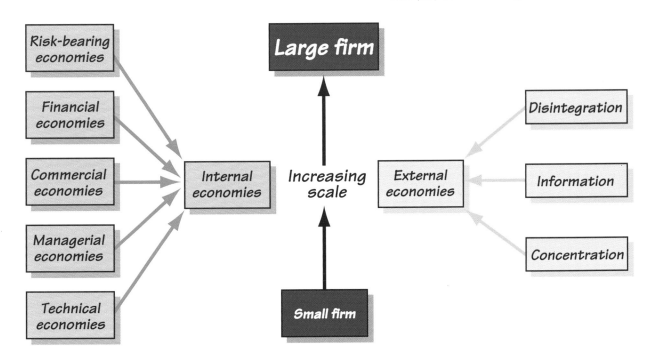

CASE STUDY

The bus tour operator

David Curry set up Jorvik Tour Bus Ltd in York in 1984 after reading in his Sunday newspaper about tourist buses in London. Realising that the idea could work in other locations, he immediately set about forming a company to offer bus tours around the historic city of York. At the time, David was in his early twenties and had recently passed his Public Service Vehicle and Heavy Goods Vehicle driving tests.

In order to get the company off the ground he needed a licence from the Department of Transport. There were no other tourist bus companies in York, and the National Bus Company opposed the setting-up of his business. However, David won his case at a public hearing.

He set up in business with one (closed-top) bus and charged tourists £1 each for the tour. The National Bus Company hit back by setting up its own tour service, charging 10p. In 1986, David decided to improve his service and removed the top of his own bus by hand with a metal grinder.

The company went from strength to strength. By 1990, David had eight open-toppers and was considering offering tours to places like Harrogate, the Dales and Herriot Country.

However, in the early 1990s things started to go wrong. The Gulf crisis reduced the number of tourists to York. As the recession began to bite, consumers began to spend less. Scenic tours became one of the luxuries that consumers were less prepared to spend money on.

David responded by cutting the price of tickets from £3.50 to £2.50. He sold two buses and scrapped one. But by August 1992 he was running buses with very few passengers, and in October 1992 he stopped trading.

  TASK

1 Was the Jorvik tour bus idea a good one? Explain your answer.

2 What factors led to the growth of the company?

3 What factors led to its fall?

4 What does the Case Study tell us about the environment in which businesses operate?

5 What does the Case Study tell us about the difficulties of growth?

Technical economies

Large-scale producers can employ techniques and equipment that cannot be used by small-scale producers. For example, a bakery may have two ovens producing 1,000 loaves a day. As the firm gets larger, these two ovens could be replaced by one oven producing 2,500 loaves a day at half the cost. This means less labour, lower energy costs – and higher profits for the owner.

Labour and managerial economies

Large organisations can employ specialist staff such as accountants and researchers. Such expertise will help to increase output and lower costs. The ratio of managers to staff is also likely to be lower in a large organisation since each manager is responsible for more staff.

Commercial economies

Commerce is concerned with the buying and selling of things. As firms grow larger they are able to buy their inputs such as raw materials or finished goods in bulk. When you buy in bulk, you can negotiate discounts. The cost of transport per unit will be much lower with larger loads. Larger firms are also able to organise the selling of their products more effectively. For example, if you can sell all your output to one or a few buyers, the cost of making the sale will be a lot lower than if you are dealing with thousands of separate customers.

Financial economies

Large firms tend to be a more secure investment than smaller firms and find it easier to borrow money. Their reputation and reliability can often help them to borrow money at lower rates of interest.

Risk-bearing economies

Large firms have the possibility of carrying out a range of activities, rather than 'putting all their eggs in one basket'. We call this **diversification**. They may decide to produce several products rather than one, or they may sell goods in different markets, e.g. France, Spain, Greece, and India as well as the UK. Or, instead of just selling goods to one age range, they may produce products which appeal to different age-ranges – for example, one breakfast cereal for young children, another aimed at teenagers, a third aimed at the weight-conscious middle-aged.

TASK

If Ron Rust buys a new car crusher, this is known as a _____ economy of scale.

External economies of scale

External economies of scale are those shared by a number of firms in the same industry in a particular area. Examples are:

Economies of concentration

As firms within an industry grow larger in a locality, a concentration of special services develops. These may include local college courses, a skilled workforce and a growing reputation for the area's products.

Economies of information

Larger industries can set up special information services to benefit producers, e.g. *The Building Trade Journal*, the Motor Research Association, etc.

Economies of disintegration

Other firms may be attracted to areas where specialised industries already exist – for example, firms producing components or offering help with maintenance and processes. Examples are the many software houses supplying the big computer companies in the Thames Valley.

Integration

Organisations can take advantage of economies of scale by ploughing back profits and gradually expanding their operations. Organic growth of this kind is, however, often a slow process.

A quicker and more dynamic route is through **mergers** or **take-overs**. These involve combining a number of businesses under a single organisation. Merging increases size and enables companies to benefit from economies of large-scale production. Some firms merge in order to increase the benefits of specialisation. Others do so in order to diversify and so cut down risk.

Horizontal integration

A company may take over another which produces similar goods and which is involved at the same stage of production. An example of **horizontal integration** is shown on the page opposite.

Vertical integration

Some products are made in stages which may be carried out by separate firms. **Vertical integration** therefore involves the joining together of firms at different stages of production.

TASK

Can you help Frankie and Cleo to classify the following as **internal** or **external** economies of scale?

Can you also say what **type** of economies are involved in each case (e.g. technical economies, economies of information, etc.)?

- A tin box factory makes use of a new automated production line.

- A new university opens in Lincoln, offering courses for local business people.

- Shell UK is able to borrow millions of pounds for a short period from a British bank at a low rate of interest.

- A food processing firm is able to sell all of its output to Marks & Spencer.

- Several new journals are published, providing details of the latest developments in computing.

- A number of new companies start to locate close to the terminals for the Channel Tunnel.

- The growth of an insurance company enables it to attract top specialist managers.

- Virgin starts to move into a number of new product lines such as insurance and cola drinks as well as its traditional lines.

- An airline purchases some jumbo-sized new aeroplanes.

- Component manufacturers set up in the areas where new port construction work is taking place.

Horizontal integration

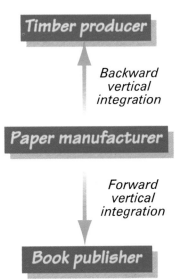

Vertical integration

Backward vertical integration would be the take-over of a supplier, and **forward vertical integration** would be the take-over of a firm at a later stage of production.

Lateral integration

This is a merger between two businesses which produce similar products. For example, a book publisher might acquire magazine and newspaper publishers, or even television and other media products *(right)*. The reasons might be to spread risk or to allow products to share the same channels of distribution.

Conglomerate integration

Another way of maximising risk-bearing economies is for a firm to acquire businesses which are not connected in any way with its present activities. A conglomerate integration *(below)* can provide wide diversification.

Multinationals

Large companies will seek to expand their markets overseas, and this often leads them to manufacture or assemble goods abroad. In many cases they will develop by taking over companies in other countries.

Above: Lateral integration

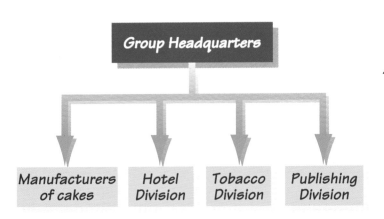

Left: Conglomerate integration

Diseconomies of scale

However, there are some drawbacks to being big. These are called **diseconomies of scale**.

Alongside the enormous advantages associated with being large, weaknesses of large firms include:

◆ **Human relations.** Large numbers of employees are often more difficult to organise. Contact between management and shopfloor will be reduced, and this can lead to industrial relations problems.

◆ **Decisions and co-ordination.** The size of a firm may limit the management's ability to make changes quickly in order to maximise sales. Improving products may involve delay and costs. Decision-making may be hampered by excessive paperwork and meetings. It is also difficult for large organisations to take a personal interest in the needs of customers.

◆ **External diseconomies.** If an organisation is big enough to affect whole marketplaces, public opinion can sometimes turn against it. Examples include the boycott of goods from Nigeria following widely publicised human rights abuses; the campaign for 'dolphin-friendly' tuna, and the campaign for real ale (CAMRA).

Downsizing

Today, a popular business word is **downsizing**. Many of the UK's big companies such as Shell UK, British Gas, ICI and the high street banks are downsizing. They have recognised that employing too many people makes them inefficient and less competitive. Downsizing often leads to **delayering**. This means the loss of layers of managers and supervisors whose services are no longer required.

One of the most important reasons for downsizing has been the spread of information technology in the workplace. Another has been competition from the Pacific Rim and other groups of countries. Companies which are very large tend to be slow-moving. Decisions are made at the top and slowly filter down. In the world of the electronic marketplace, this is unacceptable.

In small organisations where employees are allowed to make decisions for themselves, changes can be put into place quickly. Giving power to people to make decisions is called **empowerment**. Downsized companies are often described as being 'leaner and fitter' than old fashioned 'top-down' companies.

Can you help Frankie and Cleo to match the following terms and definitions?

Empowerment	Companies reducing in size in order to become more competitive
Commercial economies	The advantages a large firm has in buying and selling operations
Internal economies	Firms at different stages of production of the same product joining together
Technical economies	Diversifying into a range of products so as not to be disadvantaged by over-specialisation
External economies	The advantages enjoyed by all firms in an industry or region from the growth of that industry or region
Risk-spreading economies	Firms joining together which are at the same stage of production of a particular product
Managerial economies	Spreading out the responsibility for decision-making to lower levels in an organisation
Vertical integration	The joining together of firms producing similar and in some ways related goods and services
Horizontal integration	The internal benefits to an organisation resulting from the growth of that organisation
Lateral integration	The advantages resulting from employing specialist managers in larger firms
Conglomerate integration	The negative effects resulting from being too large an organisation
Downsizing	The benefits which large firms are able to enjoy from using better techniques and equipment
Diseconomies	The joining together of firms producing a range of quite different products

2 12 Sole Traders

Hairdressing, baking, gardening – three typical sole trader enterprises

What is a sole trader?

A sole trader is the most common form of business ownership and the easiest to set up. A sole trader is a business owned by one person – though this business may employ a large number of people. Many new sole trader businesses are currently being set up by young people.

The table below shows some of the advantages and disadvantages of setting up as a sole trader rather than as a larger business.

'If a business is a sole trader, does this mean that there is only one person working in that business?'

Unlimited liability

When you set up in business you will need **capital** to run the business. For example, you will need premises to work in, machinery and equipment, and you will need to buy supplies.

Below: Advantages and disadvantages of being a sole trader

Advantages	Disadvantages
Easy to set up as no special paper work is required	Having unlimited liability endangers personal possessions
Generally these are small businesses, so less capital required	Finance can be difficult to raise
Speedy decisions can be made as few people are involved	Small scale limits discounts and other benefits of large-scale production
Personal attention is given to business affairs	Prices are often higher than those of larger organisations
Special services can be offered to customers	Ill-health/holidays, etc., may affect the running of the business
Can cater for the needs of local people	–
Profits do not have to be shared	–
Business affairs can be kept private	–

CHAPTER 12

CASE STUDY

Jenny Prescott, signwriter

Jenny Prescott is a sole trader. After leaving art college in 1990, she worked for a signwriting firm and gradually built up her skills and speed. In 1993 Jenny felt that she had developed her abilities and understanding to the stage where she could start her own signwriting company. So she did a business course at college and learnt about the problems and pitfalls of setting up on her own.

Her first task was to find out, by producing a business plan, whether it was worth setting up at all. The business plan covered costs and receipts. **Costs** included paint, labour, heating and lighting, telephone, materials, publicity material, running a van, etc. **Receipts** were based on the number of hours worked and the hourly rate she could charge.

Jenny had decided to operate from home using a shed next to the house for her carpentry and artwork. This reduced her overhead costs considerably.

Businesses need time to get established, and Jenny calculated that at first she would only be working for 5–10 chargeable hours a week. By the end of the first year, she estimated that this would rise to 25 hours.

Taking into account the costs of her materials, she calculated that if she charged £12 an hour, she could make a **reasonable return**. This means that her revenue would more than cover her costs, leaving room for profit.

TASK

1   Do you think that being a sole trader is a suitable type of business for Jenny's signwriting enterprise?

2   What would be the main advantages and disadvantages to Jenny of this type of business organisation?

3   Give six examples of businesses that might suitably operate as sole traders. Explain why in each case.

4   Ron Rust says: 'In making and selling clothes there is no room for sole traders. Producing clothing is for people with big ideas and plenty of money! Sole traders haven't a chance!'

Do you agree?

Sole traders have only their own resources to draw on, because nobody else is an owner of their business. The sole trader therefore has to use past savings and will usually need to borrow money – probably from a bank.

Sole traders hope to make a profit. However, if a sole trader runs into debt, they will have to pay the money they owe from their own pocket.

The business term we use to describe this position is **unlimited liability**.

''Isn't it a bit risky being a sole trader?'

For example, if a sole trader has business and equipment worth £10,000, and they run up debts of £50,000, the debt is not limited to the £10,000 which they have already put into the business. This means they may have to sell their house and any other possessions they have to meet the debts. The answer to Frankie's question *(right)* is: 'Yes, running a sole trader business carries a high risk, but the rewards can also be great.'

'If you don't take risks, you don't make profits!'

MATCH IT! Can you help Frankie and Cleo to match the following terms and definitions?

Sole trader	Finance available for running a business
Reasonable return	Situation in which there is no restriction to the debts that owners of a business run up
Capital	A form of business where there is a single owner
Unlimited liability	A situation in which revenues more than match costs with a cushion of profit

13 Partnerships

What is a partnership?

A partnership is a business association between two or more owners of an enterprise. Partnerships usually have between 2 and 20 members, though there are some exceptions.

Partnerships are common in many types of business. They are usually found in shop ownership and in professional practices such as vets, doctors, solicitors and dentists.

'A partnership sounds as if it should have just two people in it. Is that right?'

How is a partnership formed?

The usual way to start a partnership is to ask a solicitor to draw up a **Deed of Partnership**. This lays down how profits and losses are to be shared and sets out the duties of each partner – for example, how much capital they should contribute, their roles and responsibilities, how profits will be taken out of the business, and procedures for introducing new partners and settling disputes.

The **Partnership Act of 1890** sets out rules which partners can refer to if they are not already covered in the Deed of Partnership (or if a Deed has not been drawn up).

Limited or **'sleeping' partners** can be introduced to a partnership. They have **limited liability** as long as they take no active part in the running of the business. However, there must always be at least one partner with unlimited liability.

Limited liability

Limited liability means that if a partnership runs into debt, the maximum amount in law that they are expected to lose is what they put into the business. In other words, the limited partner is not expected to sell off their house and possessions to meet the business debts.

 TASK

Set out a Deed of Partnership between yourself and a friend for a small enterprise that you could set up, such as washing cars, making toffee, etc.

The agreement should cover these topics:

- Who will provide the capital?
- Share-out of profits and losses
- Duties of partners
- How profits will be taken out of business (e.g. weekly, monthly)
- Procedures for bringing in new partners and settling disputes

The advantages and disadvantages of a partnership

Advantages	Disadvantages
Capital from partners	Unlimited liability (except for sleeping partners)
Larger-scale opportunities than for the sole trader	Disagreements between partners
Members of family can be introduced to the business	Limitation on number of partners
Affairs can be kept private	Partnerships have to be re-formed if partner dies
Risks and responsibilities spread among partners	

Can you help Frankie and Cleo to match the following terms and definitions?

Partnership Act, 1890	A formal agreement setting out the legal details of a partnership
Deed of partnership	A business association of between 2 and 20 owners who have clear rights and responsibilities to each other
Partnership	A partner who is not involved in the day-to-day running of a partnership.
Sleeping partner	An arrangement whereby the debts of a part-owner of an organisation are restricted to how much they have put into the organisation
Limited liability	Law introduced in 1890 governing how partnerships can and should be set up

14 Limited Companies

What is a company?

The word 'company' suggests a group of companions who have come together to set up a business. In practice, many companies are not like this today because the owners (share-holders) may be quite far removed from the decision-making.

Private limited companies (Ltd)

The owners of limited companies are called **shareholders**. This is because they each own a share in the business. Private limited companies must have at least two shareholders. There is no upper limit to the number of shareholders they can have, and companies can grow by selling more shares.

The shares of private limited companies are not quoted on the Stock Exchange. Private limited companies are also not allowed to advertise the sale of shares publicly.

'I'd never have a private company. You can't control who becomes a part-owner. Give them a small share and they think they own it!'

Is Ron right in what he is saying?

Private limited companies face the danger of issuing too many shares and so having to divide the profits between too great a number of shareholders. The liability of shareholders is limited to the value of their shareholding. To warn creditors about the dangers of dealing with these companies, the word **Limited** (or **Ltd**) appears after their name.

All private limited companies must comply with the **Companies Acts** of 1948 and 1980 and register with the Registrar of Companies. In order to register a company, two documents have to be completed. These are the **Memorandum of Association** and the **Articles of Association**.

◆ The Memorandum of Association outlines the relationship of the company with the outside world. For example, it states the name of the company, the purpose of the company and what the company actually does.

◆ The Articles of Association state the internal rules governing the company's organisation, including rules about meetings and the voting rights of shareholders. Also included is a list of directors and information on other internal matters. Shareholders can vote to change the articles.

Once the articles and memorandum have been received by the Registrar of Companies, together with some other paperwork, he or she will provide a **Certificate of Incorporation** and the private limited company can start trading.

Advantages	Disadvantages
Money from shares	Cannot sell shares on the Stock Market
Firm grows bigger	Accounts not private
Limited liability	Limitations on capital
Specialist managers can be employed	A lot of administrative work is required

Above: The advantages and disadvantages of being a private limited company

Below: The process of setting up a private limited company

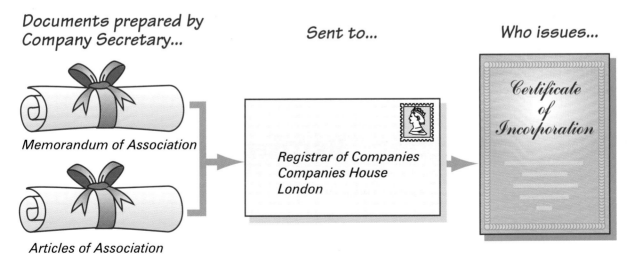

Documents prepared by Company Secretary...

Memorandum of Association

Articles of Association

Sent to...

Registrar of Companies
Companies House
London

Who issues...

Certificate of Incorporation

Buying and selling shares at the Stock Exchange in London

Public limited companies (PLCs)

PLCs have the chance to become larger than private business organisations. They are allowed to raise capital through the Stock Exchange, where shares are bought and sold.

Only two people are needed to form a public limited company, and there is no legal limit on the number of shareholders.

Forming a public company is very similar to forming a private company.

A Memorandum of Association and Articles of Association, as well as a number of other legal documents, have to be approved by the Registrar of Companies. The Registrar issues a Certificate of Incorporation as evidence that the company is registered.

The public company then issues a **prospectus**. This is an advertisement or invitation to the public to buy shares. The issuing of shares then takes place, and the Registrar of Companies issues a Certificate of Trading. Business can then start, and share prices will be quoted on the stock market.

TASK

Read the Case Study opposite then complete the following tasks:

1   List the four main stages in the growth of Marks & Spencer.

2   Explain why Marks & Spencer went through these four stages of growth. (For example, why did Michael Marks need to take on a partner? Why did the business need to become a private company and later a public company?)

3   What are the advantages and disadvantages of bringing more people into a company?

4   What do the following terms mean?

a) slogan

b) hire

c) specialise

d) administration

e) shareholder

f) executive director

g) non-executive director

h) discount

i) manufacturers

j) wholesalers

k) Stock Exchange

Some well-known PLCs

Marks & Spencer PLC

Michael Marks arrived in the north of England in 1881 as a Jewish immigrant from Russia. He started off as a hawker (a person who sells from door to door), going around mining villages selling buttons, needles, ribbons and other small items. He adopted a slogan which he tied on his tray: 'Don't ask the price, it's a penny.' He used this slogan to avoid complications as he could not speak much English.

The business quickly grew and soon Marks was able to afford a stall at Leeds market. As this brought in profits, Marks started to hire stalls at different markets. He decided that to become more successful, he would have to find a partner. In 1894 he became partners with Tom Spencer. Spencer put in £300 to become a partner.

Soon they had 24 market stalls and 12 shops. They each began to specialise in different jobs. Spencer would mainly work at the warehouse and organise administration. Marks specialised in buying goods and looking for new places from which to sell. Their shops were all 'penny bazaars'.

Unfortunately, Spencer became an alcoholic and less reliable. The partners decided to form the business into a private company, with themselves as the major shareholders. Marks stayed with the business, while Spencer left to run a chicken farm. Marks was, therefore, an executive director and ran the company, while Spencer remained a non-executive director.

An early Marks & Spencer store

Michael Marks and Tom Spencer died and Michael's son Simon and his boyhood friend Israel Sieff began to play an important part in running the company. Simon married Israel's sister, and Israel married Simon's sister.

In the early 1920s, Simon Marks went to America to learn about retailing. On his return he decided to change the company image, giving it a more up-market look, and to expand by opening a whole chain of stores. Instead of buying from wholesalers, he also started buying in bulk from manufacturers, who gave him a discount.

To raise the capital for doing this, Marks & Spencer became a public company with shares quoted on the Stock Exchange. From here, the company grew to its present size and developed the image and reputation that it enjoys to this day. There are now a large number of shareholders and the company is controlled by a board of directors.

Type of business	Ownership	Control
One-person business	Michael Marks	Michael Marks
Partnership	Michael Marks and Tom Spencer	Michael Marks and Tom Spencer
Private company	Marks and Spencer and other shareholders	Michael Marks and other executive directors
Public company	Shareholders	Directors, including the Sieff family

The four stages in the growth of Marks & Spencer

Benefits to shareholders

The benefits of being a shareholder include:

1 Possible increases in the share price (a **capital gain**).

2 Dividends received. The **dividend** is the shareholder's share of the company profits which are usually paid at six-monthly intervals (an **interim dividend**) or at the end of the year (a **year-end dividend**).

3 Being a part-owner of a business concern, with the right to attend and vote at shareholders' meetings.

4 Perks associated with some shares, e.g. reduced costs of company goods, travel discounts and so on.

Advantages	Disadvantages
Limited liability for shareholders	Formation can be expensive
Easy to raise capital	Decisions can be slow. 'Red tape' can be a problem
Operates on a large scale	Problems of being too large
Easy to raise finance from banks	Employees and shareholders distanced from one another
Employs specialists	Affairs are public

The advantages and disadvantages of being a PLC

Multinationals

A **multinational** company is one that operates in a number of countries. Most multinationals are public companies but there are also a few large private multinationals, such as Mars. Because of their size and their ability to switch operations between countries, multinationals have great powers to control prices. As major employers they can sometimes influence decision-making at government level.

MATCH IT!

Can you help Frankie and Cleo to match the following terms and definitions?

Share

Multinational

Certificate of Trading

Articles of Association

Memorandum of Association

Certificate of Incorporation

Private limited company (Ltd)

PLC

Dividend

Company whose shares are traded on the Stock Exchange

The return to the shareholder of a company

Part-ownership of a company

Organisation which operates and trades in a number of different countries

Company controlled by individuals and restricted groups

Document confirming that an organisation has company status

Document enabling a PLC to commence trading

Document setting out the internal rules and relationships of an organisation

Document setting out the external rules and relationships of an organisation

15 Franchising

What is a franchise?

A franchise is a 'business marriage' between an existing, proven business and a newcomer. The newcomer (known as the 'franchisee') buys permission to copy the business idea of the established company.

For example Frankie's Auntie Meena franchises her hairdressing business from an established company, 'TopCuts'.

The franchisee (Auntie Meena) commits her capital and effort. The franchisor (TopCuts) commits the trading name and management experience, and often supplies materials and equipment.

For example, TopCuts may help to train Meena's stylists, and sell Meena a range of quality supplies and equipment at a good price.

'You hear a lot of talk about franchising these days. My Auntie Meena franchises her hairdressing business from a well-known hairdressing company, TopCuts. Does this mean that Meena doesn't own the business?'

CASE STUDY

Mary Watson, plumber

Mary Watson had worked for a local builder as a contract plumber for several years. She worked long hours and the work was irregular. Then in September 1990 she saw the newspaper advertisement below for SuperRod, a nationwide plumbing and drain-clearing franchise.

Using her savings and a loan from the bank, Mary was able to buy a franchise and set up in business. SuperRod provided her with a three-week training course, a van and an electronic plumbing device that quickly unblocks drains and pipes. She was given an exclusive right to sell her services within a 10-mile radius, and the right to trade and advertise 24 hours a day. In return, Mary had to hand over 12 per cent of her profits to SuperRod.

The SuperRod franchise advertisement

 TASK

1   List six advantages and six disadvantages to Mary of taking on the franchise.

2   List what you consider to be the main advantages and disadvantages for the company granting the franchise.

  TASK

1   What lines of business is franchising most suitable for? Why?

2   Are there businesses for which franchising is inappropriate? If so, why?

3   If you needed a plumber in a hurry, how would you go about getting one? What might tempt you to choose a franchise plumber?

4   Identify an area of retailing which would be suitable for franchising. How would you go about organising such an operation?

The franchisee buys a licence to copy the franchisor's business system. In return they promise to pay them a percentage of their sales.

The franchisee needs to work hard, put in long hours and use a lot of initiative to get the business started and develop it. In 1996, there were over 700 franchise opportunities in the UK. The *UK Franchise Directory* lists and describes all established franchise opportunities in the UK. The *Franchise Magazine* provides up-to-date information about franchising.

Both of these publications are available for reference at all JobCentres. Copies can be obtained from:

The Franchise Development Service Ltd
Castle House
Castle Meadow
Norwich
NR2 1PJ

Franchising is common in the fast-food industry. Examples include Spud-U-Like and Pizza Hut. Further examples are Dyno-Rod in the plumbing business, Tumbletots, Body Shop and Prontaprint.

COURSEWORK ACTIVITIES

Identify a franchise opportunity that you find appealing. Find out:

- How much capital the franchisee would have to put into the business
- What the franchise opportunity involves
- The start-up help provided by the franchisor
- How much the franchisee would need to pay the franchisor on an ongoing basis

MATCH IT!

Can you help Frankie and Cleo to match the following terms and definitions?

Franchisee	A business marriage between an existing, proven business and a newcomer
Franchisor	The business granting a franchise
Franchise	An individual or group of individuals benefiting from using someone else's trading name and experience

16 Co-operatives

Defining a co-operative

If you look up the word 'co-operative' in the dictionary, you will find the following:

- 'Willing to co-operate; helpful'
- 'Acting jointly with others; co-operating'
- (Of an enterprise, farm, etc.): 'Owned collectively and managed for joint economic benefit'

'What is a co-operative?'

Retail co-operatives – the early days

Nowadays people tend to think of 'the Co-op' as just another supermarket chain. In fact, co-operatives are unique businesses which place special emphasis on serving the community.

The co-operative movement began with the Rochdale Pioneers in 1844. Twenty-eight weavers pooled money to buy food at wholesale prices. The food was then sold cheaply to members. Profits were shared out in the form of a dividend, depending on how much each member had bought.

In the late nineteenth century, co-ops flourished and societies sprang up all over Britain. Co-ops brought in the first supermarkets. However, the multiples like Tesco proved too competitive for the co-ops, which were organised into too many small societies and did not benefit enough from bulk buying. The co-ops also employed inexperienced managers and were not as slick as the new multiples. To fight back, small societies have merged together and the smaller shops have been closed.

The first co-op, situated in Toad Lane, Rochdale, is now a museum

Co-ops today

In 1996 the co-ops have their own Leo Hypermarkets which employ specialist managers and bulk-buying techniques, coupled with all the latest hypermarket technology. However, they continue to have small supermarkets, many of which help people in poorer communities where there are few local shops.

To become a shareholder in a retail co-op you need only buy a £1 share. Co-ops sometimes give stamps which can be collected and used in payment for goods. Other co-ops give benefits to customers by using profits to cut prices. Many co-ops aim to plough some of their profits back into the local community.

A modern co-operative superstore

Producer co-operatives

Producer co-operatives are groups which combine to produce a good or service.

They are usually registered as companies 'limited by guarantee'. This means that each member undertakes to fund any losses up to a certain amount. There are many types. A **workers' co-operative**, for example, is one that employs all or most of its members. In a workers' co-operative, members:

◆ share responsibility for the business

◆ work together

◆ take decisions together

◆ share the profits

Other examples of producer co-operatives are groups which grow fruit and vegetables, make furniture or organise child-minding.

The main problems that such co-operatives face are finance and organisation. Co-operatives sometimes find it difficult to raise capital from banks because they are not set up with the main aim of making a profit.

Marketing co-operatives

Marketing co-operatives are most frequently found in farming areas. The farmers set up a **marketing board** to take care of, among other things, grading, packaging, distributing, advertising and selling their products.

TASK

1 How do you become a member of a retail co-operative?

2 How are the principles of the co-operative societies different from those of supermarket chains?

3 How do co-operatives go about meeting social as well as profit-making objectives?

4 What arguments would you put forward in favour of shopping at the co-op?

 MATCH IT!

Can you help Frankie and Cleo to match the following terms and definitions?

Co-operative	A co-operative set up for the buying and selling of goods such as agricultural produce
Producer co-operative	A joint enterprise involving people working closely together and sharing ideas
Retail co-operative	A co-operative set up for the purpose of distributing finished goods to consumers
Marketing co-operative	A co-operative set up for the making of goods and services by a group of co-operators

17 Public Sector Organisations

What is the public sector?

The UK has a mixed economy. This means that, as well as many businesses being privately owned, there are others which are run by the state.

These state-controlled enterprises make up what is known as the public sector.

'I sometimes get confused between the terms "public sector" and "public companies". I know that public companies are owned by people who are called shareholders. But who owns the public sector?'

Public corporations

In the UK the government still owns a number of industries and businesses on behalf of the people. Most of these take the form of **public corporations**.

A public corporation is set up by an Act of Parliament. Examples of public corporations include the Bank of England and the British Broadcasting Corporation (BBC). Once a public corporation has been set up, the government appoints a chairperson to be responsible for its day-to-day running.

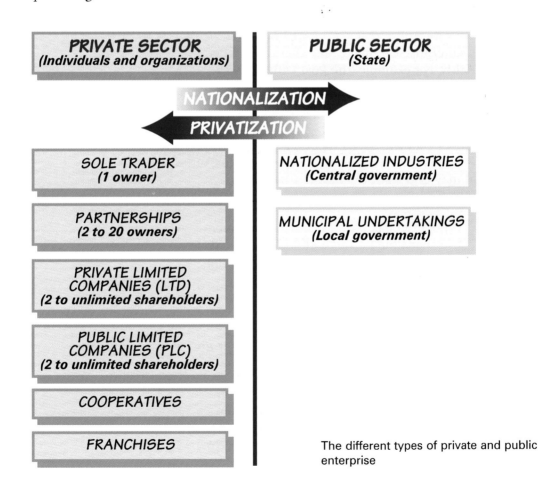

The different types of private and public enterprise

Why a public corporation?

There are a number of reasons why public corporations have been set up:

1 **To avoid wasteful duplication and confusion**
   For example, just imagine if more than one bank was allowed to print notes and coins in England and Wales. It would be difficult to control how much money each bank printed, so that the government might lose control over the money supply.

2 **To set up and run important but non-profitable services**
   For example, although the BBC makes sure that most of its programmes are profitable and popular, it also operates a loss-making service in some areas, e.g. producing special programmes for deaf people and for minority groups.

3 **To prevent exploitation of consumers**
   When there is only one enterprise providing a good or a service, it is sometimes better for it to be a government enterprise rather than a private one. Private firms will want to make a profit, while a government enterprise can make sure that consumers are treated fairly. For example, the Post Office makes sure that deliveries are made to remote parts of the UK at a fair price.

4 **To protect jobs and key industries**
   Many people feel that the government has a responsibility to protect jobs, even if this means lower profits. Government may also want to take steps to protect industries which are important to the UK economy.

Once a public corporation has been set up, a government minister is made responsible for the industry concerned. However, the minister chooses a **chairperson** to run the industry on a day-to-day basis.

The government sets targets for the industry to meet, and the chairperson and managers must then decide on the best way to meet them.

Privatisation

Since 1979, a number of public corporations have been privatised. This means that they have been sold from the public sector to the private sector, where they are owned by shareholders. (The latest privatisation in 1996 is of large parts of what used to be British Rail.)

Public corporation	Public company
Set up by Act of Parliament	Set up by issuing prospectus and inviting public to buy shares
Owned by the government	Owned by shareholders
Run by chairperson and managers appointed by government	Run by management team chosen by directors representing shareholders
Aims to provide a public service as well as having commercial goals	Commercial goals

Differences between a public corporation and a public company

Why privatise?

There are a number of reasons for privatisation:

1 Some people argue that state-run firms are not efficient because they do not have any real competition. They are also protected from bankruptcy, because the government always pays their debts.

2 It is argued that in a modern society as many people as possible should have shares in businesses. The idea is that everyone – not just the very rich – should become shareholders in enterprises such as British Telecom and British Gas. In 1979, when Margaret Thatcher became Prime Minister, there were 3 million shareholders in the UK; when she left office in 1990, there were 11 million.

3 Privatising industries raises large sums of money for the government *(see table below)*. This reduces the government's need to tax people and to borrow money.

Company	Date of sale	Proceeds (£m)
BP	1979-1990	5,273
Cable and Wireless	1981,1983,1985	1,021
British Telecommunications	1984,1991,1993	17,604
British Gas	1986,1990	7,793
British Steel	1988	2,425
Regional Water Authorities	1989-1992	3,468
Regional Electricity Companies	1990	7,997
Electricity Generating Companies	1991	2,969

Left: Some of Britain's main privatisations

Municipal undertakings

In the UK, certain services such as bus services and refuse collection are the responsibility of locally elected councils. Local councils receive money from two main sources:

◆ A grant given to them by central government

◆ Council Tax paid by local residents

Local councils often subsidise loss-making activities such as local parks which provide a real benefit to the community. Many local services have been privatised in the 1980s and 1990s. Refuse collection, leisure centres and local bus services – many of these are today in the hands of private firms who contract to carry out the work for the council. Their contracts are only renewed if the work is good and the price is not too high.

'I think that privatisation is a jolly good idea. It is only when firms are owned by private individuals like me that the best interests of all consumers will be served!'

Do you agree with Ron?

The privatisation of the electricity industry

The operations of the electricity industry can be broken down into four main parts:

- **Generation:** the production of electricity at power stations

- **Transmission:** the bulk transfer of electricity at high voltages through a central transmission system known as the National Grid

- **Distribution:** the transfer of electricity from the National Grid and its delivery to customers over local distribution systems

- **Supply:** the wholesale purchase of electricity from generating companies and its sale to the customer, using the transmission and distribution systems to deliver the power

Before 31st March 1990, the responsibility for carrying out these functions in England and Wales was in the hands of public corporations. Of these, the Central Electricity Generating Board (CEGB) produced most of the electricity generated. It also owned and operated the National Grid. Twelve area electricity boards distributed the electricity and sold it to customers within their own areas.

The new structure

In 1990 the electricity industry was privatised. A number of public limited companies were set up, with shares traded on the Stock Exchange. Under the new structure, the CEGB's businesses have been transferred to four companies. Three of these – National Power PLC, PowerGen PLC and Nuclear Electric PLC, are involved mainly in power generation. These companies now compete with each other and other generators. However, nuclear stations have been kept in the public sector under Nuclear Electric.

The National Grid is now owned and run by the National Grid Company PLC, which is itself owned by the 12 regional electricity companies. Distribution of electricity in a local area is now in the hands of the 12 electricity companies. These take supplies from the National Grid and feed power to their customers through their own distribution systems. The 12 companies have to make their systems available to private suppliers who want to supply electricity in their areas. Each of the regional electricity companies and any other supplier is now able to compete to supply customers, although the market will not be completely open until 31st March 1998. Currently, competition is mainly in the supply of electricity to large customers. In time, all consumers should be able to buy electricity from whichever source they choose.

Each of the electricity companies is required by law to supply premises within its area with electricity on request. Charges that they make are subject to the regulators' price controls.

'Does this mean that these pylons are no longer owned by the government but by private companies?'

TASK

Read the Case Study opposite, then answer the following questions:

1 Who are the main group of consumers of electricity?

2 How are they likely to have been affected by the privatisation process?

3 In what parts of the electricity industry is competition becoming fiercest? Why?

4 Do you think that competition is a good thing in the electricity industry? Make a list of the advantages and disadvantages.

5 Who owns the electricity companies?

6 What do you think that the owners of these companies will want to see them doing?

7 How do you think these aims will differ from those of the previous owners?

8 What safeguards do you think that the government needs to impose on the electricity companies to protect the public?

 Can you help Frankie and Cleo to match the following terms and definitions?

Regulator	Individual appointed by a government minister to take responsibility for running a nationalised industry
Chairperson	An organisation which runs a local service on behalf of, and is owned by, a local authority
Privatisation	That part of the economy which is run and controlled by the government
Public corporation	Independent official appointed to check on the workings of a privatised industry
Private sector	Businesses and enterprises owned and run by individuals working in their own interests
Public sector	A body set up to run a state-owned business
Municipal undertaking	Selling off government industries to private shareholders

2 18 Trends in Business Activity

A changing world

Today large firms are tending to get smaller as they reduce the number of staff that they employ. The growth of information technology means that firms no longer need large administrative departments. At the same time, the pace of technological change has increased, so that products date far more quickly than in the past.

'It's quite simple really – the larger my business becomes, the more successful it will be.'

'Small is beautiful'

In the old days, large companies dominated most markets.

These large companies had pyramid-shaped structures. Decisions were made at the top and passed down. People lower down the ladder were not usually allowed to make decisions without approval from above.

Large companies could afford expensive, state-of-the-art equipment (most notably computers), which were beyond the reach of smaller companies. They also attracted the best recruits by offering career ladders stretching for 40 years or more up to retirement, as well as perks such as company cars and private health insurance.

'But why is it that you often read in the paper about large companies cutting down the numbers they employ?'

Major changes

However, there have been two major developments in the 1980s and 1990s which have changed the picture:

1 Competition from the Pacific Rim countries
This began in the 1950s and 1960s, first in ship-building, then in car manufacture and electronic goods. In the 1970s and 1980s, the 'sunrise' countries such as Korea, Indonesia and Malaysia concentrated on more sophisticated products such as cars, cameras, fridges, etc. Their success was based partly on very competitive pricing, but more importantly on quality.

Through **Total Quality Management (TQM)**, all employees were given responsibility for setting and raising quality standards. The emphasis was on giving power to working groups rather than having a 'top-down' approach. As a result, the quality of Japanese and other goods from the Pacific Rim soon overtook those from Europe and the USA. It is only in the 1990s that the West has started to catch up by copying Japanese methods.

2 The development of information technology

Greater use of IT in organisations has transformed the way in which businesses are run. Today, desktop computers are extremely powerful and can be afforded by most companies. Small companies employing the latest information technology are now able to compete very strongly with larger companies at a fraction of the cost. This has forced larger companies to **downsize**.

'What is a small firm?'

Small and large firms

There are a number of different definitions of small firms. Under the Companies Act, a small firm was defined as one that had less than 50 employees. The Bolton Committee, which reported in 1971 on how small businesses work, defined a small company as having less than 200 employees.

◆ A small firm is likely to be a sole trader, a partnership or a private company. It is also likely to operate on one site and to have a limited amount of specialisation.

◆ Small firms often serve a small market. This means communication between members is usually good, and the company can make quick decisions.

◆ Large firms are most likely to be public limited companies, although some private companies and even partnerships are large. Mars, for example, is a private company and some very large groups of accountants are partnerships.

◆ Large companies may operate from several locations in more than one country. They may employ many people, be highly specialised, and use large quantities of capital. All this means that they can produce larger outputs with lower unit costs.

The growth of self-employment

It seems inevitable that more and more people will start working for themselves rather than working for very large organisations.

The diagram on the right shows that as we move into the 21st century, growing numbers of people will set up as **self-employed** , and that they will make up a larger proportion of the total working population. (The figures are derived from research carried out by the Institute for Employment Research in 1994.)

Interview someone you know who works in a small company. What do they see as being the advantages and disadvantages of small size?

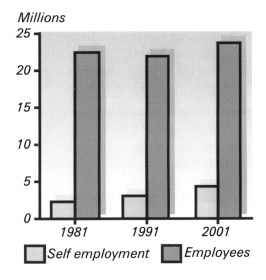

Graph showing the growth in the number of self-employed as a proportion of the working population

The need for enterprise

'Enterprise' was a favourite word of the 1980s. It is often associated with starting and running a business. But every kind of job or activity needs enterprising people. Nobody should be put off starting a business by fear of failure, or of losing interest. If you do have to give up and start working for somebody else again, you will almost certainly find that your enterprise and skill can still flourish to everyone's benefit. You will also be wiser for your experience.

Today, small businesses are seen as playing a vital part in the growth of the economy, but in the 1950s and 1960s things were very different. In 1967, for example, Michael Shanks wrote in a popular Pelican book, *The Innovators*:

> 'The trouble is… that a large proportion of British Industry consists of small firms and, while there is no necessary relationship between size and efficiency, many of the trends in modern technology do appear to favour large units.'

The trend to globalisation

An important trend associated with large firms is the spread of what is known as **globalisation.**

If you can produce millions or even billions of products, then you can spread your costs over a very large output. Coca-Cola is a classic example of this. Every day millions of cans of Coke are sold throughout the globe.

To achieve maximum benefits from this, firms need to make products which are instantly recognisable. A firm with a **global brand** is able to use the same packaging, the same advertising and the same images throughout the world. This greatly reduces costs.

Today, most products which are sold throughout the world make use of this kind of global branding. For example, Mars changed the name of one of its products from Marathon to Snickers so that it would be recognisable throughout the globe and could be easily pronounced by people whatever language they spoke.

Of course, sometimes there are product names that do not easily translate, such as Pschitt! lemonade from France and Plop chocolates from Denmark. In parts of Australia, people use the word Sellotape to mean a condom. Choosing a global brand therefore involves careful research!

COURSEWORK ACTIVITIES

Study the annual report and accounts of a large company. A useful source of information for this is *The Times 100* CD-ROM which is available in most schools and colleges.

• Where does the company operate?

• How many people does it employ?

• What is the size of its total sales?

• How much profit does it make?

• What evidence is given in the report that it benefits from being large?

Global branding ensures that Coca-Cola is known and recognised all over the world

The opening up of huge markets

Another major factor influencing business activity today is the opening up of huge new markets. Countries like India and China are made up of millions of potential consumers. Many people in these countries are now earning more money than in the past and are keen to buy branded goods. This means that instead of buying a local alcoholic drink, they may prefer a bottle of Teacher's or Johnny Walker whisky. These type of goods are often much in demand because they give the buyer added social status.

As a result, there are tremendous opportunities for large multinational companies to sell to the huge new markets of Asia and the former Soviet Union, as well as to emerging markets in Pacific Rim countries such as Thailand and Singapore.

COURSEWORK ACTIVITIES

Do you know anyone who used to work for another organisation but who has recently (in the last five years) started their own business? Why have they set up their own business? Interview them to find out.

 TASK

Set out a short chart showing the factors that in recent times have encouraged firms to grow larger or smaller.

Where do you think the balance lies between these two forces?

MATCH IT!

Can you help Frankie and Cleo to match the following terms and definitions?

Pacific Rim	Person who runs their own business or is 'their own boss'
Huge market	Using the same public face or image throughout the world
Global branding	The group of countries which includes the Western seaboard of the Americas, Japan, East Asia (including China) and Australasia
Globalisation	Taking risks and showing initiative and imagination
Self-employed	A mass market made up of hundreds of millions of consumers
Entrepreneurship	Organising a business so as to operate and trade in a standard way throughout the world

2 19 Specialisation

The growth of specialisation

Very early on in the history of the human race, people discovered that, rather than everyone meeting their own needs for food, clothing and shelter, it made sense for some tasks to be performed by specialists.

Some people could specialise in hunting, others could go and gather berries, while others built shelters or made weapons.

In this country until fairly recent times you would have found a blacksmith, baker, butcher and many other specialist trades in every village.

As the economy became more developed, individuals were able to sell their specialist skills in return for money or a salary or wage. They could then use their income to buy items or services produced by other specialists. If we concentrate on what we do best, we can all gain from this process of specialisation.

The division of labour

The **division of labour** is one example of specialisation which is very important in modern economies. Division of labour involves breaking down a production process into a number of clearly defined specialist tasks. The reason for doing this is that the total output of a group can be increased, if, instead of each person trying to do everything, each one specialises in a particular skill or activity.

The most famous early example of division of labour was in a pin factory, described by Adam Smith in his book *The Wealth of Nations* (see Case Study opposite). Smith noted that where operations were divided and where workers specialised, output was far greater than it would otherwise have been.

Other forms of specialisation

◆ Specialisation of **equipment** – e.g. specialist machines performing specialist tasks and processes

◆ Specialisation of **plant** – e.g. different factories specialising in making different things

◆ Specialisation by **firms** – different firms concentrating on different lines, e.g. Shell on oil, gas and chemical products, Virgin on air travel, contraceptives, soft drinks.

TASK

Frankie and Cleo are making a quick list of 10 specialist jobs involved in bringing tinned fruit to people in supermarkets. Help them to list the specialists.

'There are the lorry drivers that bring the products to the supermarket... And of course the people that pick the fruit in the first place... Who else is there?'

◆ Specialisation by **region** and by **nation**. Many regions still specialise in producing certain products. For example, Scotland is famous for whisky; parts of France, Germany, Spain, Australia and South Africa focus on wine; coastal areas of Portugal on fishing, Nigeria on oil production, Uganda on sisal, etc.

Comparative advantage

Specialisation is often explained in terms of the theory of **comparative advantage**. This states that resources are used in the best (most cost-effective) way when they are used in areas where they are most efficient.

For example, a golf professional may be good not only at her sport but also at being a solicitor. However, she will be well advised to concentrate on her golf, because golf is her **best line**, i.e. the area in which she is most talented.

As a solicitor, she may be able to earn £40 an hour. But as a golf professional, she can earn £50 an hour. She can then pay a solicitor to handle her legal business and pay the solicitor out of her golf earnings. For every hour that she hires a solicitor at £40 an hour, she is making a £10 profit from concentrating on what she does best.

The same rule applies to any form of specialisation. For example, it makes sense for countries to use their land to grow crops which earn them the most revenue, rather than things which they can import cheaply.

The advantages of specialisation

The advantages of specialisation are:

1 Resources can be concentrated where they are most productive.

2 Factors of production become more efficient if they are concentrated on a set task. For example, the more skilled the worker becomes at a particular task, the more they produce.

3 Specialisation allows a larger output to be produced at a lower unit cost.

4 Concentrations of specialists can lead to sharing of skills and experience. This is why footballers will improve their game far quicker when they play for a top Premier League club rather than playing in the Diadora League!

CASE STUDY

Pin-making in Adam Smith's day

'...To take an example from a very trifling manufacture... the trade of pinmaker. An inexperienced workman, unfamiliar with this business, could scarce, with his utmost effort make one pin in an entire day. But in the way in which this business is now organised, not only is the whole work in a particular trade, but it is divided into a number of individual branches, each of which can be considered as a particular trade of its own. One man draws out the wire, another straightens it, a third cuts it, a fourth points it, a fifth grinds it at the top in preparation for the head; to make the head requires two or three distinct operations; to put it on is a peculiar business; to whiten the pins is another; it is even a trade by itself to put them into the paper; and the important business of making a pin is, in this manner, divided into about eighteen distinct operations, which in some manufactories, are all undertaken by separate people.'

From *The Wealth of Nations* by Adam Smith, 1776

TASK

1 How was it possible to produce pins using lots of specialists?

2 What examples of division of labour can you think of today?

The disadvantages of specialisation

However, there are also several drawbacks to specialisation:

1 Specialisation can lead to monotony. If workers repeat the same task over and over again, they may become bored and demotivated.

2 Where tasks are closely linked, delays or hold-ups in one area can disrupt the whole production process.

3 Specialisation may lead to workers becoming little more than machine operators. This can lead to a loss of skills over time.

4 Narrow specialism may make it difficult for factors of production to respond to change. The employee who has done the same task for ten years will have problems when suddenly required to do a different task.

5 **Multiskilling** is often more useful than specialism. Someone with many skills, rather than just one, is often in a better position to look at the various parts of an organisation and come up with good ideas for change and improvement.

'Specialisation is the way forward! There's no point in people being able to do a lot of different tasks and trades. They should specialise in what they do best, just like in Adam Smith's day! Good old Adam!'

Do you agree with Ron?

 Can you help Frankie and Cleo to match the following terms and definitions?

Specialisation	Production method in which individual employees carry out particular tasks
Generalism	The benefit to be gained from individuals or other units concentrating on their best lines
Division of labour	Situation in which factories and other productive units focus on specific lines
Regional specialisation	General term used to describe the concentration of factors of production, regions and nations on specific lines
Comparative advantage	Ability of individuals, groups, areas, or productive factors to do a range of different tasks, or produce a range of different products
Specialisation of plant	A geographical concentration on specialist lines

20 Business Organisation

What is a business organisation?

It is not easy to come up with an exact definition of the word 'organisation' that will fit all organisations. However, the following features help us to arrive at a working definition of the word.

'What exactly is a business organisation?'

Organisations are:

◆ Made up of several people, who see themselves as being members of the organisation and who generally are willing to co-operate

◆ Mainly long-term. New people come into the organisation, and other members leave the organisation

◆ Made up of different people who do different tasks

◆ Run and organised according to some basic rules and procedures

Features of business organisations

We have already seen that business organisations take a number of forms, from sole traders through to multinational companies. Below *(left)* is one possible description of a business organisation. The diagram on the right shows the same definition applied to an actual company, Marks & Spencer:

TASK

Do the following have the features of an organisation described on the left?

* Your school or college
* A church
* Manchester United Football Club
* Marks & Spencer
* A street corner gang
* Your local cinema
* Passengers on a railway train

A group of people

form

A structure with rules and authority

pursuing

An objective or set of objectives

using

Resources

to meet

Customers' needs and wants in exchange for monetary reward

Shareholders, directors, managers and employees of Marks & Spencer

form

The public limited company Marks & Spencer in which there are rules and people holding posts and offices

pursuing

Customer satisfaction; quality products; profits for shareholders; and challenging, enjoyable jobs for employees

using

Many different types of inputs such as bought-in foodstuffs and clothes

to meet

The wants and needs of Marks & Spencer customers

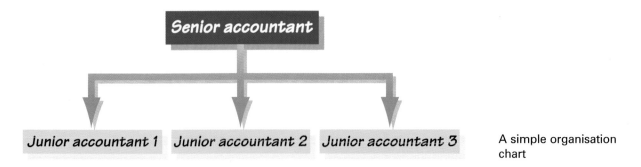

A simple organisation chart

Organisation charts

An **organisation chart** is a drawing to show the roles of various individuals in an organisation, and the relationships between them. For example, the diagram above shows that a senior accountant has three junior accountants working for her.

Every organisational structure can be charted in this way, to show the departments, how they link together and the main lines of authority between them. This gives us a 'snapshot' view of how the organisation is made up. It shows lines of decision-making and tiers of responsibility. Looking at an organisation chart may also help us to see any weaknesses in the organisation.

Levels within an organisation

When drawing an organisation chart, it is usual to show posts which have roughly equal amounts of responsibility on the same level. In the example below, the

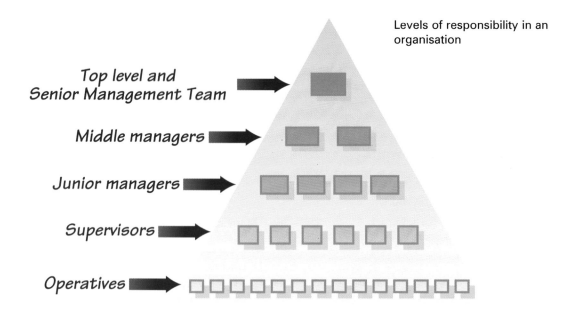

Levels of responsibility in an organisation

managing director and the senior management team are at the top level. At the next level are the middle managers. Then there are junior managers, supervisors, and finally operatives at the bottom level.

Span of control

The **span of control** of an individual is the number of people he or she manages or supervises directly. The diagram on the right shows an organisation with a narrow span of control. No one member of this organisation is directly responsible for more than two subordinates.

There is a limit to the number of people who can be supervised well by one person. Choosing the best span of control means striking a balance between having control over people below you (subordinates) and being able to trust them.

Tall and flat organisations

A narrow span of control makes it possible to control people and to communicate with them closely. However, the disadvantage is that this may lead to too many levels of management. This kind of **tall organisation**, as it is called, can be difficult to run.

Having a wider span means managers must have far more trust in subordinate staff. Fewer managers are needed, and this gives a hierarchy with fewer levels, i.e. a **flat organisation**.

How many people should managers have within their span of control? It is hard to say. Generally speaking, the higher up an organisation an individual is, the fewer people he or she should have in their direct span of control.

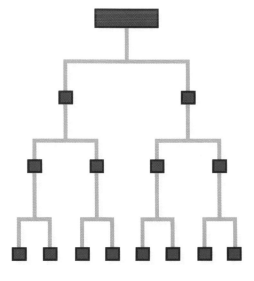

A narrow span of control

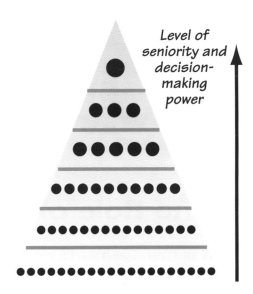

A tall organisation

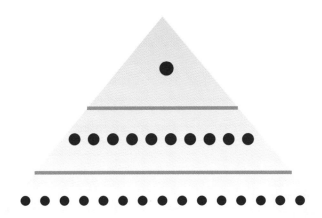

A flat organisation

MATCH IT!

Can you help Frankie and Cleo to match the following terms and definitions?

Subordinate	A diagram illustrating the roles and relationships within an organisation
Hierarchy	An organisation with relatively few layers between the top and bottom
Organisational level	A highly structured pattern of offices and posts involving a number of layers of command
Span of control	A system having an established structure in which people work and deal with one another in a co-ordinated and co-operative way to meet certain objectives
Organisation	Posts involving similar levels of power and authority
Flat organisation	A person working at a junior level to someone else
Tall organisation	The number of people that a person manages or supervises directly
Organisation chart	An organisation with many different levels in a hierarchy

21 The Role of Management

What is management?

Every organisation has objectives. Managers are people who help to steer the organisation in the direction of meeting these objectives.

Management has been described as:

'...the process of planning, organising, leading and controlling the efforts of organisation members and of using all organisational resources to achieve stated organisational goals.'

Or, to put it more simply:

'... getting things done by other people.'

A manager's job is to maintain control over the way an organisation does things, and at the same time to lead, inspire and direct the people under them.

'What do managers do? Well, in my business, almost everything!'

POSDCORB

A few years ago, business schools used the mnemonic POSDCORB to help students learn the key elements of management:

P   is for **planning.** Planning involves making decisions today about what you are going to be doing tomorrow.

O   is for **organising.** This means making sure that every last detail is organised, with nothing left to chance.

S   is for **staffing.** This means getting the people to do the jobs that the organisation requires in the best way possible.

D   is for **directing.** Directing involves giving the orders and directions so that things are done in the way that the manager requires.

Co-   is for **co-ordinating.** This means making sure that all the various parts of an organisation pull in the same direction.

R   is for **reporting.** Managers need to produce a lot of verbal and written reports, setting out what is and what should be happening in an organisation.

B   is for **budgeting.** A budget is a future plan, forecasting how resources (particularly financial resources) will be used.

  TASK

Read the Case Study below, then show how Fizzo's managers have thought carefully about:

1   The company's long-term objectives

2   The products on which it plans to concentrate

3   Its future strategy and how to build an advantage over rivals

4   Meeting customer needs

5   The resources the company will need in order to achieve its objectives.

CASE STUDY

Fizzo soft drinks

Fizzo is a world-famous maker of soft drinks. Its aim is to maximise sales worldwide so as to make the maximum possible profit for its shareholders and employees, while satisfying its customers with quality refreshing drinks.

Fizzo is famous for its lemonade and citrus drinks. It recognises that it will never be a major player in the global cola markets, which are dominated by Coca-Cola and Pepsi. So it has decided to try and be market leader in the non-cola fizzy drinks market.

A recent step for the company was to take over Grandma Salts, which is one of the most popular soft drinks in the world. By taking over Grandma Salts, it has instantly become the largest non-cola soft drinks manufacturer in the USA. The US market is the biggest in the world, so the firm is now able to produce very large quantities at far lower cost than its rivals. Top managers see this move as being an important stepping-stone to gaining global dominance in the non-cola market. Fizzy drinks are bought globally, particularly by the under-35s, and consumption is higher in hotter countries (depending on the season). In order to carry out this expansion programme Fizzo has borrowed several million pounds from a number of international banks.

Departmental organisation in a large business

Large organisations in the UK are mostly private companies, public companies or public corporations *(see Chapter 14)*. Here we focus on a large public company.

The company will be owned by **shareholders** who appoint a committee known as a **board of directors** to represent their interests. The board of directors then appoint a **managing director**. Like a head teacher in a school or the principal of a college, the managing director has the job of making sure that all the various departments are running well.

Every organisation is different and has different needs and objectives. The example on the opposite page may be found in some company structures, but many variations are possible.

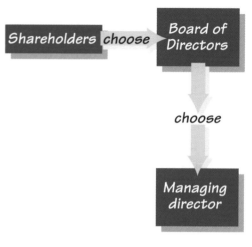

The control structure of a large public company

Management responsibilities

The company secretary and the legal department
The **company secretary** is responsible for all the legal affairs of the company. If paperwork is not done properly, he or she could end up in court. He or she must fill in and periodically amend official company records and documents such as the Memorandum and Articles of Association. He or she must also keep the share register. Departmental managers may consult the company secretary on legal matters.

The administration department
Many large firms have a central office which is responsible for controlling the general paperwork of the firm. This department may handle the filing of materials, the sorting of the company's mail, word-processing and data-handling facilities. Modern offices use information technology to service all these key areas.

The chief accountant and the accounts office
The **chief accountant** is responsible for running the accounts department. The accounts section must keep a detailed record of all money paid in and out, and present the final balance sheet at the end of the year. Modern accounts are stored on computer files, and procedures are greatly simplified by the use of computers.

The production department
The **production manager** is responsible for making sure that raw materials are provided and made into finished goods as cost-effectively as possible. He or she

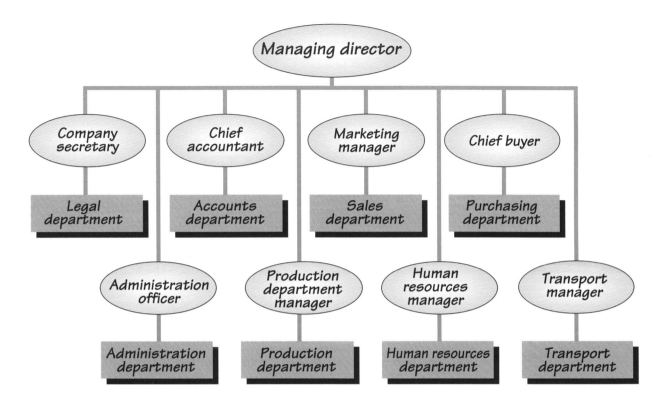

Above: An 'organogram' showing the structure of a typical large public company

must make sure that work is carried out smoothly and supervise procedures for maximising efficiency.

The marketing manager and the marketing/sales department

Marketing may be combined with sales, or the two functions may be separate.

◆ Marketing is concerned with finding out what people want and then meeting their wants and needs at a profit.

◆ Sales is concerned with all aspects of selling to customers.

In a combined sales/marketing department, the manager will be responsible for market research, promotions, advertising, distribution and organising product sales.

The human resources manager and the human resources department

The **human resources department** (sometimes called the **personnel department**) is responsible for the recruitment and training of staff. It is also responsible for health and safety at work, trade union negotiation and staff welfare. It also makes sure that the organisation focuses on meeting the needs of its human resources.

The chief buyer and the purchasing department
The **purchasing department** of a firm is responsible for all items bought by that firm. It sends for quotations from suppliers, issues orders and keeps track of the delivery of goods. It also checks the price, quantity and quality of goods received.

The transport department
This department is responsible for obtaining supplies and making sure that goods are delivered in good condition, in the right place and at the right time.

MATCH IT!

Can you help Frankie and Cleo to match the following terms and definitions?

Budgeting	Making sure that an organisation has the right people to do the jobs required
Co-ordinating	Person responsible for human resource aspects of an organisation
Staffing	Person responsible for ensuring that all legal affairs and official documents of an organisation are in order
Planning	
Marketing manager	Taking responsibility for people, materials, machines, money, information and time management in an organisation
Resource management	Manager responsible for anticipating, identifying and meeting consumer requirements at a profit
Company secretary	Forecasting future requirements of an organisation in order to help forward planning
Personnel manager	Making decisions today to meet tomorrow's requirements
	Making sure that plans, activities and actions of an organisation coincide and meet agreed objectives

22 Business Decision-making

Who makes the major decisions in a business?

Business decisions can be made and carried out in a number of ways.

Top-down decision-making

In some organisations all major decisions will be taken by senior managers and passed down to junior employees.

This type of organisation is said to be **hierarchical.** Each employee knows who their line manager is and takes commands from them. There may be just a few layers in the hierarchy, or there may be many.

This can be an effective arrangement when work is very routine and easy to predict, but it also has its problems:

1 Lower-level employees may become discontented because they are not allowed to show initiative. They may grumble about the 'hierarchy' (by which they mean people above them) and become unco-operative.

2 When decisions need to be made quickly, junior employees may be unwilling or unable to react. They may say things like, *'I can't do anything about it. It's not my job. You'll have to wait until Mrs X comes back.'*

3 Hierarchical organisations can be costly to run, if there are a lot of people wasting time reporting to each other.

Flow of communication

Senior managers

Middle managers

Supervisory staff

Operatives and other employees

Flow of communication in a hierarchical organisation

'You can't beat a top-down company. The manager needs to be the "gaffer". That way everybody is happy because they know exactly what is expected of them. It works every time. If somebody doesn't like it they can always be replaced by someone better!'

What weaknesses can you see in Ron's argument?

Democratic decision-making

In contrast to an hierarchical system, an organisation may be arranged on more **democratic** lines. Here, individuals are appointed to carry out tasks according to their skills and experience. They are expected to think and act for themselves. One way of representing an organisation like this would be as a circle. Each member is an independent decision-maker, but consults regularly with the others. An example might be a group of vets working as a partnership.

Centralisation and decentralisation

Centralisation

Centralisation means keeping major responsibilities in a business at the centre of the organisation, e.g. at head office. With this system, you have a big head office with small branches and other operating units. This was the picture in many UK companies until recently.

Decentralisation

Decentralisation involves giving decision-making power to an organisation's operating units, e.g. regional offices, factories, retailing units and plants. Today, most large companies are shedding a lot of staff from their central offices.

To make decentralisation possible, operational units must be linked by modern communications facilities such as networked computers, organisation-wide databases, fax communication systems, and so on.

The illustration *(below right)* shows a much smaller head office with relatively bigger branches.

Reasons for decentralisation

There are a number of reasons for decentralisation:

1 People at the top of an organisation cannot be expected to know everything. It may be helpful therefore to give more responsibility to experts lower down the organisation, who can see the picture 'on the ground'.

2 Decentralisation makes possible a quick response to local needs and conditions.

3 Decentralisation may help to motivate employees to make decisions for themselves.

4 Decentralisation can reduce costs, making an organisation more competitive.

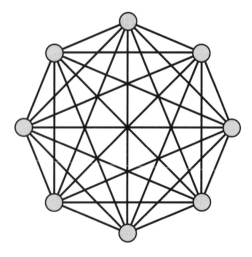

A circular or democratic network

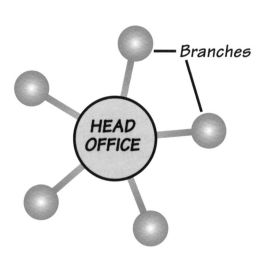

A centralised structure

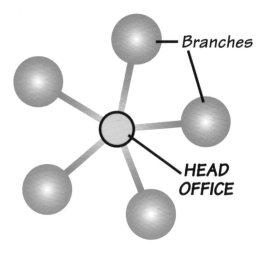

A decentralised structure

CHAPTER 22

Strategic and tactical decision-making

Strategy

Every company should be clear about its **strategy**. Strategy is about the big decisions that a company makes. It covers major decisions about:

◆ What?

◆ How?

◆ When?

◆ Where?

For example, a supermarket chain may have a strategy to become the market leader in out-of-town super-market sales in the UK.

To do this, it may set itself the target of having a store near every major town and city in the UK by the year 2000 and offering the best-value-for-money prices to be found in that locality.

Tactics

Having established its basic strategy, it will need to operate on a day-to-day **tactical** basis to meet these aims. In the short term it will need to alter its working practices and policies.

For example, when a rival sets out to undercut its prices, it may for a time enter into a price war over key items. When rivals offer free car parking for customers who spend more than £50, it may retaliate by offering free car-parking for customers who purchase goods worth over £10 and so on. The day-to-day tactics should not deflect the company from its overall strategy.

CASE STUDY

Decentralisation at Shell

One form of decentralisation is shown by recent developments at Shell UK. The organisational hierarchy of the company has been 'flattened' by removing layers, so that each divisional head now reports directly to the managing director, rather than via other directors.

Another way has been to create separate profit centres: sections of the overall business are given the responsibility and resources to operate as if they were independent. For example, Shell's bitumen business is now run by Shell Bitumen UK, a separate profit centre within Shell Oil UK.

TASK

1 Why do you think that an organisation like Shell is decentralising?

2 What are the main advantages and disadvantages of such decentralisation?

TASK

Strategy or tactics?

Which of the following decisions by a supermarket chain are strategic in nature and which are tactical?

* The decision to send Christmas cards to head office staff

* The decision to convert from a private to a public limited company

* The decision to alter the layout of the car park in the company's Watford store

* The decision to close the dry-cleaning service in one of the company's stores

* The decision to introduce in-house bakeries throughout the chain

* The decision to open ten new stores a year

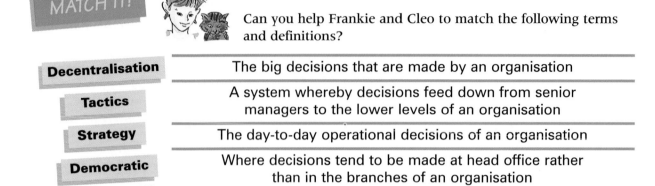

MATCH IT!

Can you help Frankie and Cleo to match the following terms and definitions?

Decentralisation	The big decisions that are made by an organisation
Tactics	A system whereby decisions feed down from senior managers to the lower levels of an organisation
Strategy	The day-to-day operational decisions of an organisation
Democratic	Where decisions tend to be made at head office rather than in the branches of an organisation
Top-down	Giving decision-making powers to lower levels within an organisation
Centralisation	An organisation in which everyone is involved in the decision-making process

23 New Technology and Business

What do we mean by technology?

Technology simply means using our knowledge to develop tools, products and processes for human purposes.

At any one time we are able to use our existing knowledge to make goods in a certain way. By learning new ways of doing things, however, and using new technology, we can change and improve the way we do things.

'People are always talking about "the latest technology" – but what exactly do they mean by technology?'

Techniques of production

A **technique** is a way of making things, using available resources such as human labour, machines, etc.

For example, a cook may have special techniques for using equipment and ingredients to produce a dish in a special way. This technique may differ from that of other cooks. One may use a gas oven, another an electric oven; one may use different spices and ingredients, another may beat the mixture for longer and so on.

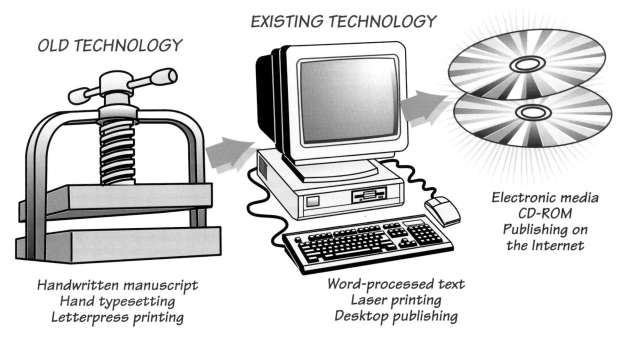

OLD TECHNOLOGY

EXISTING TECHNOLOGY

FUTURE TECHNOLOGY

Handwritten manuscript
Hand typesetting
Letterpress printing

Word-processed text
Laser printing
Desktop publishing

Electronic media
CD-ROM
Publishing on
the Internet

New technology has transformed the printing and publishing industry

Understanding technological change

Technological change occurs when new techniques of production are added to the ones we already know. For example, a cook who goes on a training course may learn new ways of preparing dishes. A UK factory manager who visits Japan may learn new techniques for producing electrical goods – and so on.

Defining high-tech industries

When asked to define modern technology, most people will mention microchips, computers and telecommunications equipment. High-technology products generally involve a high concentration of scientific and engineering skills.

High-tech industries are generally thought to be those that employ large numbers of scientists and engineers, or spend heavily on research and development. But a broader view is that modern technology involves rapid changes in techniques of production.

We can see that this definition would apply to a wide range of businesses. For example, the banking and insurance industries are being transformed by information technology, and motor manufacture and electronics are being transformed by automatic production techniques and the use of robots.

'What do we mean by "high-tech"?'

CASE STUDY

Moving from 2D to 3D seismic surveys

In the earliest days of the oil industry, an oil company would bore holes in the ground to discover deposits of oil. However, since 1936, two-dimensional (2D) seismic surveying has been the principal method of locating and mapping underground structures likely to contain oil. Nearly all the world's current oil and gas fields were first located by 2D seismic surveys.

The technique works by creating a shockwave of sound which passes downwards through the rock layers before being reflected to the surface, where it is captured by detectors similar to microphones *(right).* The returning pattern of soundwaves is then analysed and interpreted in map form.

It is essential that the results of such surveys are accurate, because every North Sea oil well costs between £5 million and £20 million. Digging a well that turns out to be dry would be a tremendous waste of money.

The breakthrough into 3D seismic surveys has been a great technological leap forward for the oil industry. The difference has been likened to the crackle of the earliest wax-cylinder gramophone, compared to the pure clarity of today's CD player.

The density of data rises by a factor of 1,600 in a typical case – with immense advantages in terms of clarity and accuracy. When processed by computer, this mass of data can be converted into visual form, with colours and shading used to highlight the complex features being studied. The chances of mapping out potential oil and gas fields accurately is much higher with 3D than with old-fashioned 2D methods.

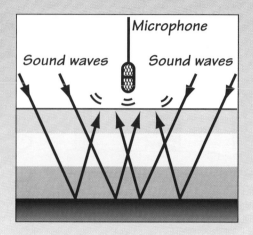

2D seismic surveying

Maps produced using 3D seismic survey techniques

  TASK

1 Identify three stages of technology used in identifying potential oil fields.

2 What is the latest technology in this field?

3 How is this technology of greater use to an oil company than previous technologies?

4 Why is it so important to develop new technologies?

5 Can you identify a similar technological breakthrough in another field?

A revolution in information technology

Go into a modern bank and you will find that the person who serves you over the counter has instant access to information just by pressing a few keys on a computer keyboard. Even a junior bank employee has access to far more information than a branch manager in the 1970s.

New technology has been the major driving force behind this change, and every business student should be aware of this. You must make sure that your information technology skills are of a high standard. Knowledge of IT is essential for most of the jobs that will be available in the next century.

The impact of IT on business

One of the major results of the IT revolution is that small companies can compete with large companies on far more equal terms. The so-called **information revolution** has also led to massive changes in the way businesses are run:

1 Company databases are no longer the exclusive property of head office. Everyone with a laptop or pocketbook computer has access to them – and, via the Internet, to a world of information beyond.

2 Computer-aided manufacturing has raised levels of quality and accuracy. Factory robots have taken over many routine, repetitive, noisy and dirty jobs, leaving people free to supervise and manage.

3 Sales specialists are able to offer customers a complete range of personalized options, with computers taking care of registering orders, requesting items from stock, scheduling delivery, etc.

4 Global IT networks allow users to communicate instantly around the world. This is especially true of the financial markets, where currency transactions take place twenty-four-hours a day.

5 Routine accounts work can be done anywhere in the world.

6 Even highly skilled work requiring close working contact with managers can be contracted-out to sites thousands of miles away. For instance, engineers in Aberdeen designing offshore oil platforms can work with qualified draughtsmen and women in India. The time difference enables the work to be carried out overnight.

COURSEWORK ACTIVITIES

It is easy to take for granted the vast range of products that we use every day involving new technology.

1 Make a list of products which you use in your household which you would describe as 'high-tech'.

2 Explain how each of the products you have mentioned contributes to improving your way of life.

Can you help Frankie and Cleo to match the following terms and definitions?

Technology	A way of combining existing resources to make a product
Technique	The application of knowledge to make products and carry out processes
High-tech	Technology involving a high input of research, engineering and scientific skills
New technology	The production, storage and communication of information using computers and micro-electronics
Technological change	Applying new knowledge to change the way of making things, and making new products
Information technology	Adding new techniques of production to those already known

24 Market Research

The importance of marketing

Many companies today claim that their main aim is to satisfy consumer needs. Instead of having to use hard-selling techniques to persuade customers to buy, these market-led companies sell goods easily because they produce what consumers want.

In its simplest form marketing answers the question:

'What does the customer want to buy?'

A definition of marketing which you should learn is:

'Marketing is the anticipation and identification of consumer wants and needs in order to meet these needs, and to make a profit.'

Researching the market

Market research means systematically gathering, recording and analysing data about the market for goods and services.

To find out what the customer wants, a wide variety of market research techniques are used. These involve asking the kind of questions shown in the diagram below.

MARKET RESEARCH QUESTIONS

| What is the target market? | Where are they? | What do they want? | When do they want it? | Can we satisfy them? | How can we improve it for them? |

MARKET INFORMATION
TRENDS
CUSTOMER PROFILES

CASE STUDY

A bright idea

Frankie and Cleo have come up with a bright idea. They have produced a new kind of shortbread which is very popular with their friends. Their plan is to sell the shortbread to the people of Midtown in packets that Frankie is designing. However, they are not sure whether the shortbread will be bought by enough people, or what price to charge or where to sell from.

They want some evidence to prove that their shortbread will be a success. This means carrying out some market research!

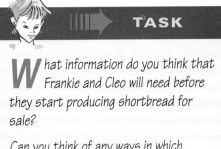

TASK

What information do you think that Frankie and Cleo will need before they start producing shortbread for sale?

Can you think of any ways in which Frankie and Cleo might collect the information they need?

Methods of market research

A firm can employ either its own (in-house) marketing department, or an outside specialist organisation. Market research can be classed under two headings:

◆ **Desk research.** This involves using existing sources of information to research the market. It is sometimes called **secondary research.**

◆ **Field research.** This is the process of gathering new information about the market by going into the 'field' (e.g. house-to-house or street surveys). It is sometimes called **primary research.**

Desk research

A popular form of desk research is for a company to study its own sales figures for trends. Or it may analyse requests from customers for changes in existing products. It may also explore customer requests for new models or lines.

An organisation can also investigate its competitors' products to find out their popular and unpopular points. This can help them develop new and improved products of their own at a competitive price.

For example, Frankie and Cleo might go to another town to investigate sales of shortbread by a rival firm.

An organisation can also study published sources of information. These include:

1 Government statistics

   Useful sources of information include census data produced by the Office of Population Censuses and Surveys. A full census is carried out every ten years. It shows numbers of people in different age groups, and where they live.

   Business Monitor, published quarterly, provides a lot of useful information about different markets.

2 Published market research information

   Today there are a number of market research organisations such as Mintel, which work full-time to produce statistics about different markets. In return for a fee, Mintel provides a monthly journal. This contains reports on consumer markets ranging from bread and alcoholic drinks to insurance.

3 Quality newspapers and magazines

   Papers like *The Independent* and specialist marketing magazines provide a lot of useful information about market trends.

COURSEWORK ACTIVITIES

Write to some companies to ask for promotional literature which shows how they go about identifying and meeting the needs of their customers.

Can you identify specific statements which show that they are focused on marketing?

'Market research is a waste of time. It is a costly business, and by the time you have collected your information, it is out of date!'

Do you think Ron Rust might be making a mistake?

CHAPTER 24

Desk research has two key advantages over field research:

◆ It is cheaper

◆ The information already exists, so it is quicker and easier to obtain.

Field research

There are several field research methods which are used by businesses. Each method involves using one or more of the following:

1 Questionnaires

These are lists of questions designed specifically for a task. Questionnaires can be completed by holding an interview. This can take place either face-to-face, over the telephone, or through the post.

2 Test marketing

This is when a product is marketed to just a small part of a total market to see if it is suitable for wider release.

3 Consumer panels

This is where a selected group of people are given a product and asked to comment in detail.

TASK

Which of the following are primary and which secondary market research sources?

• Conducting a survey of every fifth person who passes you in the street

• Looking up information about people buying different types of insurance in a Mintel survey

• Asking each of your classmates 20 questions

• Copying out information from your local evening newspaper

• Interviewing people through a phone survey

• Sending a questionnaire through the post

Can you help Frankie and Cleo to match the following terms and definitions?

Marketing	Trying out the product in just one part of a total market
Market research	Finding out opinions from a small group of people
Test marketing	Anticipating, identifying and meeting consumers' wants and needs in order to make a profit
Desk research	The systematic collection and analysis of information about markets
Field research	Commercial organisation providing detailed statistics about different markets in regular publications
Government statistics	Research which uses secondary sources of information
Mintel	Information provided by the Central Statistical Office and other public sector departments and bodies
Consumer panels	Original research involving the collection of primary information

3 25 **Consumer Behaviour**

What makes people buy?

In business it is important to have a clear idea of why consumers buy goods. This is an important part of marketing. Find out what drives consumer buying decisions and you will be well placed to meet consumer needs.

'How do people go about making a buying decision?'

The buying decision can be broken down into a number of stages:

1 A consumer recognises that there is a problem, e.g.:

   'We're running out of breakfast cereal, so we will have to buy some more soon'.

   Or, the consumer identifies an opportunity, e.g.:

   'It's time for the January sales. If we look carefully we may be able to buy some electrical goods at bargain prices.'

2 The consumer will then search for information enabling them to make a good buy. For example, they may go round several shops comparing prices, looking in catalogues, etc.

3 The consumer then weighs up the alternatives, e.g.:

   'Coca-Cola costs 45 pence in a garage, 30 pence in the corner shop, and only 25p in a supermarket.'

4 The consumer then decides what to buy and where, and purchases the good.

5 After buying, the consumer reviews the purchase, e.g.:

   'I thought I was getting a bargain when I bought that Hoover in the discount store. But the problem is, there's no after-sales service. Next time I may buy from a more expensive shop which offers after-sales service.'

This simple model can be set out in a diagram, showing that there is feedback between each of the stages in the decision process:

Below: The purchasing process

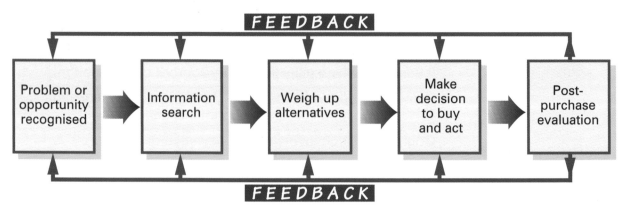

TASK

*T*hink of an item that you have recently bought. Draw a flow chart showing each of the stages involved in making the buying decision. For example, in the first box of the flow chart you might write:

'I needed to buy a new pair of jeans to go to a party!'

Individual consumer requirements

Because consumers are human, they are all different. Only a few companies (for example, made-to-measure tailors and hairdressers) can provide products designed specifically for each individual customer.

But there are two ways in which a business can get as close as possible to meeting the individual needs of its customers:

◆ Market segmentation

◆ Customer service

1 Market segmentation

Market segmentation is the process of dividing a market up into different groups of customers, in order to create different products to meet their specific needs.

Primary segmentation

The most obvious type of segmentation is between customers who buy entirely different products. For example, a firm like Colgate-Palmolive will make toothpaste and soap to meet quite different customer needs. There are not many people who clean their teeth with soap!

Segmentation by demographics and psychographics

Further segmentation can be based on **demographic** and **psychographic** factors:

◆ Demographics segments people according to facts about them as members of the population, e.g. their sex, their age, the size of their family, their income, where they live, the type of work they do, etc.

◆ Psychographics segments people according to their **lifestyle.** A person's lifestyle is their individual pattern of behaviour, made up of their attitudes, beliefs, interests and habits.

'Segmentation sounds as if the market is being divided into segments – just like an orange.'

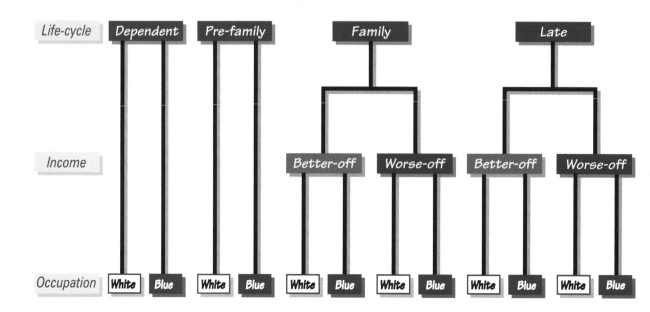

Life-cycle	Dependent	Pre-family	Family				Late			

Income			Better-off	Worse-off	Better-off	Worse-off

Occupation	White	Blue	White	Blue	White	Blue	White	Blue	White	Blue	White	Blue

◆ **Sagacity lifestyle grouping** combines psychographic and demographic segmentation. This approach works on the principle that people behave in different ways as they go through life. Four main stages of the life-cycle are identified, and these are sub-divided according to income and occupation groups (white-collar and blue-collar occupations).

The life-cycle stages can be grouped in the following way:

◆ **Dependent** – mainly under-24s, living at home or full-time students

◆ **Pre-family** – under-35s who have established their own household but have no children

◆ **Family** – parents under 65 with one or more children in the household

◆ **Late** – includes all adults whose children have left home, or who are over 35 and childless

The occupation groups are:

◆ **White** – head of household in the ABC1 occupation group where A is upper/upper middle class, B is middle class, C is lower middle class.

◆ **Blue** – head of household in the C2DE occupation group, where C2 is skilled working class, D is working class, E is the lowest level of subsistence.

Above: Segmentation by life-cycle, income and occupation

COURSEWORK ACTIVITIES

If you live near a multi-screen cinema, carry out some research to find out what type of people watch the films that are showing at the moment.

Group the audiences by age and sex, and present your results in the form of graphs and charts, using a computer package.

2 Customer service

The second technique used by companies aiming to achieve a 'one-to-one' relationship with customers is **customer service**.

Customer service describes the way a customer is treated by sales staff on the telephone, in the shop and at the check-out. It covers the way queries and complaints are handled, and the use of the latest technology to personalise even the most large-scale promotional campaign letters. All these affect the relationship between customer and business.

Types of purchases

We can identify a number of purchases that people make which involve different levels of decision-making.

1 Routine purchases

These are everyday purchases which do not require much thought. For example, a routine purchase will be the bread and butter that goes into a family's sandwiches. Every six months the family will need to renew the car tax licence and every year the television licence – again these are routine purchases.

2 Limited-decision purchases

These are purchases which are less routine and involve more careful thought.

For example, if a new flavour of crisps becomes available, a purchaser will carry out a limited amount of research before deciding whether or not to buy it. Once they are familiar with the product, it may then become a routine purchase.

3 Extensive decision-making

These are purchases which involve considerable thought or prior research – for example, buying a new car or computer. The buyer will want to have a lot of information before committing themselves to a decision.

4 Impulse purchases

These are purchases made on the spur of the moment. For example, while paying for petrol at a service station shop, a customer may notice a magazine, some attractive sandwiches, and a packet of sweets which are all temptingly displayed. On impulse, they may buy far more than they had originally intended.

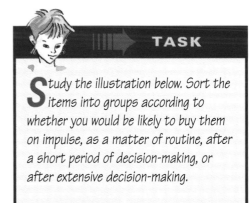

TASK

Study the illustration below. Sort the items into groups according to whether you would be likely to buy them on impulse, as a matter of routine, after a short period of decision-making, or after extensive decision-making.

Making the buying decisions

When planning an advertising campaign, it is important for businesses to know who has most influence over the buying decision, as well as who actually makes the purchase.

For example, in a family, children may not spend much money themselves, but they can still have a considerable influence over what their parents buy. Similarly, in a typical household, women often have a considerable influence over the choice of the family car, tending to value environmental factors, design qualities and safety. Manufacturers need to bear this in mind.

Can you help Frankie and Cleo to match the following terms and definitions?

Limited decision purchases	Purchases which are made regularly as a matter of course
	Unplanned purchases which are made on the spur of the moment
Demographic segmentation	Dividing up a market according to population character- istics of buyers
Routine purchases	Dividing up people according to the broad age grouping that they are in
Psychographic segmentation	The categorisation of people by their behaviour and attitudes
Sagacity life- style grouping	Purchasing decisions that require a certain amount of balanced consideration
Impulse purchases	

26 The Marketing Mix

Creating the right mix

When marketing their products, firms need to create a successful mix of:

◆ **The right product**

◆ **Sold at the right price**

◆ **In the right place**

◆ **Using the most suitable promotion**

The 'Four Ps'

The ingredients of the marketing mix are often referred to as the **Four Ps**: PRODUCT, PRICE, PLACE and PROMOTION.

A mix is made of ingredients which are blended together to meet a common purpose. As with a cake, no ingredient is enough on its own: it has to be blended together to produce something very special. In the same way that there are a many cakes to suit all tastes, a marketing mix can be designed to suit the precise requirements of the market.

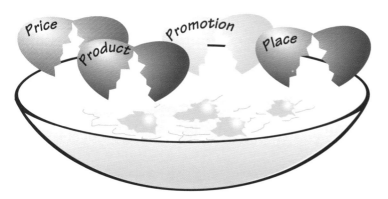

'Yes, I understand. This is the way to cater for the needs of our customers!'

'All this talk about a "marketing mix" is nonsense. There is only one factor that makes products sell, and that's price. If you charge the lowest price, then none of the other things matter!'

Do you agree with Ron?

A perfect mix

To create the right marketing mix, businesses have to meet the following conditions:

◆ The **product** has to have the right features – for example, it must look good and work well.

◆ The **price** must be right. Consumers will need to buy in large numbers to produce a healthy profit.

◆ The goods must be in the right **place** at the right time. Making sure that the goods arrive when and where they are wanted is an important operation.

◆ The target group needs to be made aware of the existence and availability of the product through **promotion**. Successful promotion helps a firm to spread costs over a larger output.

CASE STUDY

Great marketing disasters

The two case studies below highlight some great marketing flops of recent times. Can you identify which elements of the marketing mix went wrong in each case?

WHAT A FIASCEAU!

French mineral water company Perrier today announced that it would be withdrawing its sparkling water from worldwide sales after tiny amounts of the cancer-inducing chemical benzene were picked up by scientists in the US. The problem was traced back to a careless employee at the company's plant in Vergeze who splashed the wrong cleaning fluid on to a bottling machine. The company estimates that around 140 million bottles will be taken off the shelves over the next two months.

QE2 STEERS FOR TROUBLED WATERS

Unfinished bathrooms, workers drilling at all hours, equipment strewn around the corridors – and that was just the first-class accommodation!

The QE2 set sail from Southampton sailing to New York and the Caribbean, its £30m refit still incomplete. "It was like being in an unfinished Spanish hotel except that we were about 900 miles west of Ireland and couldn't get off", said one disgusted passenger, who had paid £7,400 for the privilege of being awoken at 8am by noisy workers. The dream holiday turned into a nightmare and a public relations disaster for the liner's owner, Cunard…

COURSEWORK ACTIVITIES

What about promotion?

Is the price right?

Can consumers get it when and where they want it?

Does the product meet consumer requirements?

Think of a product which you buy regularly, such as an item of confectionery or a teenage magazine. How effective is the marketing mix for this product?

Before you start, make sure you know who the product is supposed to sell to (the target market). Is the product aimed at teenagers? Male or female?

Now choose a sample of 30 people to interview from the appropriate group, e.g. females in the age range 13-18. Ask your sample to compare your selected product with three or four rival products. Rule up a table similar to the one below and then compare the brand you use with its competitors.

Now suggest how the marketing mix could be improved for the product you buy.

Product A	Very good	Good	Average	Poor	Very poor	Comment
Place						
Promotion						
Price						
Product						

MATCH IT! Can you help Frankie and Cleo to match the following terms and definitions?

Product	Advertising and other means of enticing customers to buy a product
Target market	The audience at which the marketing mix is aimed
Promotion	Getting the product to where consumers want to buy it
Place	A subtle combination of the 'Four Ps'
Price	The good or service that is being sold
Marketing mix	The amount charged for a good or service

27 Product Life-cycles

What is a product life-cycle?

During its life, every plant and animal goes through a series of stages, involving birth, growth, maturity and eventually decay. In the same way, products have a life-cycle, although the pattern varies.

The life of a product is the period over which it appeals to customers. We can all think of goods that everyone wanted at one time but which have now gone out of fashion. Obvious examples are drainpipe trousers and winklepicker shoes.

'The life-cycle of a person involves a series of ages. Is it the same for a product?'

'I'm surprised drainpipes and winklepickers went out of fashion. I used to wear mine a lot!'

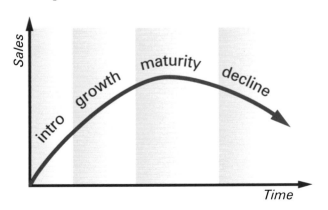

Left: The classic product life-cycle

Sales performance and profitability

The sales performance of any product rises when the product is introduced to the market, reaches a peak and then goes into decline. Most products have a limited life-cycle. Initially the product may flourish and grow, but eventually the market will mature and the product will move towards decline.

At each stage in the product life-cycle, there is a close relationship between sales and profits, so that as organisations or brands go into decline, their profitability decreases.

Injecting life into the product life-cycle

The product life-cycle may last for a few months or for hundreds of years. To prolong the life-cycle of a product, an organisation may inject new life into the growth period of the product by adjusting the ingredients of its marketing mix.

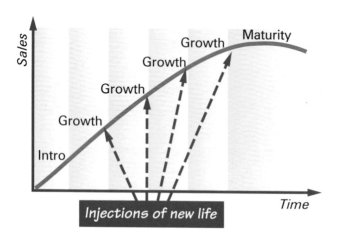

Periodic injections of new life

The changing music market

In September 1989, sales of LPs accounted for over a quarter of all album sales in the UK. By September 1992, the figure had fallen to just over 6%.

While total sales in the market had fallen, the sale of compact discs had almost doubled.

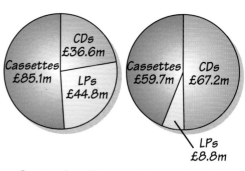

September '89
Total: £166.5m   *September '92*
                          Total: £135.7m

Album sales in September 89 and September 92

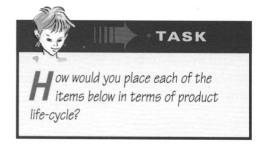

TASK

How would you place each of the items below in terms of product life-cycle?

Ways of altering the marketing mix to inject new life into the product might include:

1 **Changing or modifying the product** to keep ahead of the competition. For example, Nestlé Rowntree, makers of Smarties, responded to competition from other brands of sweets by introducing a number of improvements to Smarties.

◆ In 1989 they brought out a blue Smartie

◆ In 1991 they introduced printing on sweets

◆ In 1992 they introduced green-coloured chocolate

◆ In 1995 they relaunched the standard range of Smarties with new colourful packets.

2 **Altering distribution patterns** to create more attractive retail outlets for consumers. For example, in 1989, the clothing retailers Next introduced *Next Directory*, a catalogue enabling shoppers to buy Next goods by mail order from their own home.

3 **Changing prices to become more competitive.** During the 1990s, sales of national newspapers have fallen as people have switched to alternative sources of information. This has led to a price war as newspaper companies have competed for greater market share.

4 **Promotional campaigns.** Another way to inject new life into a product is by promoting the product through methods such as advertising, special offers, 'Buy one, get one free' promotions, trial offers, etc.

The Smarties range

COURSEWORK ACTIVITIES

Frankie needs your help with some research.

Identify an example where the marketing mix has been altered to inject new life into a product. What aspects of the marketing mix have been altered, and how successful have the changes been? Set out your findings in a 400-word report.

TASK

What would the life-cycle for each of the following products look like?

The VW Beetle, cat and dog food, Action Man toys, Lee and Perrins sauce, stiletto heels, sledges, body piercing, National Lottery tickets , Easter eggs, the TV programme Eldorado, condoms, bicycles, rave Music, Lo-Lo balls, the Bible, Pretty Polly tights, shell suits.

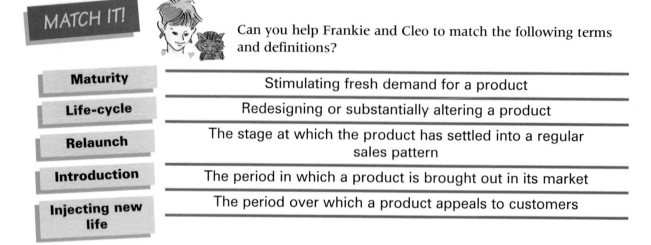

MATCH IT!

Can you help Frankie and Cleo to match the following terms and definitions?

Maturity	Stimulating fresh demand for a product
Life-cycle	Redesigning or substantially altering a product
Relaunch	The stage at which the product has settled into a regular sales pattern
Introduction	The period in which a product is brought out in its market
Injecting new life	The period over which a product appeals to customers

28 Products, Brands and Packaging

Meeting consumer needs

The most important part of the marketing mix is the product itself. The product must meet an identified consumer need.

There is no point in spending a fortune on promoting, charging a competitive price and getting your product to a good selling place unless people want to buy it.

Before launching a product, you must make sure it has the right **benefits** that consumers require.

Product benefits

Benefits are the advantages gained by buyers from the goods or services that they buy.

For example, on a hot day you receive the benefit of refreshment from a long cool drink. At the end of a long week, you get the benefit of entertainment from going to the cinema on a Friday night. In the same way, your milkman gives you the benefit of convenient, reliable doorstep delivery. The benefits offered by a product or service can include:

◆ Convenience and accessibility

◆ Good after-sales technical support and advice

◆ Reliability

'What do you mean by benefits'?

◆ Comfort and ease of use

◆ Accountability – the knowledge that if things go wrong, the manufacturer will put them right

◆ Courtesy and helpfulness of staff

◆ Attractive, appropriate and efficient design and packaging

◆ Peace of mind – the knowledge that you can trust the company, that your needs are understood and the good or service you have purchased will not let you down.

The more benefits that you can provide for customers, the more likely you are to be able to sell your product and get a 'good price' for it. Competition is all about creating more benefits than rival products.

The product mix

Many organisations produce more than one product. The **product mix** is the complete range of items made by the organisation.

Branding

A **brand** is a product with a unique, consistent and easily recognisable character. For example, we all recognise the Coca-Cola brand, not only by its logo, but by the shape of its bottles, the colour of its cans, the taste of the product and other features.

The uniqueness of a brand comes from its physical characteristics (e.g. the taste and unique ingredients of Coca-Cola), plus its image (i.e. its logo, advertising, etc.) – which are usually created by the manufacturer through advertising and packaging.

When we talk of a product's **consistency**, we mean not only the consistency of its quality and performance, but also of its design, advertising and packaging.

The importance of image

Our **image** is the way that others see us. Whether we like it or not, it is our public face. People quickly form opinions about us from the way we dress, walk and talk, from where we live and work, and our interests.

In the same way, every product conveys an image to the consumer. This can be a positive or a negative image, depending largely on how the product is designed and presented.

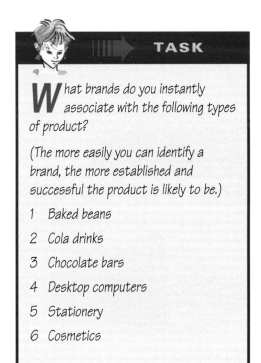

TASK

*W*hat brands do you instantly associate with the following types of product?

(The more easily you can identify a brand, the more established and successful the product is likely to be.)

1   Baked beans

2   Cola drinks

3   Chocolate bars

4   Desktop computers

5   Stationery

6   Cosmetics

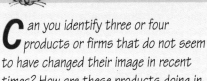

TASK

*C*an you identify three or four products or firms that do not seem to have changed their image in recent times? How are these products doing in comparison with other ones that have moved with the times?

Packaging

Packaging is the way that goods and services are presented to the customer. It can give added benefits to a product, such as an attractive design, protection during transport, ease of access and so on.

However, packaging can also add considerably to the cost of production. The heavier and bulkier the packaging, the higher the cost of moving the goods around. The more packaging you use, the more material that needs to go into the packets, etc. And of course, the more packaging you create, the greater the environmental cost of disposing of it. Firms therefore need to think very carefully about the advantages and disadvantages of packaging.

COURSEWORK ACTIVITIES

Study the packaging of five commonly used products.

Analyse ways in which the manufacturer could reduce the cost of packaging whilst continuing to make the package look attractive.

  TASK

*T*he Case Study below sets out information about the new Eurostar passenger service. Study the information, making notes on what you see as being the main benefits of the Eurostar service.

1   What factors are most likely to persuade consumers that the benefits are worth paying for?

2   Make a ten-minute presentation outlining the benefits of travel by Eurostar:

CASE STUDY

Eurostar

European Passenger Services (EPS) operates and markets international passenger train services in co-operation with other European railways. These high-speed Eurostar services operate from London to Paris and to Brussels, serving Ashford, Calais and Lille. Direct Eurostar services also run to and from Disneyland Paris.

Eurostar train at Waterloo International

Eurostar trains

Interiors
Eurostar trains provide a high degree of comfort for travellers. Footrests, reading lamps and magazine racks are allocated to each seat. Luggage racks are available in each coach and exceptional items of luggage can be carried in a separate compartment.

All passenger seats are provided with controlled air conditioning. Train to shore public telephone systems are available. Connecting doors between coaches open simply by pressure on a handle or push button.

Family arrangements
Special family compartments consist of a bay of four seats with a table which can fold away, leaving a floor area for a pushchair or a play area. Private baby changing facilities are provided close by.

Catering facilities
There are two buffet-bar coaches, one in each half of the train, where hot and cold snacks are available. Snacks can be eaten at the buffet bar or taken back to passenger seating. Refreshments are served from a trolley service. First class passengers have an at-seat meal service included in the price of the ticket.

Start of services
There has been a gradual build-up of Eurostar services, with the launch of the Discovery Service on 14 November 1994.

The Discovery Service began with eight trains (two departures a day in both directions, between London and Paris, London and Brussels). On 23rd January 1995, service increased substantially and it will build up to one train an hour in each direction between London and Paris. There will be additional trains at times of peak demand. The introduction of Eurostar regional services is scheduled for 1996.

Above: First class accommodation

Below: the Eurostar buffet/bar

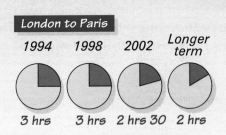

London to Paris

1994	1998	2002	Longer term
3 hrs	3 hrs	2 hrs 30	2 hrs

Intercapital journey times are fast: London to Paris in 3 hours.

Technical specifications
Eurostar trains operating between London and Paris, London and Brussels and London and Lille are just under 400m long. They reach a maximum speed of 300 kilometres per hour on the French high-speed line and are formed of a power car at each end and 18 coaches. In the event of an emergency in the Tunnel, the trains can be uncoupled at 3 points – in the centre of the train (between coaches 9 and 10) and at each end of the train between the power car and the adjoining coach.

The trains are electrically powered, making them clean, quiet and efficient. They are fitted with an advanced suspension system and a continuous welded rail helps eliminate noise at source.

 MATCH IT!

Can you help Frankie and Cleo to match the following terms and definitions?

Packaging	The diversified range of goods and services made by an organisation
Product mix	The way in which a product is presented
Branding	The way in which someone or something is perceived
Image	The range of advantages to consumers provided in a good
Benefits	Giving a product a unique, consistent and easily recognisable character

29 Pricing

What is the best price for a product?

Charging the right price is a very important part of the marketing mix. In setting a price for your product you will almost certainly want to cover your costs and make a profit as well.

The pricing decision

The actual price that a business charges for its products will depend on whether they are trying to win a massive share of the market, or whether they want consumers to buy their product because it is different and better than rival products. The main pricing decision for a firm, therefore, is whether to charge:

◆ A **low price** in order to attract sales. This makes it possible to sell large quantities at a low average cost.

◆ An **average price**. If you charge an average price, you will need to compete with your rivals by other means, e.g. by having a better-quality product, or better promotion and advertising, etc.

◆ A **higher price**. Firms can charge a high, or **premium price** if they are seen as being better than their rivals in meeting the needs of a chosen group of customers.

'You should always charge a little less than your competitors. Then you wipe them out and rule the market!'

Do you think that Ron will always be right in this opinion about pricing?

Pricing techniques

1 Cost-plus pricing

A common way to make pricing decisions is to calculate how much it costs to do a particular job or activity, and then add on a given percentage as a return for the job or activity. This is sometimes known as a **mark-up**.

For example, a business may decide that it will cost £100 to do a small repair job on a car, including parts, labour, use of premises and equipment, etc. The business works on the basis of making a 20% return on all the work that it does. It therefore charges the customer £120.

2 Hour-based pricing

Many small businesses are able to work out what their typical costs are for every hour of work they do, e.g. for gardening, signwriting, photography, etc. The business owner is then able to charge a standard charge per hour.

3 Penetration pricing

When a firm brings out a new product into a new or existing market, it may feel that it needs to make a lot of sales very quickly in order to establish itself and to make it possible to produce larger quantities. It may therefore start off by offering the product at quite a low price. When market penetration has been achieved, prices can be raised.

4 Skimming

When you bring out a new product, you may be able to start off by charging quite a high price. Some customers may want to be the first to buy your product because of the prestige of being seen with it, or because they want to be associated with your product before anyone else.

The word **skimming** comes from the idea of skimming the top layer of cream first, allowing the cream to build up again, skimming off the second layer, and so on.

For example, you could sell an exclusive dress at an exclusive price to wealthier customers. The next season, you could lower the price, making it accessible to a less wealthy group of customers. Later on, you could mass-produce the dress so that it is available at a low price to the mass market.

TASK

For each of the following brands, try to explain whether the manufacturer/retailer is going for a low price, an average price, or a high price. Explain why you think they have chosen the price that they have:

- Chanel No. 5 perfume
- Charlie perfume
- Rolls Royce motor cars
- Ford Escort motor cars
- Dime bars
- Mars bars
- Lion bars
- Mars ice cream
- Freezepops
- Own-brand supermarket goods
- Heinz baked beans
- Market stall clothes
- Etam clothes
- Benetton clothes

5 Destroyer pricing

Destroyer pricing involves selling your good at a very low price in order to destroy new competitors or existing competitors. For example, in the mid-1990s *The Times* newspaper engaged in a price-cutting campaign to take sales away from rivals. Other newspapers followed suit, and the eventual result was that in November 1995 the *Today* newspaper went out of business.

COURSEWORK ACTIVITIES

Frankie is carrying out some research to compare different types of teenage magazines and the prices charged for them. She has found out the following information:

• **Teenage Hits**

Price: £1.40, published monthly by Attic Futura

Target age group: 11-19 year olds

Average readership age: 14.4

Circulation in December 1995: 189,000

Typical features: Heavy emphasis on pop, film and television features and advice column.

• **Sugar**

Price: £1.40, published monthly by Attic Futura

Target age group: 13-18 year-old girls

Circulation 262,000

Typical features: Interviews with pop and soap stars, fashion and real-life stories

• **Mizz**

Price: 85p, published fortnightly by IPC

Target age group: The older teenager

Circulation 195,000

Typical features: Fashion and pop news, plus a regular column which explains sexual slang terms

• **Just Seventeen**

Price: 85p, published weekly by Emap

Target age group: Claimed to have the broadest range of readers in the teen market, but clearly focussed at 13-17-year-olds

Circulation 269,000

Typical features: Fashion and pop news, plus environmental features

• **Shout**

Price: 90p fortnightly, published by DC Thompson

Target age group: 12-15 year olds

Circulation: 200,000

Typical features: Adopts the safe approach. Gossip on television and pop stars, real-life stories

Frankie is trying to assess why these magazines choose to sell at different prices. Carry out some further research into these teenage magazines to find out why they price in the way they do. You will also need to compare the style of the magazines, as well as finding out some typical readers' views about the prices charged.

Alternatively, choose another market and analyse price differences of similar products.

TASK

What type of pricing is involved in each of the following examples?

- Frankie and Cleo have decided to work out how much it costs them to produce their biscuits per hour. They will then add 10% to this cost in order to make a reasonable return.

- Ron Rust has managed to wipe out some of his rivals who have tried to set up in local towns. As soon as a new scrapyard opened up, Ron started selling scrap at a much lower price than these yards could afford to sell at.

- Suzanne is a signwriter. She charges her clients according to the time it takes her to do a job.

- When Honton Winrab brought out his book about the life of the well-known aristocrat Lady Ophelia McStarkers, the original edition was in hardback and sold at £25 per copy. A second Christmas edition of the book was brought out at £20 per copy. Then the book was brought out in paperback at £10 a copy.

- A Belgian company introduced a new breakfast cereal in the UK originally selling at 50p less than similar brands. Once the new cereal had developed a good hold on the market, prices were raised to comparable levels with rival cereals.

 Can you help Frankie and Cleo to match the following terms and definitions?

Destroyer pricing	Charging customers according to the time it takes to do a job
Cost leadership	Producing large outputs cheaper than your rivals
Market share	Adding a percentage on to your costs in order to make a reasonable return
Penetration pricing	Initially charging a low price in order to establish a good position in a market
Cost-plus pricing	Undercutting rivals in order to force them out of business
Hour-based pricing	The percentage of the overall market in the hands of a particular firm

3 30 **Reaching the Market**

What is meant by distribution?

Delivery, or distribution as it is commonly called, makes products available to customers where and when they want them. Place is a very important part of the marketing mix.

Something like 20% of the total production cost of a product is taken up with **freight charges**. These are the costs of moving the raw materials to the producer and then transporting 'finished' products to the end-user.

'In the scrap metal business transport costs take up more than 20% of the total production cost!'

Do you think that Ron is likely to be right in saying this?

Transport

Different forms of transport have their own advantages and disadvantages.

1 **Pipelines** are expensive to construct and repair, but are a cheap way to transport oil and gas.

2 **Roads** give door-to-door delivery, are fast over short and some long distances, and make it possible for firms to use their own fleet of vehicles relatively cheaply.

   However, road travel is also subject to traffic delays and breakdowns, and drivers may only drive their vehicles for a certain number of hours in a day.

3 **Rail transport** is relatively cheap and quick over long distances, particularly between major cities.

   However, rail is not always a good way of reaching out-of-the-way destinations. Guaranteed speedy deliveries by rail can also be costly.

4 **Air transport** is very fast between countries, so long as the destination is not too far from a major city. Air is generally used for carrying important, urgent, relatively light and valuable loads.

5 **Sea transport** is a cheap way of carrying heavy and bulky loads when speed is not a factor.

Place

In marketing terms, the **place** is where the final exchange occurs between the seller and the customer. An important marketing decision is where this exchange takes place and how. For example, at one time, all bank services were provided 'across the counter', but in recent years banks have moved to cashpoints and increasingly towards telephone banking.

Below: Changing place for banking activities

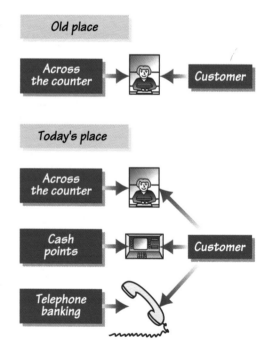

CHAPTER 30

CASE **S**TUDY

Geest PLC

Geest PLC is a major producer and distributor of fresh fruit (including bananas, apples, pears and grapes) and fresh vegetables (including carrots, mushrooms and cabbages). Geest's own fleet of lorries play an important part in distributing its products in the UK. The diagram below shows how Geest can distribute its products to reach the final consumer within 24 hours.

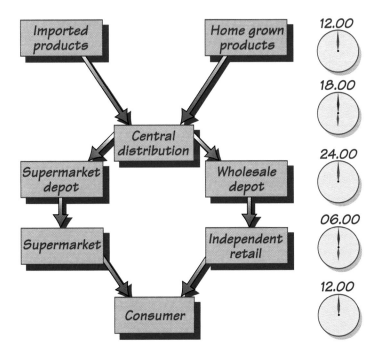

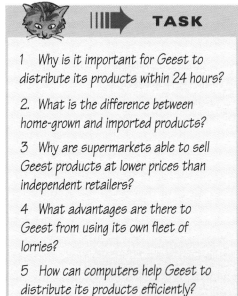

12.00

18.00

24.00

06.00

12.00

TASK

1   Why is it important for Geest to distribute its products within 24 hours?

2. What is the difference between home-grown and imported products?

3   Why are supermarkets able to sell Geest products at lower prices than independent retailers?

4   What advantages are there to Geest from using its own fleet of lorries?

5   How can computers help Geest to distribute its products efficiently?

The Geest 24-hour distribution cycle

Channels of distribution

A **distribution channel** is the means by which an organisation and its customers are brought together at a particular place and time for the purpose of buying and selling goods. This may be in a shop, office, via a computer link, or by television shopping.

The organisations that are involved in the distribution chain are:

◆ **Manufacturers** – i.e. the firms that make products.

◆ **Wholesalers** – i.e. the firms that store goods in bulk which they purchase from manufacturers before selling them on to retailers

◆ **Retailers** – i.e. the firms that sell goods to final consumers

COURSEWORK ACTIVITIES

Interview people and use your own personal experience to identify three products for which the 'place' has changed in recent times.

Why do you think these changes in place have occurred? (Show how the place has changed.)

The diagram on the right shows a traditional distribution channel from the manufacturer to the final consumer.

The diagram at the foot of the page shows how there can be a number of different types of channels of distribution between the manufacturer and the eventual consumer.

◆ In **Channel A**, the manufacturer sells direct to consumers by mail order. Examples are clothing manufacturers like Racing Green and Laura Ashley, who have their own mail order networks.

◆ In **Channel B**, the manufacturer distributes direct to their own warehouses and company shops which supply consumers. Examples are products which are produced directly by large supermarket chains in their own factories. Here, the manufacturer is entirely responsible for the distribution of their own products.

◆ **Channel C** is sometimes called the 'traditional channel of distribution': a manufacturer makes goods; a wholesaler buys lots of different goods from several manufacturers. The wholesaler sells on to retailers. The manufacturer, wholesaler and retailer are all independent organisations. This was the pattern for most goods in the UK until the 1960s.

◆ In **Channel D**, retailers buy directly from manufacturers. This is easiest when the retailers have a very large storage area, or when goods can be bought in bulk.

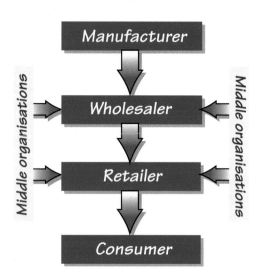

A distribution channel

Interview the owner of a retail outlet to find out what channels of distribution they use for the various items they stock. (You will normally find that they use more than one channel of distribution).

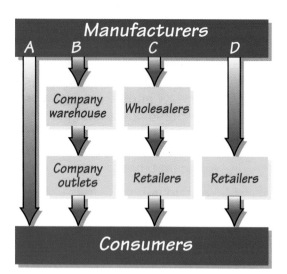

Left: Examples of distribution channels

MATCH IT! Can you help Frankie and Cleo to match the following terms and definitions?

Distribution	The person who enjoys the final good or service
Wholesaler	Organisation that makes goods
Retailer	Where the final exchange takes place between the seller and buyer
Consumer	A middle organisation that is responsible for storing goods in bulk before selling them on in smaller quantities
Manufacturer	Making products available to consumers where and when they want them
Place	Person or organisation who sells finished products to end-users

31 Advertising and Publicity

The role of advertising

There are many parts of the promotional mix. In this chapter we deal with advertising and publicity. In the next chapter we deal with selling and sales promotion.

One of the best forms of advertising is the product itself. But advertising still plays a very important role. Advertising is the presenting or promoting of a product to the public to encourage sales.

It can have spectacular results. For example, in 1996 jeans manufacturers like Levis suddenly switched to using female models in their television adverts. Jean sales shot through the roof.

Adverts don't always have to be popular to be successful. For example, in 1995 one advert sent TV viewers into a frenzy. The zany commercial for 'Chicken Tonight' was listed as the 'most irritating advert on the box'! Viewers' love-hate relationship with a TV advert can mean that the product sticks in their mind. Advertisers know this, and often go out of their way to make an advertisement 'daft but memorable'.

'But surely if a product is good enough then you won't need to advertise it?'

CASE STUDY

Using sex to promote ice cream

Contestants in Europe's $7 billion-a-year ice cream market are using sex to turn on the public. The use of naked flesh to advertise products is nothing new, but fierce competition in the 'adult' market is inspiring advertisers to new heights. In the UK, campaigns by two manufacturers in the gourmet market have raised eyebrows as well as brand awareness.

The UK's television watchdog, the Independent Television Commission, recently banned a series of erotic advertisements for ice cream, saying they were 'too hot' for British viewers. The Advertising Standards Authority has also received complaints about the use of sex in ice cream adverts.

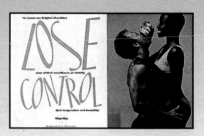

Haagen-Dazs advertisement

Unilever's best-known adverts featured the pan-European Cornetto gondola. It, too, has recently turned to sex appeal with the 'girl-licks-lolly' formula to help it to double the sales of Magnum, the chocolate-covered ice cream on a stick. With predicted sales of £300 million-plus in Europe each year in the late 1990s, it shows that the proof of the pudding is in the eating!

  TASK

1 *Why might the use of sex to sell ice cream be considered against the public interest?*

2 *Outline the benefits of using such methods to (a) sellers of ice cream and (b) consumers.*

3 *What other methods of promoting ice cream might also be successful? Working in groups, consider what themes you would emphasise if you had to promote a new ice cream product in the luxury 'after-dinner' segment of the adult market.*

Publicity means any technique or process used to attract public attention to people and products. Unlike advertising, however, publicity is usually free. Any type of publicity is advertising.

Informative advertising

In the UK, the highest spender on advertising is the government. Most government advertising is aimed at giving information to the public. This passing on of information is a very important part of advertising.

Persuasive advertising

Most adverts, however, try to do more than just inform the public. The soap-powder manufacturers spend almost as much money on advertising as the government, and their advertisements are blatantly designed to attract people to buy their products.

A government health warning

CASE STUDY

Creating a strong public image at Eurostar

The Eurostar service began in the Summer of 1994, providing the first-ever high-speed rail link between London, Paris and Brussels. A key aspect of the new service was a detailed attention to all aspects of public relations. Design is a key element in promoting the right public image.

The world-famous French designer Pierre Balmain was commissioned to design the uniforms for the Eurostar services with the Eurostar colour.

Around 750 people working for Eurostar, from drivers to reception staff, wear the new uniforms which are wholly designed and made in Europe.

The Eurostar brand identity has been awarded a prize for excellent design in a French national design competition. The communication industry award was given for best visual identity in the 'services' category.

A key element in developing the Eurostar public image is the distinctive name branding that communicates well across Europe, symbolising a breakthrough in travel. The 'E' of Eurostar symbolises the three European railways working together, while the star

The Eurostar logo and uniform

symbolises their common goal as well as pointing to the future and reflecting the high quality Eurostar will offer. The soft, flowing design of the logo symbolises the ease and enjoyment Eurostar customers will experience.

A **persuasive** selling message is one that promises a desirable and believable benefit to the people to whom it is addressed. There are many different types of advert that can be used to persuade, including the following:

◆ Adverts showing a 'personality' using the product

◆ Adverts comparing one product with other products

◆ Adverts using sex appeal

Many firms aim to develop strong **brand images** for their products. If people associate a brand name with a product, then this will help create loyalty for the brand.

Public relations

The aim of public relations is to create, promote or maintain goodwill and a favourable image of a company or institution among the public.

  TASK

*R*ead the Case Study above then answer the questions below:

1 What do you see as being the key strengths of design at Eurostar?

2 Why is it important for the company to develop good public relations?

3 What will be the long-term benefits to the company?

4 What aspects of the design would encourage you to use the service?

Advertising agencies

Running an advertising campaign is very expensive, and firms need to make sure that their money is well spent. Generally firms will use an advertising agency to carry out the campaign. For advertising to be successful it must:

◆ Reach the right audience

◆ Be attractive and appealing

◆ Be cost-effective in relation to the extra sales

Control over advertising in the UK

Advertisers cannot just say anything they like when preparing an advert.

1 They must keep within the law. For instance, the **Trade Descriptions Act** lays down that goods advertised for sale must be as they are described (e.g. a 'waterproof' watch must be waterproof).

2 The advertising industry has its own **Code of Practice** which advertisers must obey.

The British Code of Advertising Practice

This is a voluntary agreement by firms in the advertising industry to keep their adverts up to certain standards. It covers newspapers, magazines, cinema adverts, leaflets, brochures, posters and commercials on videotape, but not TV or radio advertising.

The Advertising Standards Authority (ASA)

The ASA is responsible for supervising the British Code of Advertising Practice, except for Independent Television. You may have seen the advert on the right in national newspapers and magazines.

The advert goes on to say that if you have any complaints about adverts in the paper, you should write to the ASA, who will take up your complaint and force the advertiser to make changes if necessary.

Of course, some of the complaints received by the ASA are frivolous, like the man who complained that he had poured Heineken lager over his pot plant and it had died!

The Independent Television Commission

Following the 1990 Broadcasting Act, the Independent Television Commission (ITC) was set up to replace the Independent Broadcasting Authority (IBA). It now exercises control over television advertising.

COURSEWORK ACTIVITIES

Watch television commercials and list six examples of what you consider to be 'sit-up-and-notice' commercials. Then survey 20 people to find out if they can remember the advertisement and what it is advertising.

Find out what people's views are of the advertisement and whether they have actually purchased the article recently.

Are you:

Legal ☑

Decent ☑

Honest ☑

Truthful ☑

Advertisers have to be.

ASA press advertisement

MATCH IT!

Can you help Frankie and Cleo to match the following terms and definitions?

ASA	Projecting a positive image of an organisation
Advertising	Body responsible for making sure that adverts are legal, decent, honest and truthful
Persuasive advertising	Voluntary agreement regulating behaviour in the advertising industry
Informative advertising	Presenting or promoting a product to the public
Public relations	Setting out basic factual information about a product or service
British Code of Advertising Practice	Enticing consumers to buy a product through advertising techniques

32 Selling and Sales Promotion

Selling v. marketing

It is important to understand the difference between selling and marketing.

◆ **Marketing** begins by identifying and anticipating what consumers want and need. Once these wants and needs have been identified, products or services can be developed to meet them.

◆ **Selling** and **sales promotion** are concerned with persuading potential customers that your solution is the best one to fulfil their needs.

For example, market research might indicate that there is a big market made up of households that want to buy a computer with a CD-ROM drive, bundled with an encyclopaedia on CD-ROM. It is the job of the salesperson to convince potential customers that your particular computer CD-ROM and encyclopaedia are the best way of meeting this need.

'How is selling different from marketing?'

Stages in selling

The diagram on the right shows the various stages which are involved in the selling process.

Making sales

At the point of sale, the aim is to persuade the customer to take the step from wanting a product or service to actually buying it. The more closely the product matches their needs, the easier this will be. The key thing for the seller to remember is that customers are not so much looking for particular products or services as for the **benefits** those products or services will bring *(see pages 104–105)*.

Sales promotion

Sales promotion refers to a set of methods used to encourage customers to buy a product, usually at the point of sale.

Sales promotion is used along with advertising, personal selling and publicity. It can include the use of point-of-sale materials (e.g. leaflets and brochures), competitions, offers, product demonstrations and exhibitions.

A distinction is often made between promotion into the pipeline and promotions out of the pipeline:

◆ **Promotions into the pipeline** are methods which are used to sell more products into the distribution system – i.e. they are aimed at wholesalers and retailers rather than final consumers. Examples are 'dealer loaders', such as thirteen for the price of twelve, point-of-sale materials, dealer competitions, extended credit to dealers, sale-or-return and promotional gifts.

COURSEWORK ACTIVITIES

When you visit a supermarket, you will often find sales representatives encouraging you to taste or try a product e.g. wine, cheese, biscuits, etc., as part of a sales promotion.

List and describe five other types of sales promotion that you have seen in a supermarket recently.

THE SELLING PROCESS

Preparing to make the sale
The salesperson needs to know everything possible about a particular product and how it can meet different customer needs.

↓

Contacting and meeting customers
Choose a moment when the customer has plenty of time to discuss their problem and will be receptive.

↓

Finding out the problem/need
If you sell the customer a product which does not really meet their needs, you are unlikely to make a repeat sale.

↓

Providing the solutions
This should meet all the customer's needs.

↓

Closing the sale
This should be done in a business-like and friendly way.

↓

Dealing with objections
Unless objections are dealt with in a systematic way the customer may go away to 'think about it' and never return.

↓

After-sales service
This can include a service and repair agreement.

TASK

What do you see as being the strengths and weaknesses of the following sales promotions?

- A manufacturer of a new type of disposable razor advertises the product on television and then gives out thousands of free razors to people visiting the cricket Test matches in a series against the Australians.

- To boost falling sales, the manufacturer of an exclusive brand of perfume offers free sample bottles of the perfume nationwide in a chain of well-known chemists.

- The manufacturer of a new type of cheese runs a 'free' promotion one week before the cheese goes on sale nationwide. Taster pieces of the cheese are given away free in supermarkets for one week prior to the national launch.

- A national newspaper runs its own 'lottery-style' promotion for five weeks. Every week there is an expensive car as first prize in the competition, which is only open to purchasers of the newspaper.

◆ **Promotions out of the pipeline** help in promoting and selling products to the final consumer. These include free samples, trial packs, coupon offers, price reductions, competitions, demonstrations, charity promotions and point-of-sale materials.

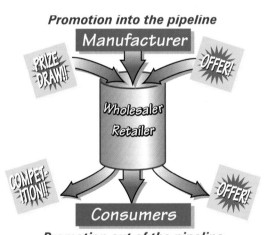

Promotion into and out of the pipeline

'Sales promotion is a complete waste of time. Whoever heard of someone buying a good because they were given a free sample? If people want to try a good, they should pay for it!'

Do you agree with Ron?

The effectiveness of promotions

The effect of sales promotions varies widely. Though most promotions using free samples lead to an immediate (if temporary) increase in sales, sales promotions are a short-term measure on the whole and have little effect on brand loyalty over a longer period.

MATCH IT!

Can you help Frankie and Cleo to match the following terms and definitions?

Sales	Promotions aimed at intermediaries such as wholesalers and retailers, rather than end-consumers
Marketing	Meeting customers' needs by presenting them with ways of solving their problems through goods and services
Solutions	Different ways of meeting customer needs
Sales promotions	Promotions aimed at the final consumers of products
Promotions 'out of the pipeline'	Identifying, anticipating and meeting consumer needs whilst making a profit
Promotions 'into the pipeline'	A range of methods used to encourage customers to buy products, e.g. free gifts, samples, demonstrations and exhibitions

33 Protecting the Consumer

Meeting standards

Every good or service that is bought or sold must meet certain standards. Some of these standards are laid down in law, some in voluntary codes of practice within an industry, and others are set by individual businesses.

Businesses supply goods or services for consumers in return for payment. The legal system sets out a fair framework for trading, and also to help to settle disputes that may arise.

'In my business it's a case of "let the buyer beware!"'

Buying goods

The **Sale of Goods Act 1979** says that goods must be:

◆ 'Of merchantable quality' – i.e. free from significant faults, except defects which are drawn to your attention by the seller (for instance, if goods are declared to be 'shop-soiled').

◆ 'Fit for the purpose' – including any particular purpose mentioned by you to the seller. For example, if you ask for a jumper that is machine-washable, you should *not* be sold one that has to be hand-washed.

◆ 'As described' – i.e. on the package or sales literature, or verbally by the seller. If you are told that a shirt is 100% cotton, then it should not turn out to be a mixture of cotton and polyester.

Any good that you buy from any sort of trader (e.g. shop, street market, mail order, or door-to-door sales-person) should meet these basic requirements. They also apply to food and goods bought in sales.

What to do if things go wrong

If there is something wrong with what you buy, you should tell the seller as soon as possible. Exactly what you are entitled to depends on how serious the fault is and how soon the goods are returned.

If you take faulty goods back straight away, you should be able to get your money back. You have not legally 'accepted' the goods, and this means you can 'reject' them (i.e. refuse to accept them). You can still reject goods even if you have taken them home, provided that you examine and try them out as soon as possible, and then take them back at once (or within a few days of purchase).

What is acceptance?

When you take faulty goods back to the seller you may be offered a replacement or a free repair. You do not have to agree to this. You can insist on having your money back. If you agree to a repair, you may have problems getting all your money back later if the fault is not sorted out, because, in law, you will have **accepted** the goods. If you accept a credit note, you will not usually be able to exchange it for cash later on.

Once you have 'accepted goods' in the legal sense, you lose your right to a full refund. You can only claim compensation.

'Acceptance' normally happens when you have kept the goods beyond a reasonable time. The law does not lay down any fixed periods for what is considered 'reasonable' – it depends on the goods and the circum-stances. But you would generally be expected to make it clear to the seller that you are rejecting the goods as soon as possible after purchase.

TASK

Frankie wonders whether the Sale of Goods Act has been broken in the following cases. Can you help her?

'Last year was a bit of a disaster for my Christmas shopping. First of all I bought my Auntie Amber a beautiful micro dress. The first time she washed it, it shrank so she couldn't wear it again. The label said "guaranteed shrinkproof"...

'...Then I bought my sister Juniper a pair of gloves which had one of the fingers missing. I think we should have taken that back to the shop...'

'...Then I bought my brother Ossie a multi-purpose football pump adaptor, but it wouldn't fit any of his footballs.'

Buyers' rights

Buyers should not be put off by traders trying to talk their way out of their legal responsibilities. The law says that it is up to the seller to deal with complaints about defective goods, so the seller should not try and lay the blame on the manufacturer.

As a buyer, you have the same rights even if you lose your receipt. A receipt, however, is useful evidence of where and when you bought the goods.

You may be able to claim compensation if you suffer loss because of faulty goods – for example, if a faulty iron ruins your shirt or trousers.

Buying a service

When you pay for a service – for example, from a dry cleaner, travel agent, car mechanic, hairdresser or builder – you are entitled to certain standards.

A service should be carried out:

◆ **With reasonable care and skill.** The job should be done to a proper standard of workmanship. If you have a dress made for a special occasion, it should not fray or come apart at the seams for no reason.

◆ **Within a reasonable time.** If you have to have your hi-fi system repaired, it should not take weeks and weeks. You can always agree upon a definite completion time with the supplier of the service.

◆ **At a reasonable charge**, if no price has been fixed in advance. However, if the price is fixed at the outset, or you have agreed some other way of working out the charge, you cannot complain later that it was unreasonable.

Always ask a trader how much a particular job will cost. The trader may only be able to make an informed guess at the cost and give you an estimate. If you agree a fixed cost, it is usually called a **quotation.** A fixed price is always binding.

'I frequently get asked to pick up cars which have been smashed up in accidents. I never quote a price to the customer at the time, just in case they think it's too high. When they get my bill, they have a bit of a shock, but then they can't do anything about it!'

Is Ron Rust keeping within the law? What do you think?

Other consumer laws

1 The Trade Descriptions Act

The description given of the goods forms part of the contract between the buyer and the seller. This Act makes it a criminal offence for a trader to describe goods falsely. A type of case frequently prosecuted under this Act is the turning back of the 'clock' on a used car to disguise the mileage.

2 The Weights and Measures Act

This Act aims to ensure that consumers receive the actual quantity of a product that they believe they are buying. For example, pre-packed items must have a declaration of the quantity contained within the pack. It is an offence to give 'short weight'.

3 The Food and Drugs Act

This Act covers the contents of food and medicines. The government needs to control this area of trading so that the public is not led into buying anything that might be harmful. Some items have to carry warnings – tins of kidney beans, for example, must carry clear instructions that they need to be boiled for a fair length of time before eating. The Act also lays down minimum standards for certain food products. For example, a sausage can only be called a sausage if it contains a certain amount of meat.

4 The Food Safety Act

This Act gives Environmental Health Officers powers to shut down premises where food is not being prepared in a hygienic way. Regulations cover such things as refrigeration temperatures.

Help and advice for consumers

There are a number of bodies providing advice and help to consumers:

1 **Trading Standards** departments of local authorities (also known as Consumer Protection departments) have powers to investigate complaints about false or misleading descriptions or prices, inaccurate weights and measures, consumer credit and the safety of consumer goods. They will often advise on everyday shopping problems.

2 **Environmental Health** departments deal with health matters such as sub-standard food and drink, and dirty shops and restaurants.

3 **Citizens' Advice Bureaux** offer help with many consumer problems, including shopping complaints.

4 **Trade Associations** often have written codes of practice. A code of practice is not legally binding, but it can be a guide to whether traders have broken their own rules. The trade association can put the case before an independent person who will decide in favour of either the seller or the buyer.

  TASK

What do you think the legal situation would be in the following cases?

1 Frankie's mum buys her a new school blazer in a department store on a Saturday afternoon. When she gets the blazer home, she realises that it is black, not dark blue as required. On Monday Frankie's mum takes the blazer back to the store.

2 Instead of returning the blazer straight away, Frankie's mum lets Ossie wear it for a few days. However, it is too large for him, so the next week she takes it back.

5 **Utilities watchdogs.** If you have a complaint about gas, water, electricity or telephones, you can call a customer service helpline (the telephone number will be on your bill). In addition, the four utilities each have a regulator who has the power to investigate complaints brought by consumers.

6 **The Consumers' Association** is a well known and powerful consumer group. It produces the monthly consumer magazine *Which?*, and is funded by subscriptions from members who buy the magazine. The Consumers' Association uses its funds to test a wide variety of products, which are then reported in the magazine. It also produces books on consumer-related matters.

MATCH IT!

Can you help Frankie and Cleo to match the following terms and definitions?

Terms	Definitions
'Acceptance'	Law stating that adverts and labelling of goods must be accurate
'Fit for the purpose'	Law stating that goods must contain the quantities and weights that they are advertised as having
Trade Descriptions Act	Of goods: free of significant faults
	Legal consequence of having kept goods beyond a certain time
Trading Standards Department	Body having powers to investigate complaints about false or misleading descriptions or prices, inaccurate weights and other matters
Trade Association	Group set up by commercial organisations to set their own codes and standards
Weights & Measures Act	Of goods: able to serve the purpose which the seller has mentioned in any way to the buyer
Food & Drugs Act	Act setting out requirements for the contents of foodstuffs and medicines
'Of merchantable quality'	

34 Production and Marketing

Understanding customer needs

The production and marketing of products should be seen as two parts of the same important process.

An organisation's **product** is the good or service it offers to consumers. The goods and services that firms produce must meet consumers' needs. They can only meet these needs if the manufacturer or producer first finds out what consumers want.

Product-led or market-led?

A criticism of many UK firms until the late 1980s and 1990s was that they were **product-led**. People in organisations came up with good ideas or carried on with existing ideas without finding out what the consumer wanted. Not surprisingly, many products flopped.

Today, far more companies are **market-led**. They first identify what consumers want, then set about trying to create the kind of benefits that will satisfy them.

The importance of meeting consumer needs

When you produce a product or service, you must make sure that it genuinely meets consumer needs. You are unlikely to be successful if you try to persuade customers to buy a product which fails to meet their needs. You 'may fool some of the people some of the time, but you can't fool all of the people all of the time'.

The message is clear: produce a real product which provides the benefits which consumers require, and then promote those benefits in a genuine way.

Frankie says:

'We first find out what benefits our customers want and need. We then set out to make sure that we provide these benefits.'

Above: a market-led approach

Below: a product-led approach

Ron Rust says:

'I produce the goods that I'm good at producing, and supply them to the market. I expect customers to buy them because of the knowledge I have about the scrap metal business.'

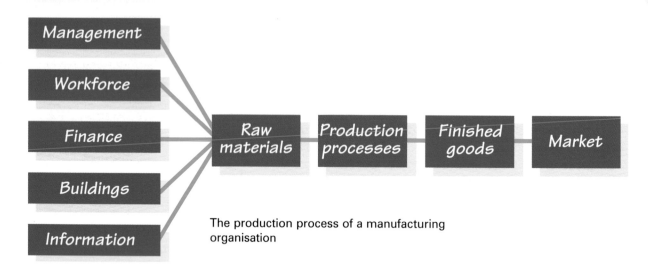

The production process of a manufacturing organisation

The production function

Production is the process of using resources to add value to a product or a service and so meet the customers' needs. In a manufacturing company, this will involve buying-in raw materials and then transforming them through a series of processes and stages into finished products which can then be distributed to the market (*see diagram above*).

In service industries, the production function involves organising resources efficiently to offer the final consumer the best value and quality. The finished good may be a haircut, a night's entertainment, an enjoyable visit to a leisure centre or theme park, or any of a thousand and one other services on offer today.

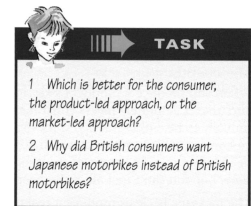

TASK

1 Which is better for the consumer, the product-led approach, or the market-led approach?

2 Why did British consumers want Japanese motorbikes instead of British motorbikes?

CASE STUDY

A classic case of ignoring the customer

A classic example of UK manufacturers' failure to find out what customers want comes from the motorcycle industry.

Thirty years ago, British roads seldom saw a foreign motorbike. Great names such as BSA, Triumph, and Norton graced the roads with heavy, slow-revving, large-capacity machines. Imports from Italy in the form of lightweight, high-revving machines were hardly given a second glance by British manufacturers – they did not make them, so customers could not possibly want them.

However, someone had noticed these machines, and thousands of miles away research and development were underway: the Japanese were about to enter the market.

Today the transformation is complete. Motorbikes on British roads are nearly all Japanese and there are very few British manufacturers left. If the British had only taken the trouble to research their market and find out what their customers really wanted, the position might be very different today.

Can you help Frankie and Cleo to match the following terms and definitions?

Product	Producing a good or service because you are good at making that product
Product-led	Providing goods and services which genuinely meet consumers' needs and wants
Market-led	The good or service offered to consumers

35 The Production Function

What is meant by 'value added'?

One of the most important terms in business is 'value added'. All businesses prosper in direct proportion to their ability to add value to their 'input' materials. The more value they add, especially in comparison with competitors, the better they do.

Value is added at each stage of production. A simple example is the carpenter converting relatively inexpensive materials into furniture. The difference between the cost of the wood and the price of the finished article is the wealth which he or she has created. The illustration below shows the simple stages involved:

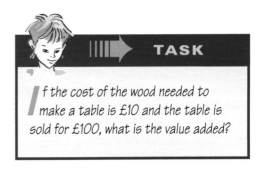

TASK

If the cost of the wood needed to make a table is £10 and the table is sold for £100, what is the value added?

Adding value in making furniture

Forest

Stage 1

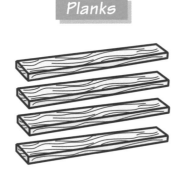

Planks

Stage 2

Chairs

Stage 3

At Stage 1 trees are grown in a forest. At Stage 2 they are converted into seasoned wood in a sawmill. At Stage 3 they are converted into finished chairs by a carpenter. At each stage value is added.

◆ Perhaps the forester buys £100,000 worth of small trees from a tree nursery, and they eventually grow into £500,000 worth of trees for sale. The value that is added is £400,000.

◆ The £500,000-worth of trees are seasoned and eventually converted into finished planks by the sawmill. The planks are worth £1 million.

◆ A furniture factory then converts the wood into chairs which are sold in the factory shop for £2 million.

We can show value added at each stage of production in the following way:

Stages of production	Input	Output	Value added
Tree nursery	0	£100,000	£100,000
Forestry	£100,000	£500,000	£400,000
Sawmill	£500,000	£1,000,000	£500,000
Furniture factory	£1,000,000	£2,000,000	£1,000,000

You can see that the final value of the chairs is £2,000,000, and that this value has been created to a greater or lesser extent at each stage in the chain of production. We can represent this in another table (right).

The importance of adding value

Businesses compete with each other. They are all involved in adding value. However, if your rivals are more successful at adding value than you, then they are more likely to win sales.

Creating consumer benefits

A **benefit** is an advantage gained by a customer from a product or service. Consumers will buy those products which give them the greatest benefit.

Adding value therefore should involve creating and adding benefits which consumers want and then producing them at an acceptable price and in an environmentally acceptable way.

A well-run business will produce the maximum benefits at the lowest possible cost. The way in which value is added is the key to business success.

TASK

1 Frankie and Cleo are setting up a biscuit-making business. How can they make sure that they add more value than all their rivals?

2 Think about the way in which a top-quality company works e.g. Shell UK, Eurostar, Mars, or Marks & Spencer. Show how this organisation adds value to its products.

Value added and chain of production	
Value added by tree nursery	£100,000
Value added by forestry	£400,000
Value added by sawmill	£500,000
Value added by furniture factory	£1,000,000
Total value added in production	£2,000,000

'The only benefit that I know that customers want is low prices. In business, low price is all that counts. Give customers the lowest price and they will be happy!'

The chain of production

For every product there is a **chain of production**. Some products go through many stages in the chain of production, while for others the chain is a lot shorter.

In tea production, for example, we can identify a number of clear stages, as shown in the diagram on the right.

At each stage, value is added. The stages need to be very closely linked together to avoid wastage and ensure that maximum value is added.

Other products may have a much shorter chain of production – for example, when fresh vegetables are grown by a farmer and sold over the garden gate.

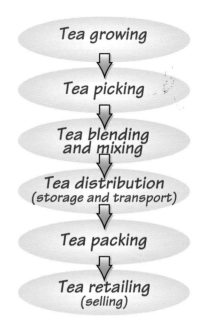

Chain of production for tea

Links in the chain of production

A crucial part of adding value successfully is the way in which each stage in the chain is linked. If we look at how a business operates we can see that it requires:

◆ Excellent links with suppliers

◆ Excellent internal links between activities inside the company

◆ Excellent links with customers

Links with suppliers
A business needs to make sure that it gets inputs of the right quality, at the right price, and at the right time. For example, a company like Marks & Spencer will insist that the goods it buys from outside sources meet very high standards. If suppliers cannot meet these standards, it will no longer buy from them.

Internal links
Within a company there need to be very good links between each activity involved in a production process.

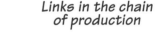
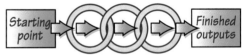

Links in the chain of production

Links with customers
Finally, there needs to be very close liaison with customers, so that the goods can be transferred smoothly to the next stage in the chain with no hold-ups or complications. There also needs to be a very good relationship with firms later on in the chain of production, so that everybody involved works together to create maximum consumer benefits.

Links in the chain of production can be illustrated as a **value chain**, as in the illustration on the right.

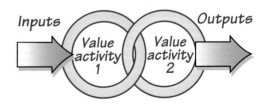

A value chain

Can you help Frankie and Cleo to match the following terms and definitions?

Value added	The various stages involved in creating final goods
Value chain	The links involved in creating effective consumer benefits through production
Benefit	Advantages gained by consumers from goods and services
Chain of production	The increase in the benefits of a good which are created at each stage of production

36 Methods of Production

Maximising efficiency

All businesses need to organise their methods of production efficiently so as to meet the needs of their customers.

The key to doing this successfully is through **operations** or **production**. Operations or production are the processes and methods an organisation uses to produce something or to make a service.

The methods of production

Most businesses use one of the following methods of production:

◆ Project production

◆ Job production

◆ Batch production

◆ Line production

◆ Continuous flow production

It is easiest to relate these methods to manufacturing operations, but the same classifications can quite easily be used for services.

'Creating a service is not production. How can it be? Where is the end product?'

Do you agree with Ron?

1 Project production

A **project** involves bringing together a number of people and resources to complete one product, e.g. building a new hotel or motorway, making a Hollywood movie, developing a new CD-ROM and so on.

When you do a GCSE project, you will look at it as a 'one-off' assignment. You will need to carry out operations in a set order, e.g.:

◆ Choose a project title

◆ Decide how to collect information

◆ Start collecting information by interviewing and writing letters

◆ Start to assemble and make sense of information

◆ Design front cover for project

◆ Write up introduction, etc.

Project production works in exactly the same way. For example, a project may be to produce a film for a television company. There will be a sequence of steps that need to be followed. The success of the operation depends on:

◆ Planning the tasks

◆ Carrying them out in the right sequence

◆ Making sure that all the steps in the project fit together closely

◆ Ensuring that the steps are carried out successfully

The term we use to describe this is **project management**.

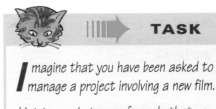

TASK

*I*magine that you have been asked to manage a project involving a new film.

List ten main types of people that you will need to bring together for the project. Set out a rough sequence of tasks that will be involved in producing the film.

2 Job production

Job production is the term we use to describe a situation where an organisation produces one or a small number of items, where the product is smaller than in a project – for example, a designer dress or hand-made suit. The product would normally be made on the producer's premises and then transported to the purchaser.

The producer might work on several jobs at the same time for different groups of customers. Firms operating in this way need to make sure that they keep having orders for new jobs to replace the ones which are nearly completed.

CASE STUDY

Automation in a modern brewery

In the UK today, the beer and lager market is dominated by a few large breweries. These firms are able to produce high outputs at a low average cost per unit. The brewing process is controlled by a central computer which checks that the mixing of ingredients has taken place correctly and takes regular readings on temperature and fermentation.

An automated bottling plant

Used bottles from pubs and other outlets are returned on pallets containing several crates at a time. The crates are lifted off the pallet automatically and a machine picks up the bottles before passing them down a line into a washer. The bottles are then checked for faults by an electronic device. The bottles are automatically filled and an electronic eye checks that the contents reach a certain level in the bottle.

The machine line then automatically labels and caps the bottles. The bottles are automatically placed on crates which are passed onto a pallet which is automatically stacked on an out-going lorry.

The whole process has been designed to eliminate the need for labour. Labour is only required to manage the computer, maintain machinery and keep an eye on it in case it breaks down.

3 Batch production

This is where a number of identical or similar items are produced in a set or **batch**. The items need not be for any specific customer but are made at regular intervals in specific quantities.

Batch production involves work being passed from one stage to another. Each stage of production is highly planned.

A simple example would be the production of loaves of bread in a bakery. Every day 200 brown loaves, 100 white loaves, and 500 small buns are produced. First the dough is made for the brown loaves. While this rises, the dough is made for the white loaves. While this is rising, the dough for the brown loaves is kneaded – and so on.

A key feature of batch production is that every now and then you have to stop the production process and reset it for a different product.

Most manufacturing companies work in this way, as do most service organisations. For example, a cinema attendant at a multiplex cinema checks the tickets of a batch of cinema-goers waiting to see *Forest Gump*; he or she then checks the tickets of a batch going to see *Pocahontas* – and so on.

TASK

1 Why is the beer and lager market suitable for mass-production?

2 What other production lines can you think of that are suitable for continuous flow production?

3 Why is it that these products are suitable for continuous flow?

4 What types of products would be unsuitable for continuous flow?

4 Line production

This involves products or services passing down a **line of production**. The production process is a repeating one, with identical products going through the same sequence of operations. Car assembly lines are a classic example of line production. The work comes down the line to the worker, who carries out a set operation. Nowadays humans have been replaced by robots on many production lines. Examples of line production can also be found in fast food outlets.

Line production produces identical products. The disadvantage of this is that many customers (e.g. car buyers) want their purchase to be made different or distinctive in some way.

5 Continuous flow production

Continuous flow production takes line production one step further. Today, it is an advantage to be able to mass-produce standard items like Mars bars and cans of beer. Continuous flow involves producing for 24 hours a day, using automatic equipment in a standardised way.

An oil refinery, for example, works on a continuous flow basis, with petrol being refined around the clock. Modern breweries, paper mills and chocolate factories also use the continuous flow method.

In continuous flow, the whole operation is handled by machinery controlled by computers. Human labour does not touch the product. Continuous flow therefore does not apply in the service industries, which depend more on human labour.

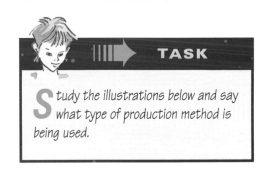

TASK

Study the illustrations below and say what type of production method is being used.

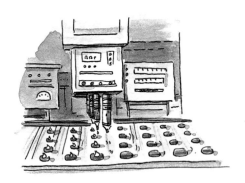

MATCH IT!

Can you help Frankie and Cleo to match the following terms and definitions?

Terms	Definitions
Operations	Producing one-off items such as a suit for an individual customer
Automation	The processes involved in converting inputs into outputs
Job production	One-off assignment for a particular customer requiring careful planning of sequential steps
Project production	A production system in which operations are controlled by computer
Continuous flow production	Products or services passing down a line of production
Line production	Mass-producing items 24 hours a day
Batch production	Producing a series of items and periodically altering the type of product being produced

37 Production Strategies

What is a production strategy?

Production strategies are the 'big' decisions that need to be made about how to make goods and services. Rather than the day-to-day details, they concern overall questions about *how* to produce.

In the last chapter we started off by looking at operations management. An important starting point in operations management is deciding how to produce.

'Why is it that different firms make similar goods in different ways?'

Transforming resources

Operations involve converting inputs into finished outputs. The illustration on the next page shows how operations management involves successfully transforming inputs into desired goods and services.

We can make a distinction between transforming resources and transformed resources:

◆ Managers, employees, machinery and equipment are a firm's **transforming resources**.

◆ The **transformed resources** are the materials and information which they process.

Mass production

The twentieth century has seen the development of **mass production** of many products, from Coca-Cola to contraceptives, Mars bars to medicines, Ford motor cars to Frosties.

Mass production has been made possible through the development of mass markets. Firms are able to produce standard products using standard parts, built on standard machines.

The greater the volume of mass production, the greater the economies a firm is able to make by cutting back production costs. Mass production can also lead to better quality, particularly where computers and robots are involved in the production process.

Mass customisation

In the last decade of the twentieth century, a number of producers have gone beyond mass production to **mass customisation**.

This is where goods are produced in very large quantities, but individual goods can be customised, i.e. produced specially for a particular customer. In Japan, in particular, robot-controlled machinery can be programmed to make a specific product such as a car for a specific customer almost as quickly as it makes a standard car.

This is possible because of the sophistication and flexibility of computer-driven equipment. Mass customisation makes it possible to produce individual items at almost the same cost as mass-produced ones.

Quality

Today we use the term **quality** to mean 'producing a good or service to customer requirements'. In UK industry there have been three stages involved in moving towards quality: quality control, quality assurance, and more recently, Total Quality Management (TQM).

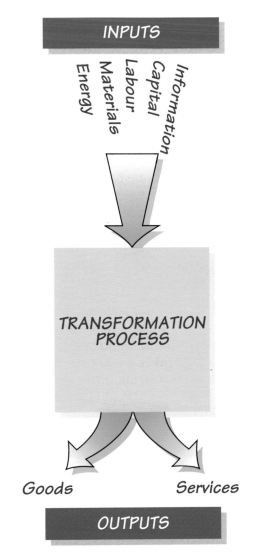

Transformation of resources

TASK

List ten items which are mass-produced.

1 Quality control

Quality control is an old idea. It involves inspectors checking finished goods and detecting and cutting out components or final products which do not meet the required standard. It can involve considerable waste as sub-standard products have to be scrapped.

2 Quality assurance

This is less wasteful than quality control. Quality assurance occurs both during and after production, and seeks to stop faults happening in the first place. Quality assurance aims to make sure that products are produced to pre-set standards. It is the responsibility of the workforce working in teams, rather than of inspectors.

3 Total Quality Management (TQM)

This is the most complete form of operations management. It is concerned with encouraging everyone in the workplace to think about quality in everything they do. Every employee sets out to satisfy customers, placing them at the heart of the production process.

Three stages in the move towards quality

CASE STUDY

'Kaizen' at Nissan

The Nissan car plant was set up in Sunderland in 1984. A Japanese company, Nissan has used its operation strategies to build up a successful plant. 'Kaizen' or 'continuous improvement' lies at the heart of Japanese operations management and TQM.

'Kaizen' requires the total involvement of all employees. It is based on the idea that in order for people to want to create quality, they must feel part of the Nissan team. The company policy is that:

- All employees have a valuable contribution to make as individuals, and this contribution is most effective when they work together as a team.

- 'Kaizen' team activity helps develop leadership skills, and the ability of people to learn from each other.

Team members discuss ways of improving quality on a regular basis. The purpose is to provide the best possible cars to satisfy customers.

 TASK

1 What do you understand by the term 'quality'?

2 Why is 'quality' so important to business?

3 How is 'Kaizen' at Nissan likely to encourage quality production?

CHAPTER 37

Just-in-time production

'Just-in-time' production is another key element in the Japanese manufacturing success story of the 1970s and 1980s. The idea is very simple: to cut costs by reducing the amount of goods and materials a firm holds in stock. It involves producing and delivering finished goods 'just in time' to be sold, partly finished goods 'just in time' to be assembled into finished goods, parts 'just in time' to go into partly finished goods, and materials 'just in time' to be made into parts.

When it works well, it is a very efficient method. However, in a mass production plant it requires a constant delivery of new parts, and employees therefore need to be highly skilled and flexible. Other disadvantages are:

◆ If you run out of stocks the plant cannot function.

◆ The workforce must be flexible or the system becomes difficult to run.

◆ The organisation is at the mercy of the quality standards of its suppliers.

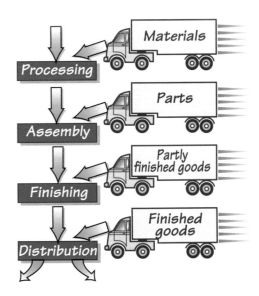

Just-in-time production

MATCH IT! Can you help Frankie and Cleo to match the following terms and definitions?

Just-in-time	Detecting and cutting out faults after they have happened
Kaizen	A process of continual improvement in production
Quality	Producing items in very large quantities
Transformation process	Creating an atmosphere where everybody in the workplace is concerned to improve quality standards
Mass production	Producing in mass quantities but catering for individual customer requirements
	Converting inputs into finished goods and services
Mass customisation	Producing goods or services to a customer's individual requirements
TQM	Managing the transformation process
Operations management	Getting stocks and components to where they are required just before they are required in order to reduce stock holdings
Quality control	

4 *38* Production Activities

The 'five Ps of production'

Production activities vary considerably depending on the product, but there are a number of components which are common to all forms of production. Together these make up the so-called 'five Ps of production' *(see below right)*.

The first 'P' is the product, which we looked at in Chapter 28. The others are:

1 Plant

In order to add value to a product or service, firms nearly always need some sort of **plant** or base.

The location, size, design, safety and layout of the plant are all very important. Managers need to think carefully about how parts and materials are to be delivered, and how finished goods will be transported away from the plant. The layout should make it easy to co-ordinate the various activities that will take place there. Time and costs involved in transferring goods, materials, information and people should be kept to a minimum.

Managers must also make sure that plant and equipment are properly maintained. A maintenance department may include electricians, plumbers and joiners, as well as many other skilled workers. The effectiveness of the maintenance department can be judged by the number of breakdowns and accidents at work. Safety is vitally important.

2 Process

In Chapter 36 we looked at various ways of **processing** inputs. We listed the various methods as:

◆ Project production

◆ Job production

◆ Batch production

◆ Line production

◆ Continuous flow production

3 Programme

Programming is mainly concerned with timetabling the use of resources. To meet orders successfully, the firm will need to plan and control activities carefully. Successful programming involves purchasing, stock control and quality control.

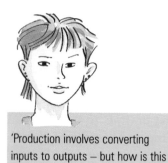

'Production involves converting inputs to outputs – but how is this done?'

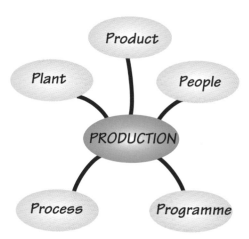

The five Ps of production.

Purchasing

Purchasing involves buying materials and other inputs. A typical manufacturing company spends one half of its income on supplies of raw materials and services. Effective purchasing is all about getting good value for money.

Stock control

Stock control involves holding stocks of raw materials, work-in-progress, finished goods, plant and machine parts and spares. The aim of the stock control system should be to keep stocks low while having enough stocks to meet requirements.

Quality control

Quality control is increasingly seen as a guiding principle for all members of an organisation. Total Quality Management (TQM) is all about thinking ahead and preventing faults and accidents before they happen.

4 People

The success of any production process will depend on the **people** involved. Just as with any other resource, the quality of employees depends on how much is invested in them. Training and development are vital. Management needs to bring out the potential of employees by helping them to develop.

In many manufacturing organisations the bulk of employees will work in production. They thus add value directly to the final good or service.

Ways of improving output

◆ **Work study** looks at the way tasks are carried out in order to improve output. For example, a work study researcher may note that some activities can be done better in a different order.

◆ **Method study** looks at the methods being employed to do a task in order to increase efficiency.

◆ **Work measurement** is concerned with measuring the work carried out by employees. Performance standards are set so that performance can be compared with these standards.

◆ **Ergonomics** is the study of workers in their working environment. It looks at the relationship between employees and the plant and machinery they use. The aim is to find out how best to motivate employees and enable them to work more effectively.

COURSEWORK ACTIVITIES

Compare two organisations producing similar types of goods and services, which are of roughly the same size, e.g. two supermarkets, two service stations, two hairdressers, two schools, two discos, two corner shops, etc.

Compare and contrast the two organisations in terms of:

- Location
- Size
- Design
- Safety
- Layout

Identify the strengths and weaknesses of the plant of each organisation.

Operations management in a service industry

Much of the discussion above relates to manufacturing. But it is a lot more difficult to measure the value of services, and to control their quality, because the 'quality' of a service depends on the expectations of consumers, which can be difficult to measure.

Services are also instantly perishable. When you enjoy a restaurant meal, you benefit from the service of the waiter. But you can't 'store' this in the way you can store a bar of chocolate. This makes it difficult for operations managers of services. If their restaurant is half-full, they are not able to store up the surplus waiter or waitress service until the restaurant is full. When a waiter is not working, you still have to pay his wages.

Customer contact

In service industries, employees are likely to have far more customer contact than in manufacturing or information processing operations. As a result, the 'people' side of the production operation is very important. In services, you need people who are able to work closely and well with customers and colleagues.

Customised services

Many services are highly customised – think of the personal relationship between a hairdresser and a client, a doctor and a patient, a teacher and a student. While some services lend themselves to mass-production, such as banking and insurance services, as a general rule the production side of a service industry needs to be organised in a far more customised way.

Personal initiative

In service industries, firms also need to rely far more on individual employees taking the initiative when dealing with customers. This means that those employees need to be given a certain amount of decision-making power.

Examples include the way in which a claims department clerk deals with a customer's claim, the way in which a bank employee deals with a customer's account, and so on. Customers want instant personal service from employees.

Labour input

The net result of these factors is that service industries tend to be a lot more **labour-intensive**, while manufacturing tends to be more **capital-intensive**.

COURSEWORK ACTIVITIES

Make a study of a small service organisation such as a hairdresser's, retail outlet, or other organisation. Show how each of the operational factors listed here relates to the organisation and its operations management.

Can you help Frankie and Cleo to match the following terms and definitions?

Ergonomics	The employees of an organisation and the way they act
Work study	All aspects of making sure that products meet customer requirements
Plant	Looking after plant and equipment
Process	Study of the relationship between workers and their environment, especially their equipment
Purchasing	The land, buildings and equipment used by a business
Maintenance	The act of transforming inputs to outputs
People	Buying materials and other inputs
Programme	Involving a high input of people relative to other resources
Stock control	Dealings between members of an organisation and customers
Quality control	A specifically arranged selection and sequence of things to be done
Method study	A study of the way in which work is arranged
Customer contact	The systematic arrangement of materials, parts, components coming into and being stored by a company
Labour-intensive	Systematic research into ways in which employees carry out tasks in order to suggest better ways of organising jobs

4 *39* **New Products**

The changing marketplace

In today's marketplace it is essential for companies to create new products to meet the needs of consumers, whose wants and needs are changing all the time.

We can illustrate this by looking at the activities of British pharmaceutical companies (i.e. firms that make medicines and drugs).

When you produce a new drug or medicine you only have the patent for that medicine for a limited amount of time. A **patent** is a government licence to an inventor assigning her or him the sole right to make, use and sell the invention for a given period of time.

Once the patent runs out, anyone can copy the product. Zantac, an anti-ulcer treatment, is the best-selling drug in the world, but its patent runs out in 1997. In 1996, British companies are therefore seeking new drugs that will prevent and cure AIDS, and others that will prevent and control 'flu to replace their current top sellers.

Testing the market

A lot of planning needs to take place before a good or service is launched. Firms need to study the market and the way it is changing. **Research and development (R & D)** is a very important business process that relies on market research information.

'One of the problems today is that people constantly want new products. Investment in new products reduces profit margins for people like me!'

'What new products can you think of that have made a big impact recently?'

Below: Planning a new product

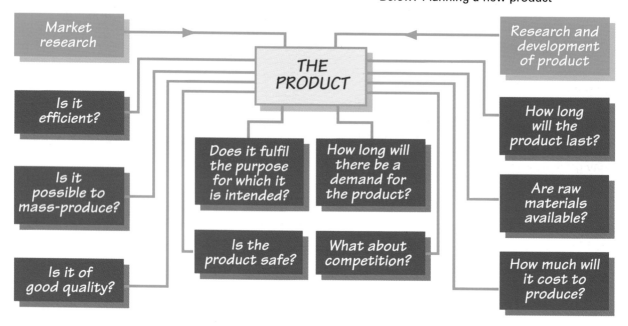

Market research

Research and development of product

THE PRODUCT

Is it efficient?

How long will the product last?

Is it possible to mass-produce?

Does it fulfil the purpose for which it is intended?

How long will there be a demand for the product?

Are raw materials available?

Is it of good quality?

Is the product safe?

What about competition?

How much will it cost to produce?

CHAPTER 39

Setting up a production line can be very expensive. You need to make sure that you have got everything right before you start. Careful work in the early stages will help to ensure that the launch will be successful and that consumers get the benefits they want.

Research and development

Once a firm is sure there is a suitable market for a product, then research and development must find out the best way of meeting demand. The product must be attractively designed to appeal to consumers and to meet their needs. The researchers need to answer many questions, including those shown on the illustration on the previous page.

An organisation may be reluctant to change an earlier design, particularly if it is distinctive or helps to give a good image of the organisation, such as the radiator grille of a BMW, or the lettering on a Coca-Cola can. Designers need also to think about the way the product will be handled. For example, consumer goods need to be easy to use, especially products for the elderly; children's toys must be safe and able to stand up to wear and tear, and so on.

TASK

*R*ead the Case Study below, then answer the following questions.

1 When was the ballpoint pen patented?

2 List two advantages the Biro has over the fountain pen.

3 What mistake did Lazlo Biro make?

4 How did Marcel Bich take the ballpoint pen forward?

The Bic Crystal – the largest-selling pen in the world

CASE STUDY

The ballpoint pen

The ballpoint pen was patented in 1938 by a Hungarian journalist, Lazlo Biro. Unlike a fountain pen, it used a runny, jelly-like ink.

A British entrepreneur, Henry Martin, spotted the potential of the invention. He bought the patents to sell the product in the UK and many other countries. Martin realised that the great strength of the ballpoint pen was that it was unaffected by changes in air pressure, so it could be used by aeroplane pilots and navigators for making calculations. The Biro Pen Manufacturing Company was set up near Reading and 30,000 pens were produced for use by the RAF during the war.

In 1945, the Biro pen cost the equivalent of £2.75 – approximately the weekly wage for a secretary. Within four years it was outselling the fountain pen.

The launch in the USA in October 1945 was equally spectacular. The New York department store Gimbells sold 10,000 Biros at $12.50 each. Unfortunately, Lazlo Biro failed to register his invention and it was soon copied.

In France, another entrepreneur, Baron Marcel Bich, took the ballpoint even further. He created the Bic Crystal, a simple plastic ballpoint which is now one of the best-known trademarks in the world. In 1957 Bich's Société Bic SA took over the Biro company. As time went on, more and more products were sold under the Bic name and fewer and fewer under the Biro brand.

Today 15 million Bic ballpoints are sold every day, making the Bic Crystal the best-selling pen in the world. When Marcel Bich died in 1994 he was the fifth richest man in France.

Today designers often allow for **planned obsolescence**, so that the product will need replacing after a time. For example, many cars are only built to last a limited number of years, and today we even have 'throw-away' cameras.

Testing and trialling

Once a design has been developed, the researchers will either build a **prototype** which can be tested, or trial the service on offer. Many prototypes will be tried and then discarded, while others may be altered and improved *(see right)*.

It is essential to look at the profits that a new product is likely to generate. This involves estimating how many it is likely to sell in a given time period, and how much costs will be during this period.

Sometimes the product or prototypes are **test-marketed** with a representative sample of consumers. This provides useful feedback and reduces the risk of a failure when the product is officially launched.

The **launch** is the final stage. This involves presenting the product to the market for the first time.

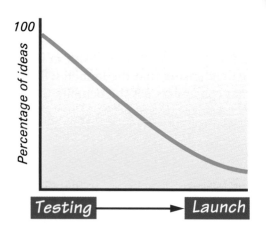

Many ideas will be discarded during the testing process

MATCH IT!

Can you help Frankie and Cleo to match the following terms and definitions?

Patent	Trying out a product in a small part of the overall market which is felt to be representative
Test market	Deliberately creating a product which will date or wear out
Prototype	A government licence to an inventor, giving them the sole right to make and sell a product for a period of time
Development	Systematic investigation to find facts or collect information on a subject
Research	The time at which a product is exposed to the full market
Launch	Bringing a product to a more advanced stage, or to completion
Planned obsolescence	Model of a good or service, produced for test purposes

40 Production Technologies

Keeping pace with changing technology

We live in an age of rapid progress in production technology. In the past, firms struggled because they were twenty years out of date. Today firms can struggle because they are a year or even a few months out of date.

'Advanced technology is a waste of time. It is always expensive to buy and rarely lowers costs. Firms are more likely to go out of business than gain an advantage from using new technology!'

Do you agree with Ron?

Advantage through technology

If we look at the development of production technology in many fields, we can see that progress often takes the form of a major breakthrough, followed by a series of less spectacular improvements. This pattern will then be repeated at regular intervals, as shown below:

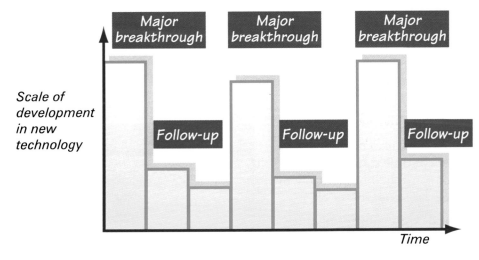

The pattern of progress in production technology

Many businesses expect to replace their plant and equipment every few years, and allow for this in their forward plans. The best time to buy new technology is immediately after a 'giant step', rather than just before one. The firm that buys plant and equipment just as it is becoming out of date may be left with old-fashioned plant while rivals are leaping forward.

Examples of recent technologies

Computer-aided design (CAD)
Computer-aided design has improved the reliability and speed with which complex structures such as aeroplanes, cars and bridges can be designed. The system works like an electronic drawing board, allowing complex two- and three-dimensional shapes to be modelled quickly and accurately on-screen, stored conveniently and copied when needed.

Micromachines

Micromachines will be the newest success story in production technology for the millennium. The Japanese have been working on a programme to invest in micromachines for the last 30 years. The project has had massive sponsorship from the Japanese government.

Micromachines are tiny intelligent machines powered by the latest laser technology. They can be programmed to perform a number of key operations. Their greatest use will be when they are put to work inside other machines.

Today, for example, when you want to clean a nuclear reactor, you have to close it down and strip it down. A micromachine would be able to climb through the pipes of the reactor and carry out cleaning operations while the reactor is still running. Micromachines will be able to get inside any mechanical device and do things where human hands are unable to reach.

Eventually micromachines may be able to enter the human body to perform complex surgery. Micromachines stand to provide huge value added to Japanese industry in the 21st century.

Machine tool developments

As well as CAD, developments have also taken place in machine tools. Many are now controlled numerically **(numerical control – NC)** or controlled numerically by a computer **(computer numerical control – CNC)**.

CADCAM (computer-aided design/computer-aided manufacturing) refers to the use of data from a CAD system to drive machines as part of the manufacturing process. A more recent development in this process is **computer-integrated manufacturing (CIM)**. Here, the CAD system not only designs the product, but also orders materials, drives CNC machine tools and has its own control system which provides data for purchasing, accounts, sales and other functions.

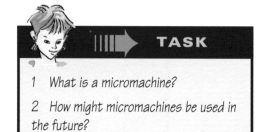

TASK

1   *What is a micromachine?*

2   *How might micromachines be used in the future?*

Robots

Robots are multi-purpose machines that can be programmed and re-programmed to perform physical tasks. An industrial robot in a car factory may be programmed to paint and then re-programmed to weld pieces together or to assemble parts.

Robots in industry are now being fitted with vision recognition systems. These make it possible for them to recognise objects by their shape and size, and to fit items like car windscreens by measuring up and centring the screen.

MATCH IT!

Can you help Frankie and Cleo to match the following terms and definitions?

Robot	Use of computer software to model complex two- and three-dimensional shapes
Micromachine	The application of science to the production of goods and services
New technology	Multi-purpose machines that can be programmed to perform physical tasks
Production technology	Use of computers in the manufacture of products
Computer-aided manufacture	Tiny robots that can get inside other systems
Computer-aided design	New scientific application, typically involving the use of computers or micro-electronics

5 *41* Accounting Processes

Monitoring performance

Whether you are at college, school or at work, you will naturally be concerned about how you are getting on. The likelihood is that you will measure your success with information or feedback.

For example, your exam results will tell you how you have performed. If you are at work, a positive word from a supervisor may be very helpful.

In the same way, business organisations need **financial information** in order to measure their performance. This information may help them to judge how successful they are in achieving their objectives.

'I now understand all about marketing and production, but I have not yet come across many figures. How do I know if my business is doing well?'

Why do we need accountants?

Different businesses have different objectives, but every business owner needs to keep an eye on the firm's finances.

The job of an **accountant** is to answer crucial questions about the financial health of the organisation, such as:

'When you can afford to buy a flash car or a nice home like mine!'

◆ How are we doing?

◆ What sort of return are we going to get?

◆ Can we meet our debts?

◆ Should we expand?

◆ What about taxation?

◆ Where does our future lie?

As well as helping managers to manage the business more efficiently, information supplied by accountants can help:

◆ Shareholders to assess the value of the money they invest in a business

◆ Suppliers to assess whether a company can pay its debts

◆ Providers of finance to know whether repayments are possible

◆ Employees to know how a company is performing

◆ The Inland Revenue to make an accurate tax assessment

These individuals or organisations are known as **stakeholders,** as they have a 'stake' or interest in the way the organisation is run. Some of the stakeholders

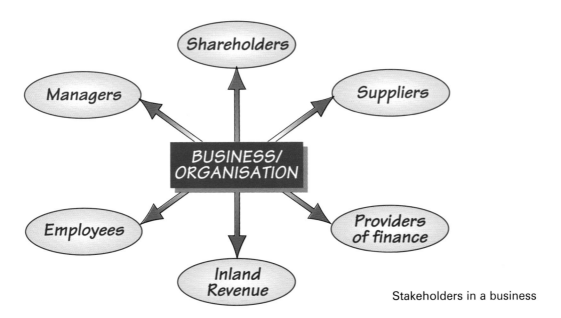

Stakeholders in a business

are within the organisation – for example, managers and employees. Others are from outside the organisation. For example, providers of finance and suppliers will want the business to do well so that they can be paid for their products and financial services.

Accounting data prepared by accountants can therefore be used by a variety of different groups of people to help them make decisions.

The accounting process

An **accounting system** consists of methods and procedures which are used to keep track of financial activities, and to summarise information for managers.

Accounting therefore acts as an information system, so that groups of individuals can understand how well or badly the organisation is performing.

The three steps in the accounting process are:

1 **Recording financial activities**. This means having an organised record of financial activities. For example, whenever a transaction takes place, even if it involves credit, it has to be recorded.

2 **Classifying information**. A jumbled list of business transactions would be too large, diverse and unwieldy for decision-makers. It needs to be classified into a series of groups and categories.

3 **Summarising data**. For accounting information to be useful, it must be summarised.

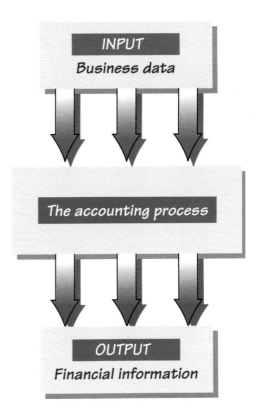

The accounting process

 **TASK**

*R*ead the Case Study below, then answer the following questions:

1 Why have managers at AT&T decided to break the company into three separate units?

2 Upon what sort of information might their decision have been based?

3 What effect might diseconomies of scale have had on the decisions taken?

Management and financial accounting

The process of accounting falls into two broad areas:

1 Management accounting

2 Financial accounting

Management accounting is concerned with giving managers information from within the business so that they can plan, control and make decisions. Management accounting may help a business to:

◆ Control its costs

◆ Monitor its operations and make day-to-day decisions

◆ Control the activities of departments

◆ Create budgets for various parts of the business

◆ Forecast future events

◆ Manage its activities efficiently

Financial accounting is primarily about recording transactions and extracting information from them. It involves:

◆ **Book-keeping** – i.e. the day-to-day recording of financial activities

◆ Preparation of **final accounts** such as the **trading account** (Chapter 45), the **profit and loss account** (Chapter 46) and the **balance sheet** (Chapter 47).

Final accounts are **summary statements** prepared at the end of a certain period. By studying these, shareholders know how the directors or managers have performed on their behalf. From the final accounts, **ratios** (see Chapter 49) can be extracted. These show fairly accurately how a business is performing.

A financial accountant must also ensure that a business's accounts provide a **true and fair** view of its activities and that they comply with the provisions of the Companies Acts.

CASE STUDY

The splitting up of AT&T

AT&T, the world's largest international telecommunications carrier, is splitting itself into three separate companies. Its main reason is to benefit the shareholders. The company has simply become too big. Financial information shows that some parts of the company are performing well while others are losing money. Accountants and analysts say that it makes sense for the various businesses to learn to live on their own.

The 'stars' could then shine and shareholders would be rewarded. The losers would be forced out into the cold where they would have to become more focused, efficient and competitive in order to survive.

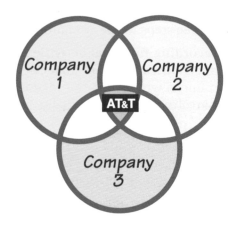

Re-organisation at AT&T

TASK

R on Rust has been told by the Inland Revenue that he must keep a better set of financial records.
He looks in the drawers in his desk and finds lots of different types of information (see below).
Which of this information might the tax inspectors want to see?

Can you help Frankie and Cleo to match the following terms and definitions?

Shareholders	Government department to which taxes are paid
Inland Revenue	Methods and procedures to keep track of financial activities
Stakeholders	People or organisations who own a financial stake in a business
Book-keeping	The grouping of business transactions
Financial accounting	The recording of financial activities
Accounting process	The providing of information for managers so that they can make decisions
Classifying information	The recording and summarising of financial information for management
Management accounting	People with a 'stake' or interest in the successful running of an organisation

5 42 Sources of Finance

Understanding cashflow

Within all organisations, money comes in and flows out. This is called the organisation's cashflow.

From time to time, business managers may pose questions such as:

◆ *'Can we afford to buy x?'*

◆ *'Are we going to be able to pay that bill?'*

◆ *'Wouldn't it be nice if we could develop y?'*

To answer such questions, they will often have to carry out some form of financial planning – and often to seek additional finance from outside the company. The key issues are:

◆ What is the finance for?

◆ How long will it be needed?

◆ Is it affordable, i.e. can the firm keep up with the repayments?

'I suppose it is a bit like organising your personal finances. I often used to run out of cash at the end of the month. I usually had to borrow money from my dad. On one or two occasions I even had to arrange an overdraft. When I bought my car, I took out a small bank loan, but before doing so I checked that I could meet the repayments.'

Below: Short-term and long-term sources of finance

Common methods of finance

Sources of finance fall into two main categories. **Short-term** finance is designed to be paid back quickly, while **long-term** loans may be paid back over many years. Below are some of the different types of finance available:

1 Trade credit

This is a useful source of finance provided by suppliers. With trade credit, a business can use the goods or service provided by suppliers before they are paid for.

The **credit period** is simply the period between receiving a good or service and paying for it. Although no charge or rate of interest is attached to trade credit, cash discounts may be lost if payments are not made within the agreed time.

2 Overdraft

An overdraft is probably the most frequently used solution to cashflow problems. The bank sets an agreed limit on the customer's bank account, beyond which they will not draw. This is called an **overdraft facility**. The amount the customer borrows is called an **overdraft**.

SHORT TERM
Trade credit
Overdraft
Factoring
Leasing and hire purchase
Loans

LONG TERM
Mortgages
Profit retention
Government grants
Venture capital
Equity

A special charge is made for setting up the overdraft facility, and interest is calculated on the level of the overdraft on a daily basis. Businesses often depend on customers paying bills promptly. Given that customers like Ron Rust may delay payment as long as possible, an overdraft can be a useful form of short-term business finance.

Factoring

Trade debts mean that money can often be tied up for as much as six months. For a business requiring cash quickly this can be a real problem. A **factoring** company may offer immediate payment of part of the amount owed to a business – normally around 80% – with the balance being paid when the debt is settled. This provides an immediate way for a business to improve its cashflow. In return, the factoring company will charge a fee which includes interest and administration charges.

Leasing and hire purchase

There are many different ways for customers to receive goods and make payments over time.

Goods on **hire purchase** remain the property of the finance company until the customer has made all the payments. Other **credit purchasing** schemes enable the goods to belong to the customer from the first payment.

With **leasing,** the lessee uses the asset while making regular payments to the lessor, who owns it. An **operating lease** is for a small amount, and a **capital** or **finance lease** is for a large item over an extended period.

COURSEWORK ACTIVITIES

Conduct separate interviews with two locally-based small business owners. Prepare a simple questionnaire about the sources of finance used for each business.

Within your coursework, label the businesses 'A' and 'B' and then compare and contrast their source of finance.

TASK

*R*on sometimes has problems getting suppliers to provide him with the goods he wants. Everybody in the scrap metal trade knows how he does business. Because of this, his suppliers tend to charge him higher-than-average prices.

Name two advantages which Ron would receive if he made his business practices more efficient.

'I never pay bills until the last possible moment. If people want to do business with me they have to accept my rules. After all, I am their customer. I want the goods now and I will pay them in three months.'

CASE STUDY

Ark Geophysics Ltd

When Ark Geophysics, a software company in the geophysics industry, was first established, its founders Richard Gleave, Kitty Hall and Andy McGrandle had to ask themselves a number of questions:

- What equipment would they need?

- Would there be enough work to generate the income they required?

- Could they meet a repayment schedule?

- How would they be affected by their competitors?

- What were their financial needs?

They began by carefully researching their **revenue expenditure**, i.e. the day-to-day running expenses of their business, such as rent, office expenses, electricity, telephone, etc. They also looked at their **capital expenditure** on large or fixed items such as computers and office equipment. They tried to work out what they would have to pay out and when their income would come in. Next they drew up projections of cashflow in a **business plan**. This outlined how their proposals would work. It was shown to several banks. Soon they were being offered help in the form of loans and leasing facilities.

Today Ark Geophysics Ltd is a successful company with a reputation throughout the industry.

Drawing up the business plan

 TASK

1   Explain the difference between revenue expenditure and capital expenditure.

2   Why was it necessary for Richard, Kitty and Andy to draw up a business plan?

Loans

Most businesses need to borrow in order to trade successfully. The charge for borrowing is called **interest**. The key to calculating interest is usually the risk involved. For example, a longer-term loan or a loan to a business with no track record may carry higher rates of interest.

Banks may offer a variety of types of loans. These include business starter loans, franchise finance and the Small Firms Guarantee Scheme, offered by banks and supported by the DTI.

Large public limited companies may issue **debentures**. A debenture is an acknowledgement of a debt made to a company for a fixed rate of interest which specifies the terms of repayment at the end of a period. Debentures are bought and sold on the Stock Exchange.

Mortgages

A mortgage is a loan secured on a property. The size of the mortgage payment will depend upon factors such as the amount of the loan, the age of the property and the income of the borrowers.

Profit retention

Probably the most important source of finance for many businesses is profit which is ploughed back from one year to the next. Although managers must first satisfy shareholders, they will also be conscious of the need to put some of their profits back into the business.

Government grants

Important sources of finance for many businesses are **soft loans** and **subsidies** from the EU or from central or local government. Soft loans are loans at lower rates of interest. Subsidies help to reduce the price of products and encourage producers to produce more.

Examples of this type of help include the **Enterprise Allowance Scheme** for people starting up in business, development agency loans in areas of high unemployment or regional selective assistance.

Venture capital

A **venture capital company** may help small firms to get established by providing investment capital in return for a shareholding in the business. 3i is the largest venture capital company of this type.

Equity

This means finance provided by the owners of the business. How easily equity can be raised will depend upon the type of business. For example, a sole trader may rely on personal sources, and extra sums of money may be difficult to raise. Sole traders may even take in partners to inject some capital into the business.

A private limited company has certain restrictions on the rights of members to transfer shares, and there are limits on their ability to extend share ownership.

A fully listed public limited company may have many different opportunities to raise fresh capital from the financial markets. However, the problem with issuing more shares is that it dilutes the control of the original shareholders.

CASE STUDY

The problem of late payment

A recent survey by a firm of accountants revealed that:

- 76% of firms wait 3 months or more for their bills to be paid

- Only 14% receive their money within the contractual limit of 30 days

- 8 out of 10 manufacturers have to wait up to 3 months for payment

- 96% of businesses say it adds to their problems, and 30% say it seriously affects their business!

Most businesses feel they are in a difficult situation. They want payment for the goods and services they provide, but they do not want to have to take their customers to court in order to get it.

TASK

1 Why do organisations delay paying their bills?

2 How might delayed payment affect the cashflow of the supplier and the customer?

3 What would you consider to be a reasonable credit period?

4 Work in a small group to discuss what action could be taken to stop late payment.

Can you help Frankie and Cleo to match the following terms and definitions?

Mortgage	Practice of delaying payment of bills and invoices for as long as possible
Overdraft	Repayment scheme in which goods remain the property of the finance company until the last payment is made
Late payment	Source of finance in which the customer has an agreed credit limit over which they will not draw
Hire purchase	Loan usually secured upon a property
Factoring	Organisation providing financial help to businesses in return for a shareholding
Trade credit	Government grant available to those wishing to start their own business
Enterprise Allowance	Offering of immediate payment against debts
Venture capital company	Source of finance where businesses use goods before paying for them

43 **Liquidity and Cashflow**

Organising our own finances

When it comes to looking after our own finances, we all know that we have to take some form of responsibility.

If we spend too much, we will soon run out of money. We will then either have to go without things that we need, or borrow in order to get them. But if we borrow, can we pay back the lender?

One way to predict if we are able to meet our financial commitments as and when they arise is to draw up a **cash** or **cashflow budget** showing our income and expenditure. **Cashflow forecasts** are statements which enable us to analyse our proposed expenditure and income over a period of time.

'I try wherever possible to plan my finances by working out what spending I will have to commit myself to in future months and then matching this to my forecast income. If I didn't do this, I would not be able to meet all of my financial commitments.'

'Forecasting sounds good in theory, particularly if you are working for somebody else, but for businesses like mine it just doesn't work. I have good months and bad months and I just cannot predict when the good months are likely to occur.'

'Do you set money aside for the bad months, so that you can pay your bills?'

'No, that would be inefficient. When money comes into the business I make it work by purchasing more stock. More stock helps to generate more sales.'

Just imagine the problems which face Ron Rust when he can't pay his bills *(above and right)*. You'll notice he doesn't say how he copes with not having enough money to pay his bills. Perhaps he visits his bank manager to arrange an overdraft or sells off his debts to a factoring company. Whatever solution he chooses, it can only be a short-term answer. One day there will be a crisis and he won't be able to raise enough cash to sort out his problems.

Financial forecasting and liquidity

Looking into the future will help all organisations to plan their activities so that things can happen in the way they want.

'But how do you cope if you can't pay the bills?!'

The process of financial forward planning using techniques such as cashflow forecasting is known as **budgeting.** We all budget to a greater or lesser extent. Our short-term budget may relate to how we are going to get through the next week and do all of the things we want to do. In the longer term we may be thinking about Christmas, buying a car or splashing out on a special birthday present for someone. In exactly the same way, businesses try to look into the future. The **cashflow forecast** is a financial plan or budget which tries to anticipate money coming into and going out of the business over a future period.

CASE STUDY

Planning your cashflow

Imagine that you have left school and started work. You earn £80 a week and out of this you have certain fixed weekly expenses *(below)*.

Expenditure	£
Rent to parents	20
Daily fares	5
Lunches	10
Weekends	12
Records, magazines, etc.	10
TOTAL	57

On 2nd of January you receive your wages of £80. You owe your father £40 from December. There are some clothes that you want to buy costing £15 in a sale that ends on 6th January. A deposit of £30 for a holiday must be paid during the second week. This week you are taking three friends to a cinema which will cost you £9 and you have to pay a dry-cleaning bill of £2. There are four weeks in January, and in the third week you will economise and not buy any records and magazines.

Week	1	2	3	4
Income	80	80	80	80
Expenditure				
Rent	20	20	20	20
Fares	5	5	5	5
Lunch	10	10	10	10
Weekends	12	12	12	12
Records, magazines, etc.	10	10	-	10
Clothes	15	-	-	-
Cinema	9	-	-	-
Dry cleaning	2	-	-	-
Holiday	-	30	-	-
TOTAL	83	87	47	57
NET	(3)	(7)	33	23
Loan from mother	(3) B	(7) B	(10) R	-
Loan from father	-	-	(23) R	(17) R
TOTAL	-	-	-	6

B = Borrowing   R = Repayment

A cashflow forecast will enable you to see if you can afford to do all of these things and predict how soon you can pay back the loan from your father.

Look carefully at the cashflow forecast on the left and analyse all of the different expenditures.

The cashflow forecast indicates that you need to borrow from your mother in Week 1 and 2, but you can pay her back in Week 3, and that you can finish paying your father back in the last week of the month.

Cashflow has, therefore, provided the planning necessary to cope with the timing of your various financial commitments – and the same principle applies in business.

  TASK

1 *Using a similar format to the one above, produce a cashflow forecast of your income and expenditure for the next month.*

2 *What sort of benefits would you gain if you regularly used this sort of technique for monitoring your finances?*

Profit and cash

Whereas **profit** is a surplus from trading activities, **cash** is money a business can use to pay its debts. It is thus a **liquid asset** which enables an organisation to buy the goods and services it needs in order to add value to them, to trade and make profits.

However, a business can trade and appear to be profitable, but at the same time not have enough money flowing in to pay its bills. All businesses must therefore ensure that cash coming in is enough to cover cash going out.

By budgeting, a firm can forecast the flows into and out of its bank account, so that surpluses or deficits can be highlighted. By doing this, any necessary action such as arranging an overdraft facility can be taken beforehand.

TASK

*D*oes Marie Hebden need to arrange an overdraft facility over the next six months? If so, how large an overdraft is likely to be required?

On the 1st January Marie Hebden has £350 in the bank. She expects her receipts over the next six months to be:

	Jan	Feb	Mar	Apr	May	June
	£1,250	£1,600	£1,700	£1,250	£1,230	£1,900

She has also worked out her payments and expects these to be:

	Jan	Feb	Mar	Apr	May	June
	£1,300	£1,500	£1,900	£1,800	£1,100	£1,100

Copy out and complete the template below to undertake the task:

	Jan	Feb	Mar	Apr	May	June
Opening balance	350	300				
Add Receipts	1,250	1,600				
	1,600	etc.				
Less payments	1,300					
Closing balance	300					

When you have finished this exercise, change the figures and make up another exercise of your own to complete.

MATCH IT!

Can you help Frankie and Cleo to match the following terms and definitions?

Cash budget	Liquid financial asset, enabling an organisation to buy the goods and services it needs
Cashflow	Financial plan showing money coming in and going out over a period
Cash	Financial surplus generated by trading activities
Profit	Money coming in and going out of a business
Cash forecast	Financial forward planning using techniques such as cashflow forecasting
Budgeting	Financial statement allowing income and expenditure over a period of time to be analysed

44 Accounting Principles and Records

'I am beginning to understand why I need to look after my finances. What I do not understand is how I go about doing this.'

'Ah, now I can tell you all about this. You need to set up a book-keeping system.'

The trading cycle

The trading cycle provides us with a useful starting point from which to look at accounting principles.

In a manufacturing company, the cycle starts with the purchase of raw materials. It then goes through production and the warehousing of finished goods ready for sale, finishing with the eventual sale of the goods.

The diagram on the right shows what the trading cycle might be like for a manufacturer of food products.

Of course, not all organisations manufacture products. Some provide services. The trading cycle for a service organisation will be very similar *(see diagram below right)*, except that the business may be purchasing goods which are then offered for resale, or providing a service such as gardening. When payments are made, further stock can be purchased.

The trading cycle provides a useful and easy way of thinking about how businesses operate and trade. The ultimate purpose is to meet customer requirements. But at the same time, organisations have to meet their business objectives – for example, making a profit. That is why organisations need to keep records of all the trading activities which take place. By keeping records of their activities, they can measure their performance, improve their overall financial control and take action when problems arise.

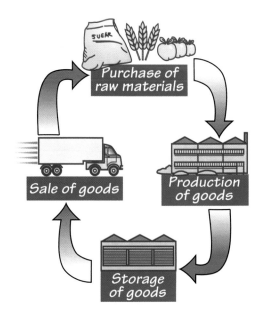

The trading cycle for a food manufacturing business

A basic accounting system

A useful definition of accounting is: *'the art of preparing accounting reports from book-keeping records in accordance with acknowledged methods and conventions.'*

Let us look more closely at this definition:

◆ **Book-keeping records.** In the past, records of account were kept in books or ledgers. These records were continually updated as transactions took place. Today most businesses – except of course Ron Rust's – record their transactions on computer.

◆ **Preparing accounting reports.** In order to be understood and analysed, entries from the book-keeping records have to be presented in a clear way.

This is done by preparing **trading** and **profit and loss accounts** and **balance sheets** based on information collected via the book-keeping system.

◆ **Acknowledged methods and conventions.** There are certain set ways of recording accounts which have grown up over a period of time. Records need to be set out according to these conventions.

Imagine the confusion if everybody presented information in a different way. It would be nearly impossible to make comparisons between one business and the next.

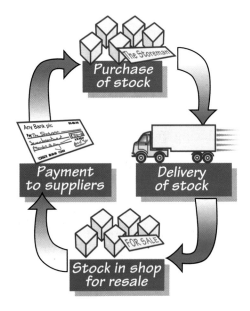

The trading cycle for a retailing organisation

CASE STUDY

Frankie and Cleo visit their bank manager

Frankie's bank manager has been providing her with advice about how to run her business. She says:

- *Keep all of your records up to date. Write them up promptly and regularly.*

- *Get professional advice if you are in any doubt about your records.*

- *Remember that the Inland Revenue and Customs & Excise will be interested in your records.*

- *Accurate and up-to-date records will help you to manage your business, as well as saving money with your accountant.*

The accounting process

There are a number of stages involved in putting together a basic accounting system:

1 Preparing, keeping and using documents

2 Transferring information from documents to records in books or on computer

3 Setting out a **trial balance** (a list of balances for all accounts)

4 Producing financial statements known as **final accounts**

We will look briefly at each of these stages in turn.

TASK

1 How often should Frankie update her records?

2 Who will be interested in her records? Why will they show such interest?

1 Business documents

When we go into a shop to buy a newspaper or magazine there is little need for documentation. Organisations, however, will usually require a lot more documentation to record each transaction. This is because:

◆ Most organisations buy goods or pay for services on credit (i.e. buy now and pay later). Documents help to record what is happening.

◆ Documents help to create records which meet the legal requirements of the Inland Revenue and Customs & Excise.

◆ Documents provide source data which forms the basis for detailed accounting records.

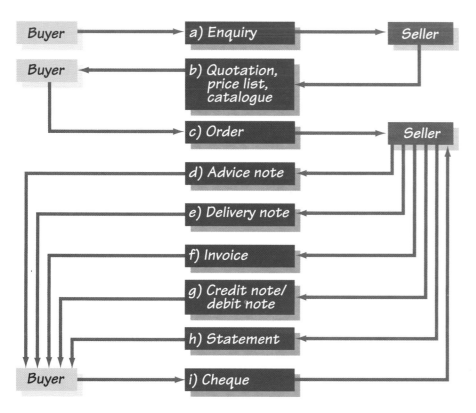

Documents produced
during a typical
business transaction

The diagram above shows the various documents
produced during a typical business transaction:

a A **letter of enquiry** will be sent to suppliers to find
   out what they can offer

b The buyer will then receive several **quotations, price
   lists** or **catalogues**.

c The buyer will then send out an **order** specifying
   their requirements.

d Before sending the goods, the seller may send an
   advice note to say that the goods are being sent and
   that they will arrive shortly.

e A **delivery note** is often sent with the goods.

f The **invoice** shows the details of the transaction.

g A **credit note** or **debit note** may be used to change
   amounts appearing on an invoice. The credit note will
   reduce the invoice price, while the debit note may
   increase the invoice amount.

h A **statement** is simply a copy of the customer's
   account in the sales ledger. It is usually sent to
   remind them to pay their bill.

i A **cheque** is sent by the buyer to the seller to settle
   the account.

COURSEWORK ACTIVITIES

Talk to somebody who either
owns or works for a local
business. Find out more about
their accounting systems.
For example, are records kept
manually or by computer?
How often are entries made?
How is the system used?
What information does it
generate?

Provide a full description of
their accounting procedures
and record-keeping processes.

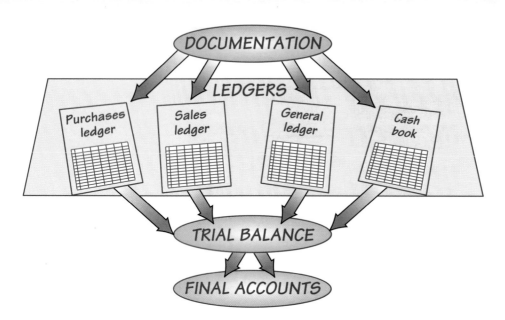

Accounting records

2 Accounting records

Book-keeping records are kept in **ledgers**. These are often referred to as **books of prime entry** as they are the first place where information is recorded. There are four main types of ledger:

a The **purchases** ledger records purchases and includes the accounts of creditors (i.e. people the business owes money to).

b The **sales** ledger records all the sales transactions carried out by the business. It contains the accounts of debtors – customers to whom goods or services have been supplied on credit.

c The **cash book** records all the cash or bank transactions within the business.

d The **general** or **nominal** ledger contains all the other records of the business.

3 Trial balance

In ledgers, transactions are recorded using the **double-entry system**. This means that for each transaction, one account is debited and another is credited. This system reflects a process of exchange.

The **trial balance** is a list of all of the accounts from all the ledgers. It should balance, because for every debit entry into one account there should have been a corresponding credit entry into another. This list provides the raw material for accountants to draw up the final accounts.

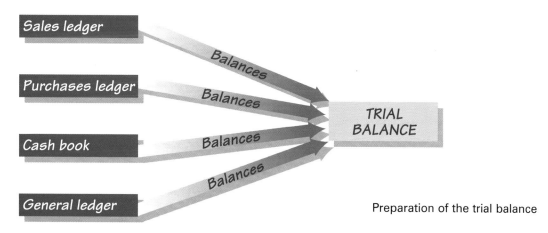

Preparation of the trial balance

4 Final accounts

Final accounts are financial statements drawn up at regular intervals by a business's auditors. They provide valuable information about the business and will help to answer many questions. They include:

◆ The trading account

◆ The profit and loss account

◆ The balance sheet

We will look at each of these in more detail in later chapters.

 Can you help Frankie and Cleo to match the following terms and definitions?

Balance sheet	Request to a supplier for information about products and prices
Credit note	Sequence of business operations, including purchase of materials, production, storage, distribution and sale
Statement	Financial summary prepared by company auditors as part of the final accounts
Invoice	Document recording an increase in the price shown on an invoice
Trading cycle	Request for payment recording the details of a transaction
Letter of enquiry	A reminder to pay, consisting of a copy of a customer's record in the sales ledger
Debit note	Document recording a reduction in the price shown on an invoice

5 45 The Trading Account

What is the trading account?

In the previous chapter, we saw that accountants use information from the ledger accounts and the trial balance to draw up the organisation's final accounts. Final accounts are the summary financial statements produced at the end of each year's trading.

There are three basic types of financial statements:

◆ The trading account

◆ The profit and loss account

◆ The balance sheet

Calculating profit

In the example of Kim Hughes *(opposite page)*, profit is simply the difference between the overall cost of all of the stock bought and the income generated through sales. Though there are one or two further complications, this simple principle works in the same way in business.

The trading account is rather like a video giving ongoing pictures of an organisation's trading activities. For many businesses, such as that of Kim Hughes, trading involves buying and selling stock. The difference between the value of the stock sold (sales) and the cost of producing those sales – which may be the production costs of manufactured goods for a manufacturing company, or the cost of purchasing supplies for a trading company – is known as the **gross profit**. The trading account simply shows how gross profit is arrived at, i.e.:

Sales – Cost of sales = Gross profit

Remember that gross profit is NOT the final profit. It is simply the profit made from trading or from selling goods, before all of the overheads and expenses have been taken into consideration.

In the Case Study, Kim starts business with no stocks and, at the end of the year, has sold all of the football kits. In practice this is clearly unrealistic. Cost of sales has to take into account the value of stocks. Opening stocks is effectively a purchase, as these goods will be sold in the current trading period. On the other hand, closing stocks must be deducted from purchases as these will be sold next year. The true cost of sales is therefore found by applying the following formula:

Opening stocks + Purchases – Closing stocks

'What sort of information do you want to find from your accounts, Ron?'

'As far as I am concerned, the only purpose of my accounting system is to tell me how much profit I am making.'

CHAPTER 45

CASE STUDY

Working out profit

Kim Hughes has a small part-time business buying and selling sports wear. He works from home and his business has no costs of operation.

He started his business on 1st April when he bought 165 football kits for £23 each. During the year he bought a further 83 kits for £25. All the kits were sold during his first year of operation at an average selling price of £40. By the end of the year he had no kits left in stock and decided to close his business.

Let us imagine that Brenda Cross sells or has a turnover of £15,000-worth of widgets, from the beginning of January to the end of December 1996. At the beginning of January her opening stock was £4,500. During the year her purchases were £9,000 and at the end of the year her closing stock was £6,400. From this basic information we can draw up her trading account as shown below:

The Trading Account of B. Cross for the year ended 31/12/96

	£	£
SALES		15,000
Less Cost of sales		
Opening stock	4,500	
Add Purchases	9,000	
	13,500	
Less Closing stock	6,400	7,100
GROSS PROFIT		£7,900

TASK

Read the Case Study on the left then complete the following tasks:

1 Work out Kim's profit for the year. (Make sure that you show all of your calculations)

2 Explain how you worked it out.

3 Kim's profits did not take into account any costs. If he had incurred £5,000 of costs such as transport and warehousing, how might this have affected his profits?

'I know I shouldn't boast, but see if you can work out my gross profit. During 1996 my turnover – or sales – was £87,000. My closing stock was £15,000 and my opening stock was £35,000. During the year I purchased £65,000 of stock.'

'You mean – that's all I've made!????'

Returns

If a firm buys goods which are faulty, these goods should be returned to the supplier and recorded as **returns outwards**. For the purpose of the trading account, they are deducted from the purchases figure. Similarly, if a firm sells goods which are returned by the customer, these are also known as returns, but this time as **returns inwards**. These are then deducted from the sales figure in the trading account.

The Trading Account of H. Ogden for the year ended 31/12/96

	£	£	£
SALES			20,000
Less Returns inwards			2,000
			18,000
Less Cost of sales			
Opening stock		3,000	
Add Purchases	14,000		
Less Returns outwards	1,000	13,000	
		16,000	
Less Closing stock		3,000	13,000
GROSS PROFIT			£5,000

TASK

*C*omplete the following examples from the information provided:

1 At the end of 1996, A. Tree had a sales figure of £23,200. His opening stock was £3,760 and his closing stock £8,564. During the year he purchased £14,530 of goods. Draw up his trading account and calculate his gross profit.

2 R. Terry runs a manufacturing business. At the end of 1996, her turnover for the year was £34,532. Her opening stock of finished goods was £3,456 and at the end of the year a stock check of finished goods revealed a cost value of £4,553. The production cost of manufacture was £18,767. Draw up her trading account and calculate her gross profit.

(Remember that the cost of manufacture will effectively appear in the same place as purchases.)

MATCH IT!

Can you help Frankie and Cleo to match the following terms and definitions?

Returns inwards	Financial statement showing sales revenues for the year, less the cost of those sales
Closing stocks	Value of stocks held at the end of the year
Gross profit	Goods returned by customers (and deducted from sales)
Opening stocks	Opening stocks plus purchases less closing stocks
Trading account	Sales revenue less cost of sales
Cost of sales	Goods returned to suppliers (and deducted from purchases)
Returns outwards	Value of stocks held at the start of the year

46 The Profit and Loss Account

What is net profit?

The profit and loss account is usually drawn up beneath the trading account and covers the same period of trading. The gross profit from the trading account becomes the starting point for the profit and loss account.

> Net profit = Gross profit + Income from other
> sources – Expenses

Net profit is the final profit of the business. It is the amount of profit made by the owners of the business at the end of the period.

Some organisations receive income from sources other than sales. This can take the form of rent, commission, discounts received, profits on the sale of assets, etc. As these are considered to be extra income, but not from trading, they are added to the gross profit.

In addition, every organisation incurs **expenses** and a range of **overheads,** and these are deducted to show the true net profit of the business.

For example, the expenses might include:

◆ Rent of premises

◆ Depreciation

◆ Gas

◆ Bad debts

◆ Electricity

◆ Interest on loans

◆ Stationery

◆ Advertising costs

◆ Cleaning costs

◆ Sundry expenses

◆ Insurances

◆ Motor expenses

◆ Business rates

◆ Accountancy and legal fees

'I now understand about trading profit. But surely it can't be my final profit – it doesn't take into account my expenses.'

'If I only made £2,000 gross profit, what am I going to have left after I deduct all my expenses…?'

Calculating net profit

In the previous chapter we looked at the example of Brenda Cross. Brenda made a gross profit of £7,900. Let us now have a look at her other income and expenses so that we can work out her net profit.

During the same year Brenda received £500 rent from a tenant. She then had to pay a range of expenses. These included electricity (£455), administration expenses (£509), insurance (£45), salaries (£3,400), advertising (£45), and interest (£55). From this information, we can draw up her profit and loss account below:

The Profit and Loss account of B. Cross for the year ended 31/12/96

	£	£
GROSS PROFIT		7,900
Add other income:		
Rent received		500
		8,400
Less Expenses:		
Electricity	455	
Administration expenses	509	
Insurance	45	
Salaries	3,400	
Advertising	45	
Interest paid	55	4,509
NET PROFIT		3,891

Bad debts

Not everybody pays their bills on time. We have seen how long it takes Ron Rust to pay his bills! Some businesses are not just late paying their bills, they are not able to pay their bills at all.

Imagine if you sold £5,000 of goods to a small business on credit and it went bankrupt. Though you might get some of that debt back, the chances are that you would not get all of your money back. If this happens the debt is declared 'bad' and entered in your accounts. **Bad debts** are simply treated as an expense and written off through your profit and loss account.

Depreciation

The things we own do not last for ever. Assets wear out for a number of reasons. For example,

◆ Consumption (they get used up)

◆ Changes in techniques and fashions

◆ Obsolescence (they no longer work)

Most businesses are realistic about the lifespan of their assets. They therefore 'write them off' over many years. This means that their value is gradually reduced to

TASK

Complete the following tasks from the information provided:

1   At the end of 1996, A. Daley has a gross profit of £17,110. During the year he incurred the following expenses: Rates £1,140, rent £861, advertising £432, salaries £4,953, light and heat £639, bad debts £45 and sundry expenses £55. Draw up his profit and loss account and calculate his net profit.

2   Copy out the following trading and profit and loss account and insert the missing figures:

The Trading and Profit and Loss Account of D. Boy for the year ended 31/12/96

	£	£
SALES		XXXX
Less COST OF SALES		
Opening stock	3,100	
Add Purchases	4,215	
	XXXX	
Less Closing stock	1,218	6,097
GROSS PROFIT		12,058
Less Expenses:		
Rent	132	
Rates	85	
Salaries	XXXX	
Advertising	327	
Interest paid	95	
Light and heat	41	2,136
NET PROFIT		£XXXX

nothing over the period of their use. This is called **depreciation**. Depreciation is charged as an expense in the profit and loss account.

There are two main methods of working out how much an asset has depreciated and what to charge to the profit and loss account.

The **straight-line** or **equal instalment method** charges an equal amount of depreciation to each accounting period for the life of an asset. The instalment to be charged to the profit and loss account is calculated by:

$$\frac{\text{Cost of asset} - \text{Residual value}}{\text{Expected useful life of asset}}$$

For example, a machine which is expected to last five years costs £20,000. At the end of its life its residual value will be £5,000.

$$\text{Depreciation charge} = \frac{£20,000 - £5,000}{5 \text{ years}} = £3,000$$

	Year 1 £	Year 2 £	Year 3 £	Year 4 £	Year 5 £
Cost	20,000	20,000	20,000	20,000	20,000
Accumulated depreciation	3,000	6,000	9,000	12,000	15,000
Net book value	17,000	14,000	11,000	8,000	5,000

The **reducing balance** method calculates the depreciation charge as a fixed percentage of net book value from the previous accounting period. This method, therefore, allocates a higher depreciation charge to the earlier years of the asset's life.

For example, a machine is purchased by a business for £20,000 and its expected useful life is 3 years. The business expects that its residual value will be £4,320 and thus wishes to depreciate it at 40%:

Accumulated depreciation	£	£
Machine at cost	20,000	
Depreciation Year 1	8,000	8,000
Net book value		12,000
Depreciation Year 2	4,800	12,800
Net book value		7,200
Depreciation Year 3	2,880	15,680
Residual value		£4,320

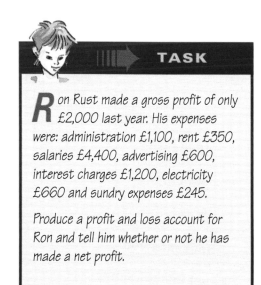

TASK

*R*on Rust made a gross profit of only £2,000 last year. His expenses were: administration £1,100, rent £350, salaries £4,400, advertising £600, interest charges £1,200, electricity £660 and sundry expenses £245.

Produce a profit and loss account for Ron and tell him whether or not he has made a net profit.

MATCH IT! Can you help Frankie and Cleo to match the following terms and definitions?

Business rate	Financial statement based on gross profit shown in the trading account
Expenses	Charging depreciation as a fixed percentage of the value of an asset
Bad debts	Payment made by firms for local authority services
Net profit	Gross profit plus income from other sources, less expenses
Rent received	Another name for overheads
Equal instalment method	Charging an equal amount of depreciation over the life of an asset
Profit and loss account	Payment received for use of premises
Reducing balance method	Amounts owing to a business which are written off as expenses

47 The Balance Sheet

What is a balance sheet?

In the last two chapters we saw that the trading and profit and loss accounts provide an ongoing picture of how a business is performing in terms of profitability – a bit like a video. A balance sheet is a snapshot of what a business owns and owes on a particular date.

Why does a balance sheet balance?

A balance sheet is a clear statement of the assets, liabilities and capital of a business at a particular moment in time – normally the end of an accounting period.

'The balance sheet is an important statement. It shows what you've got, and who you owe things to.'

The balance sheet balances simply because in book-keeping you record everything twice.

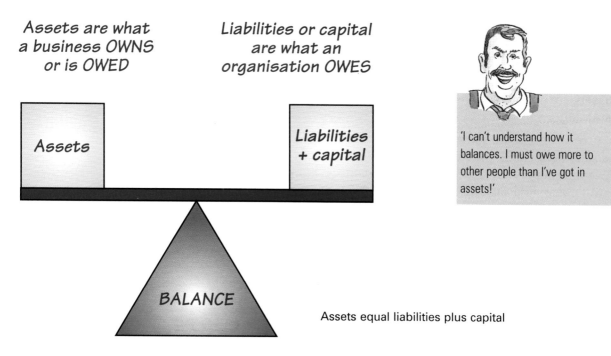

Assets are what a business OWNS or is OWED

Liabilities or capital are what an organisation OWES

Assets

Liabilities + capital

BALANCE

'I can't understand how it balances. I must owe more to other people than I've got in assets!'

Assets equal liabilities plus capital

For example, if you lent me £100 we can say that:

1 I owe you £100 (a *liability*)

2 I own £100 (an *asset*)

My balance sheet is therefore:

Asset	Liability
£100	£100

At the end of a period, a business will have a number of **assets** and **liabilities**. Whatever the nature of the individual assets and liabilities, the balance sheet will always balance.

The parts of a balance sheet

Every balance sheet has a heading, which will contain the name of the organisation and the date at which the 'snapshot' is taken.

Assets

The asset side of the balance sheet is normally set out in what is called an **inverse order of liquidity**. This means that items which may be difficult to convert to cash quickly and are therefore **illiquid,** appear at the top of the list of assets. Those which are easy to convert to cash appear further down the list of assets. At the bottom is the most liquid asset of all – cash.

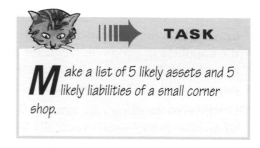

TASK

Make a list of 5 likely assets and 5 likely liabilities of a small corner shop.

Assets can be divided into **fixed** and **current**.

◆ **Fixed assets** tend to have a lifespan of more than one year. They are items that are purchased and generally kept for a long period of time. Examples of fixed assets are premises, fixtures and fittings, machinery and motor vehicles.

◆ **Current assets** are sometimes called 'circulating assets' because they are constantly changing. Examples of current assets are stocks, debtors, money in the bank and cash in hand.

Perhaps the best way of describing how current assets circulate is to refer to the **cash cycle**. A manufacturing business holds **stocks** of finished goods so that it can be ready to satisfy the demands of the market. When a credit transaction takes place, stocks are reduced and the business gains debtors. These debtors have bought goods on credit and therefore owe the business money. After a reasonable credit period, payment will be expected. Once payment is made by debtors, the business will be able to pay for further stocks. 'Cash' or 'bank' changes to 'stock', then to 'debtors', back to 'cash' or 'bank', and then to 'stock' again.

Liabilities

Liabilities can be divided into **current** and **long-term**.

◆ **Current liabilities** are debts which a business needs to repay within a short period of time (normally a year).

Current liabilities may include trade creditors, who are the suppliers of goods on credit for the business. They may also include the bank (for an overdraft) or any unpaid taxes or short-term loans.

◆ **Long-term liabilities** are not due for payment until some time in the future, normally longer than one year. Examples might be a bank loan or a mortgage on a business property.

Capital

Capital is provided by the owner of the business and is therefore treated as being something owed to the owner of the business. The balance shows an updated record of this amount.

During a year's trading the owner's capital may be increased by flows of **profits** and decreased by **drawings** (money or assets taken out of the business for

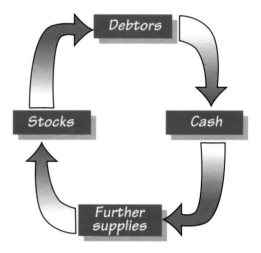

The cash cycle

the owner's personal use). After these have been taken into consideration, a new capital figure is calculated at the end of an accounting period.

Let us now finish the final accounts of Brenda Cross by completing her balance sheet:

The Balance Sheet of B. Cross as at 31/12/96

Fixed assets	£	£		£
Property	25,000		Capital	15,935
Motor vehicles	3,000	28,000	Add Net profit	3,891
Current assets				19,826
Closing stock	6,400		Less Drawings	5,510
Debtors	2,300			14,316
Bank	325	9,025	**Long-term liabilities**	
			Mortgage	20,000
			Current liabilities	
			Creditors	2,709
		£37,025		£37,025

Meanwhile we cannot ignore the plight of Ron Rust. Earlier in the chapter, Ron thought that he probably owed people more than he owned. Let's have a quick look at his balance sheet. Can you advise Ron upon the strengths (if any) and weaknesses of his financial position as shown by his balance sheet?

The Balance Sheet of Ron Rust as at 31/12/96

Fixed assets	£	£		£
Property	30,000		Capital	25,000
Fixtures and fittings	1,000		Less Net loss	6,555
Motor vehicles	10,000	41,000		18,445
Current assets			Less Drawings	10,000
Closing stock	15,000			8,445
Debtors	2,500	17,500	**Long-term liabilities**	
			Mortgage	40,000
			Current liabilities	
			Bank overdraft	10,055
		£58,500		£58,500

TASK

*P*hilip Brown is in a dilemma and has asked you for help. He understands how to work out his profit and has calculated that he has made £2,000 net profit during 1996. But he needs to draw up his balance sheet – and that's where he's asked for your help.

1 Briefly explain to Philip the importance of drawing up a balance sheet and how a balance sheet is organised.

2 Draw up his balance sheet as at 31/12/96 from the following information: land and buildings £8,150, motor vehicles £2,000, machinery £6,000, closing stock £850, debtors £400, bank £20, creditors £1,200, bank loan £6,000, capital £10,000 and drawings £1,780.

3 Philip is worried he may not be able to pay his debts. What figures from the balance sheet indicate that he has cause for concern?

MATCH IT!

Can you help Frankie and Cleo to match the following terms and definitions?

Drawings	Assets with a life of more than one year
Current assets	People or businesses that owe money to an organisation
Mortgage	Long-term loan based on using property as security
Debtors	Items in a balance sheet that an organisation owns or is owed
Assets	Short-term assets that can quickly be turned into cash
Fixed assets	Statement showing the financial position of an organisation
Current liabilities	Money or assets taken out of a business for the owner's use
Balance sheet	Debts that a business must pay in the short term

48 Company Balance Sheets

Meeting legal requirements

Companies must comply with the Companies Act and the Companies Registration Office. This means that information in their annual report and accounts must be presented in a special way.

Company accounts therefore differ slightly from the accounts of a sole trader.

Remember that:

◆ The company has a legal identity which is separate from that of its owners

◆ The owners of a company are known as **shareholders** and have certain rights and responsibilities

◆ Shareholders have limited liability

◆ Management is delegated to a board of directors who may not be shareholders (*see Case Study on opposite page*)

◆ Corporation tax must be paid on profits made

'When we set up our business, I am not sure whether we are going to be sole traders. If we become a company, will our accounts be very different?'

'I wouldn't set up as a company. Too much paperwork!'

Corporate governance

The owners of companies are known as **shareholders**. In many instances, particularly in the case of larger companies, shareholders will not be directly involved in running the business which they part-own. This task is undertaken by professional managers, some of whom may even be shareholders themselves.

This process whereby managers take responsibility for the running of the company on behalf of shareholders is known as **corporate governance**.

One of the main aims of the many different Companies Acts is to ensure that managers carry out their responsibilities properly. For example, the shareholders will want to know 'who holds the reins' in the business in which they have invested, and what decisions the managers are making.

A company AGM

Horizontal and vertical balance sheets

In the previous chapters, the balance sheet of the sole trader was presented 'horizontally', with assets on one side of the equation and liabilities and capital on the other. Most businesses today, and particularly companies, will want to present their information in a balance sheet which is displayed vertically (*see Case Study on page 181*).

The main reason for this is that the vertical balance sheet shows **working capital**. As we will soon see, this is a useful indicator of how easily a business can pay its short-term debts.

Assets

In the balance sheet of a company, the fixed and current assets are presented in the same way as in any other form of balance sheet. In the vertical style, however, current liabilities are deducted from current assets in order to show working capital.

TASK

1   What responsibilities do professional managers have to shareholders?

2   Why will shareholders want plenty of information about the activities of the company in which they have invested?

Working capital

When drawing up a vertical balance sheet, **working capital** is a very important calculation. Working capital is simply current assets less current liabilities. Having too much working capital means that the business is not using its resources well. If it has too little, it may not be able to pay its short-term debts.

Working capital is important because it keeps 'the wolf from the door'. It is the amount of money a company has available to meet its immediate liabilities. Many businesses have suffered the consequences of having too many of their assets tied up as illiquid assets.

Liabilities

The **current liabilities** of a company are similar to those of a sole trader, except that limited companies also have to show **corporation tax** due to be paid to the Inland Revenue, as well as any **dividends** (shares of profit) to shareholders. Long-term liabilities may include long-term loans raised through the financial markets such as debentures.

Keeping the wolf from the door

The 'Financed by' section

The second part of the vertical balance sheet is known as the **'Financed by'** section. This displays the capital of the company and reflects the company's relationship with shareholders.

At the top of the 'Financed by' section are details of the **authorised capital**. This will show the value and number of shares a company's shareholders have authorised managers to issue. These are in the balance sheet for interest only and their value is excluded from totals. **Issued capital** shows details of shares actually issued. **Reserves** appear below the capital and are **retained profits** *(see Chapter 42, 'Sources of finance', page 157)* that the directors and shareholders decide to keep.

'I'm beginning to understand now. Though my working capital ratio appears OK, all of my current assets are tied up in stock, which means that I have to use a bank overdraft in order to pay the bills!'

COURSEWORK ACTIVITIES

Write to a public limited company to obtain a copy of their annual report and accounts. Within an annual report there will appear a set of accounts. Describe the statements accompanying the report. Comment on other information and indicate what these statements try to show. Explain why they are important for shareholders.

A vertical balance sheet

Fixed assets			xxxx
Current assets		xxxx	
Less Current liabilities		xxxx	
= Working capital			xxxx
			xxxx
Less Long-term liabilities			xxxx
Capital employed			xxxx
Financed by:			
Authorised share capital			xxxx
Issued share capital			xxxx
Reserves			xxxx
			xxxx

The Balance Sheet of Stilton Sandwiches Ltd as at 31/12/96

	£	£	£
Fixed assets			
Land and buildings			22,000
Machinery			10,000
Motor vehicles			10,000
			42,000
Current assets			
Stocks		5,000	
Debtors		4,500	
Bank		2,000	
Cash		1,000	
		12,500	
Less **Current liabilities**			
Creditors	2,000		
Proposed dividends	4,000		
Corporation tax	2,000	8,000	
Working capital			4,500
			46,500
Less **Long-term liabilities**			
Bank loan		10,000	
Debentures		3,500	13,500
			33,000
FINANCED BY:			
Authorised share capital			
20,000 ordinary shares of £1			20,000
			20,000
Issued share capital			
20,000 ordinary shares of £1			20,000
Reserves			
Retained profit			13,000
			33,000

MATCH IT! Can you help Frankie and Cleo to match the following terms and definitions?

Corporation Tax	Part-owner of a company
Debenture	Capital which a company has been authorised to issue
Companies Acts	Shareholders' liability for debts
Shareholder	Long-term liability of a company
Authorised capital	Process of management on behalf of shareholders
Limited liability	Set of laws within which companies must operate
Corporate governance	Tax paid on company profits

49 Business Ratios

Picking out useful information

Taken on their own, figures from final accounts can be confusing. But when financial ratios are used to analyse the information more closely, it becomes more meaningful.

A number of people might be interested in a business's accounts. For example:

◆ The **owner(s)** will want to know if the business is profitable

◆ **Employees** will want to know how the business is doing and whether their job is secure

◆ **Managers** will want to use information from the records to make business decisions

◆ **Creditors** and providers of loans will want to know if the business can afford to repay them.

All these groups of people can use business ratios to pick out the information they need.

'Looking at all these financial statements is very interesting. But how do I know what all the figures in the statements mean?'

CHAPTER 49

Types of business ratio

Financial ratios are an arithmetical way of comparing different figures within a set of accounts. Using ratios helps you to answer key questions about a business organisation. But you must be clear why you are using the ratio and what it can tell you. Properly used, ratios can tell us about three main areas:

◆ Profitability

◆ Liquidity

◆ Asset usage

Profitability

1 Return on capital employed (ROCE)

If you invest £100 in a business, you will be looking at the return and comparing it with other investments. For example, if you received £30 back, you would probably be quite pleased as this would be significantly higher than any investment in a building society. But if you only received £2 from the business, you might think about putting your money elsewhere.

The **return on capital employed** simply relates profitability to an investment in a business. The ratio is expressed as:

$$\text{Percentage return on capital employed} = \frac{\text{Net profit for year}}{\text{Capital employed}} \times 100\%$$

The figure for capital is usually taken at the beginning of the year, as this is the capital generating profit for the following year. ROCE is a good measure of how effective an investment is and how it compares with others.

2 Gross profit percentage

This ratio is extracted from the trading account. It simply relates gross profit to sales revenue:

$$\text{Gross profit percentage} = \frac{\text{Gross profit}}{\text{Sales revenue}} \times 100\%$$

For example, if sales of £100,000 produce a gross profit of £50,000, then the gross profit percentage is 50%. In other words, every £1 of sales generates 50p of profit.

The gross profit percentage should be calculated at regular intervals and any rise or fall investigated. For example, if the ratio falls, it may simply mean that the price of raw materials has gone up. However, it might also mean that stocks have been stolen or damaged.

COURSEWORK ACTIVITIES

Look at the accounts of a business. Use the simple ratios described in this chapter to help you analyse and comment on their performance.

3 Net profit percentage

This is extracted from the profit and loss account and is calculated as follows:

$$\text{Net profit percentage} = \frac{\text{Net profit}}{\text{Sales}} \times 100\%$$

This takes into account any changes in business expenses. For example, if the gross profit percentage is consistent and a change occurs in the net profit percentage, this would indicate an increase in overheads (costs) as a proportion of sales revenue. This may suggest that managers need to reduce overheads.

Liquidity

Liquidity is the ability of an organisation to convert its assets to cash and meet its debts.

1 Working capital ratio

The working capital ratio is the ratio of current assets to current liabilities:

Working capital ratio = Current assets:Current liabilities

It is important for every organisation to maintain a sensible ratio. What this is depends on the type of business, and how quickly funds may be needed to meet liabilities (e.g. creditors demanding repayment quickly).

A prudent ratio is usually 2:1, but this might not necessarily be the case if stocks form the bulk of current assets. Companies have to be aware that bank overdrafts are repayable on demand.

2 Quick ratio/acid test ratio

This ratio takes into account stocks. It is simply:

Current assets less stock:Current liabilities

This is a tougher ratio than the working capital ratio and excludes stocks because they are not immediately available to pay short-term debts. A rule of thumb for this ratio is that it should be greater than 1.

Asset usage

1 Stock turnover

An organisation does not want its stock staying around too long. Stock turnover is the average period of time an item of stock is held before it is used or sold. This ratio usually depends upon the type of business. For example, a fast-food outlet *(right)* would turn over its stock many more times a year than a furniture business.

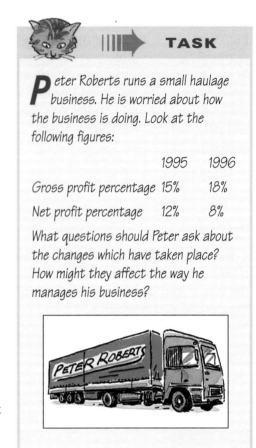

TASK

Peter Roberts runs a small haulage business. He is worried about how the business is doing. Look at the following figures:

	1995	1996
Gross profit percentage	15%	18%
Net profit percentage	12%	8%

What questions should Peter ask about the changes which have taken place? How might they affect the way he manages his business?

Stock turnover can be worked out using the following formula:

$$\text{Stock turnover} = \frac{\text{Cost of sales}}{\text{Average stock}}$$

In this formula the average stock is calculated by adding together the values of the opening stock and the closing stock and dividing the result by 2.

2 Asset utilisation

It is possible to relate the use of other things to sales in order to show how efficient an organisation is in generating sales revenue. For example, how many sales are assets generating? One way to find out is to relate sales to fixed assets. This would be measured by:

$$\text{Asset utilisation} = \frac{\text{Sales}}{\text{Fixed assets}}$$

This would show how well managers are using fixed assets like machinery and equipment to generate sales.

TASK

Help Ron to work out his acid-test ratio. His current assets are £17,500 but his closing stock is £15,000. His only current liability is his overdraft which is £10,055.

 MATCH IT! Can you help Frankie and Cleo to match the following terms and definitions?

Acid-test ratio	Gross profit divided by sales x 100
Bank overdraft	Net profit divided by sales x 100
ROCE	Ratio used to help measure the efficiency of a range of assets
Stock turnover	Cost of sales divided by average stock
Net profit percentage	Money borrowed by a business from a bank that is repayable on demand
Gross profit percentage	Ratio of current assets less stock to current liabilities
Asset utilisation ratio	Net profit divided by capital employed x 100

5 *50* **Making Comparisons**

'Now I understand about how to read accounts, let's put these skills to practical use and look at some final accounts. How about looking at your final accounts, Ron?'

'Sorry, not now, can't stop, I have an interview – with my bank manager!'

Analysing accounts

In this chapter we will look at Ice Freeze Ltd, a company owned by a friend of Frankie's *(see Case Study on opposite page)* and make comparisons between two sets of accounts.

Profitability of Ice Freeze Ltd

1 Return on capital employed

Probably the first thing Frankie's friend will want to know is whether her business has become more profitable between the years.

'Oh well, I have a friend who runs a frozen food business called Ice Freeze. I'll ask her if we can look at her accounts instead.'

$$
\begin{array}{cc}
1995 & 1996 \\
\dfrac{8,900}{70,000} \times 100 & \dfrac{4,500}{70,000} \times 100 \\
= 13\% & = 6\%
\end{array}
$$

Note: For the purpose of this example, we have called the capital employed £70,000 and not taken into account the reserves.

Frankie's friend is worried because the ROCE figure shows that the profitability of the business has halved over the two years.

2 Gross profit percentage

$$
\begin{array}{cc}
1995 & 1996 \\
\dfrac{20,000}{55,000} \times 100 & \dfrac{25,000}{70,000} \times 100 \\
= 36\% & = 35\%
\end{array}
$$

Despite the massive increase in turnover, there is virtually no change in the gross profit percentage. Like-for-like, sales seem to be generating the same amount of trading profit.

CHAPTER 50

Analysing the accounts of Ice Freeze Ltd

The Trading and Profit and Loss accounts of Ice Freeze Ltd

	1995		1996	
	£	£	£	£
Sales		55,000		70,000
Less Cost of sales:				
Opening stock	15,000		10,000	
Add purchases	30,000		45,000	
	45,000		55,000	
Less Closing stock	10,000	35,000	10,000	45,000
Gross profit		20,000		25,000
Less Expenses:				
Rent	1,400		1,500	
Rates	300		300	
Salaries	8,000		14,000	
Advertising	1,000		1,500	
Sundry expenses	400	11,100	3,200	20,500
Net profit		8,900		4,500

Balance Sheets of Ice Freeze Ltd

	1995		1996	
	£	£	£	£
Fixed assets				
Land and buildings		50,000		50,000
Fixtures and fittings		20,000		20,000
Motor vehicles		5,000		5,000
		75,000		75,000
Current assets				
Stocks	10,000		10,000	
Debtors	5,500		9,700	
Bank	3,200			
	18,700		19,700	
Less Current liabilities				
Creditors	3,000		2,000	
Bank overdraft		3,000	1,000	3,000
Working capital		15,700		16,700
		90,700		91,700
Financed by:				
Authorised share capital				
70,000 ordinary shares of £1		70,000		70,000
		70,000		70,000
Issued share capital				
70,000 ordinary shares of £1		70,000		70,000
Reserves				
Retained profit		20,700		21,700
		£90,700		£91,700

3 Net profit percentage

1995	1996
$\dfrac{8,900}{55,000} \times 100$	$\dfrac{4,500}{70,000} \times 100$
$= 16\%$	$= 6.4\%$

These figures are extremely important and reveal the main cause of the fall in profitability.

Expenses have risen from £11,100 to £20,500 and this ratio has fallen dramatically. To improve this, Frankie's friend may want to look at ways of cutting some of her expenses.

Liquidity of Ice Freeze Ltd

1 Working capital ratio

1995	1996
1:6.2	1:6.5

Ice Freeze has a comfortable working capital position and there are no real liquidity problems revealed by this ratio.

If anything, despite the fall in profitability and the bank overdraft, the ratio has become slightly stronger over the two years.

2 Quick ratio/acid test ratio

1995	1996
2.9:1	3.2:1

Again, despite the bank overdraft, Ice Freeze has more debtors in 1996, so the quick ratio shows a slight increase and no real liquidity problem.

Asset usage by Ice Freeze Ltd

1 Stock turnover

1995	1996
35,000	45,000
12,500	10,000
= 2.8 times	= 4.5 times

There is a clear change in asset usage over the two-year accounting period. Stock turned over much more frequently in 1996 than in 1995.

COURSEWORK ACTIVITIES

Is there a Young Enterprise group at your school or college? Find out how they are operating, about the goods or services they are producing and how successful they have been.

Look at their book-keeping processes and offer to help them produce their financial statements and analyse their final accounts.

2 Asset utilisation

1995	1996
55,000	70,000
75,000	75,000
= 1:1.36	= 1:1.07

With this ratio, the same amount of fixed assets are operating more efficiently because they are generating higher levels of sales.

Summary

Overall, there are few major differences over the two years, other than the rise in expenses affecting the profitability ratios. Sales have increased, the company is operating more efficiently and there are no obvious liquidity problems.

51 Classifying Costs

What is cost?

The word 'cost' has several meanings, even in everyday language. The cost of goods in the shops is something we all know about!

Organisations will want to use management accounting to control their costs and forecast future events. This helps managers to make decisions about future activities.

'So, we have looked at financial accounting by looking at financial statements and analysing them with ratios. What about management accounting?'

Costing techniques

In organisations managers frequently refer to calculating the cost of, or **costing,** an event or activity.

What they mean by this is that they are using a knowledge of past costs and expected revenues to plan something they hope to achieve. These **costing techniques** are a useful source of data for management accountants.

All businesses incur some form of cost. A sound knowledge of costs and the factors affecting them will help a business to assess its profitability. Remember that profits only begin to be made once costs are met!

TASK

Some of Ron Rust's costs are shown below. Which of these are going to be his fixed costs and which will be his variable costs?

- Purchases of scrap
- Business rates
- Electricity
- Ron's salary

- Wages to labour in the yard
- Rent
- Telephone bills
- Advertising

CASE STUDY

Johnsons Toy Company

Johnsons Toy Company produces toy trains and sells them at £12 each. Next year it expects to produce 10,000 trains. The fixed costs for the business are £14,000 and the variable cost to produce each train is £8. Below is a table to show how much profit will be made if Johnsons manage to produce and sell the 10,000 they anticipate.

Units of production	Fixed costs £	Variable costs £	Total costs £	Revenue £	Profit/loss £
1,000	14,000	8,000	22,000	12,000	(10,000)
2,000	14,000	16,000	30,000	24,000	(6,000)
3,000	14,000	24,000	38,000	36,000	(2,000)
4,000	14,000	32,000	46,000	48,000	2,000
5,000	14,000	40,000	54,000	60,000	6,000
6,000	14,000	48,000	62,000	72,000	10,000
7,000	14,000	56,000	70,000	84,000	14,000
8,000	14,000	64,000	78,000	96,000	18,000
9,000	14,000	72,000	86,000	108,000	22,000
10,000	14,000	80,000	94,000	120,000	26,000

We can see that if Johnsons Toy Company produces 10,000 toy trains they will make a profit of £26,000. Clearly, analysing costs has helped them to predict the future with more certainty.

Fixed and variable costs

There are two types of costs:

◆ **Fixed** costs

◆ **Variable** costs

Fixed costs are costs which do not increase as output increases, for example, rent, heating bills, mortgage repayments, rates and salaries. An organisation could therefore increase the number of units it produces from 10,000 to 20,000 and incur no increases in these types of costs.

Variable costs are costs which increase as output increases. This is because when more units are produced, more of these costs are incurred. For example, if you produce more items, you might need more workers on the shop floor and more raw materials.

Marginal costing compares fixed and variable costs with sales revenue at different levels of production in order to calculate the profit which will be made.

Contribution

We have seen that fixed costs have to be paid however many units are sold. A management accountant may also want to look at how much each unit sold is contributing to paying off the fixed costs of its production. This **contribution** is calculated by taking the variable cost from the selling price:

Contribution = Selling price – Variable costs per unit

This technique is particularly useful for making short-term decisions – for example, helping to set the selling price of a product, or deciding whether or not to accept an order.

  TASK

*R*ead the Case Study on Duvey Duvets Ltd (right).

1 Divide the costs listed into fixed and variable.

2 Draw up a chart to show fixed, variable, total costs and total revenue for each 1,000 units produced up to 12,000 units.

3 Duvey Duvets aim to produce and sell 10,000 duvets this year. How much profit will they make if their plans succeed?

Duvey Duvets Ltd

Duvey Duvets is a small business producing low-cost duvets. The company is run by Pauline Smithers. She employs 5 full-time employees: 1 production manager and 4 machine operators who cut out material for sending to part-time workers. The part-time workers then use their own sewing machines to make up the duvets in their own homes.

The costs of the business are as follows:

• Pauline's salary of £500 per week

• Salary of production manager – £200 per week

• Salaries of machine operators – £150 per week each

• Rent and rates – £500 per week

• Electricity – £300 per 3 months

• Sundry overheads – £100 per week

• Material costs for each duvet – £5

• Payment to workers for producing duvets – £3 per duvet.

The duvets are sold for £20 each.

TASK

Scotties Pens hope to sell 2,000 pens next year at £9 per unit. The firm's variable costs are £5 per unit and its fixed costs are £4,000.

Draw up a profit statement to show how much it will make in the year. Also, draw up a table to show how much profit it will make at each 500 units of production up to 3,000 units.

MATCH IT!

Can you help Frankie and Cleo to match the following terms and definitions?

Raw materials	Costs which increase as output increases
Variable costs	Difference between total revenue and total costs
Total costs	Selling price less variable costs per unit
Profit/loss	Example of a variable cost
Marginal costing	Used by management accountants to forecast profitability in the future
Fixed costs	The sum of fixed costs plus variable costs
Contributrion	Costs which do not increase as output increases

52 **Break-even Analysis**

When does a business break even?

Break-even extends the principles of marginal costs which we looked at in Chapter 51.

Break-even is the unique point at which an organisation makes neither a profit nor a loss. If sales go beyond the break-even point, profits are made. But if sales have not reached the break-even point, losses are incurred.

'People keep using this term "break-even". If I broke even, would that mean that I had covered my costs?'

'Don't get confused by terminology. I've never broken even and it's never bothered me!'

Calculating the break-even point

To calculate the break-even point, there are two stages:

◆ Calculate the unit contribution (selling price less variable costs)

◆ Divide the fixed costs by the unit contribution:

$$\text{Break-even point} = \frac{\text{Fixed costs}}{\text{Contribution}}$$

This shows how many units must be produced to break-even at that selling price. The **sales value** of the break-even point is calculated by multiplying the number of units at the break-even point by the selling price.

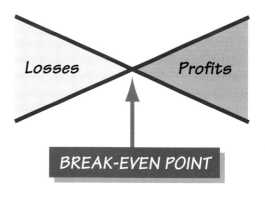

The break-even point

CASE STUDY

Trio Toys

Peter Taylor, the dynamic entrepreneurial chairman of Trio Toys, has been carefully monitoring the baby buggy division of his company. Each baby buggy sells for £12 and the variable costs in manufacture include:

• £4 direct labour per unit

• £3 direct materials per unit

• £1 other variable overheads per unit

The fixed costs of the baby buggy division are £80,000.

Peter carefully works out the break-even point for the buggy. The unit contribution for each buggy produced will be:

£12 (Selling price) – £8 (£4 + £3 + £1 Variable costs) = £4

$$\text{Break-even} = \frac{\text{Fixed costs}}{\text{Unit contribution}}$$

$$= \frac{£80,000}{4} = 20,000 \text{ units to break-even}$$

Sales value to break-even = 20,000 units x £12 Selling price

$$= £240,000$$

Peter hopes to make a profit of £30,000 on his buggies. In other words, he not only has to cover his fixed costs, but also to make an extra £30,000. To find out how many units he has to sell to achieve this, he must add a profit target to his fixed costs and divide this by his contribution.

$$\frac{£80,000 \text{ (Fixed costs)} + £30,000 \text{ (Profit target)}}{4} = \frac{110,000}{4}$$

$$= 27,500 \text{ units to achieve this target}$$

The sales value required to make this profit is therefore 27,500 units x £12 selling price

$$= £330,000.$$

Producing a break-even chart

A **break-even chart** shows the point at which a business breaks even and the profits and losses it will make at various levels of activity. It is constructed by:

1 Labelling the horizontal axis for units of production and sales

2 Labelling the vertical axis to represent the value of sales and costs

3 Plotting fixed costs (this will be a straight line as fixed costs do not rise as more units are produced).

4 Plotting variable costs. These are shown rising from where the fixed cost line touches the vertical axis. This line also therefore represents total costs. It is plotted by calculating total costs at two or three random levels of production (*see Table below*).

5 Sales are plotted by taking two or three random levels of turnover. They are shown rising from the intersection of the two axes.

A sample break-even chart based on the Case Study on page 193 is shown below.

TASK

*R*ead the Case Study on page 193 then complete the following tasks:

1 One alternative strategy for Peter Taylor of Trio Toys is to increase the price of the baby buggy to £15. At this price, market research reveals that the company should be able to sell 22,000 units. Find the new break-even point and then find out whether Peter would be able to meet his profit target at this level of production.

2 Describe the benefits of using techniques of break-even analysis.

	10,000 units £	20,000 units £	30,000 units £
Variable costs = £8 per unit	80,000	160,000	240,000
Fixed costs	80,000	80,000	80,000
Total cost	160,000	240,000	320,000
Sales £12 per unit	120,000	240,000	360,000

Left: Table showing total costs and sales for Trio Toys at three random levels of activity *(see Case Study, page 193)*

Below: the same information displayed as a break-even chart

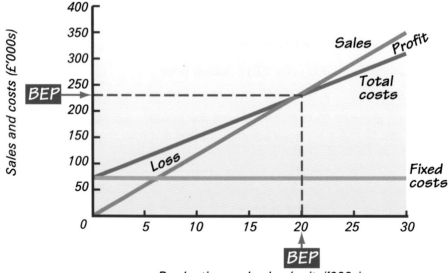

Production and sales (units/'000s)

MATCH IT!

Can you help Frankie and Cleo to match the following terms and definitions?

Unit contribution	Units produced x selling price
Total cost line	On a break-even chart, line plotted by calculating total costs at three random levels of activity
Direct materials	Selling price less variable costs
Sales value	Label of horizontal axis of break-even chart
Break-even	Example of a variable cost
Production and sales	Unique point where a business makes neither profit nor loss, calculated by dividing fixed costs by unit contribution

6 53 Communication within a Business

What is communication?

Communication is the passing on or exchange of information, ideas or feelings.

Today there are many ways of communicating. These include writing letters and articles, speaking to people face to face, telephone conversations, sending a fax, sending e-mail and using computer links such as the Internet.

Some of these communications involve written words, some involve spoken words, and others are made up of visual symbols.

Internal communication

Internal communications are those that take place within an organisation – for example, between a manager and a supervisor, between two employees, etc.

'What is meant by internal communication?'

It is very important to have good, clear communications so that the organisation can run smoothly.

Purposes of internal communication

A number of purposes of internal communication are set out in the diagram below:

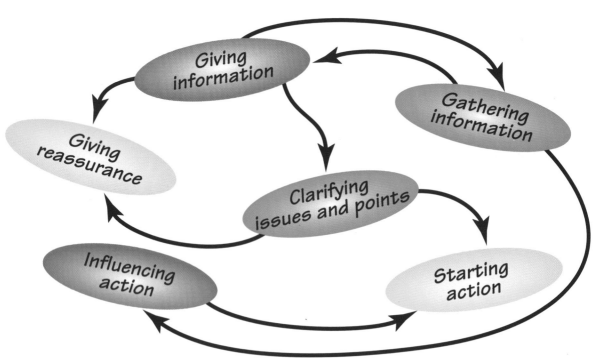

Purposes of internal communication

1 **To give information**

A common reason for communication is to give information. For example, a manager may want to tell people when a meeting has been arranged, or to inform people of Health and Safety requirements.

2 **To gather information**

People in organisations need information to help them make decisions. For example, the managing director may ask for sales figures from different regions. Or the personnel manager may want information about accidents and injuries in the workplace.

3 **To give reassurance**

Information is needed to reassure people that they are doing things correctly, or that things are happening in an organisation. For example, employees may feel better if they are given a written report on their work. A manager may want a report to reassure him or her that safety checks are being carried out properly.

4 **To clarify issues and points**

Communications are required to clarify anything that may be confusing in an organisation. For example, if employees are not sure who they should report to after being absent from work, then this can be made clear in a written notice.

5 **To start action**

Communications are important in getting new ideas off the ground. For example, if managers want to introduce a major change in an organisation, they may call everyone together to tell them what will be happening.

6 **To influence action**

Communications are required to make sure that things happen in a desired way. For example, if output is falling and costs are rising in a company, managers may need to warn staff that if things don't improve the business may fold.

Types of communication

We will now look at a number of ways of communicating within an organisation.

1 Written communications

Written communications are used to pass on inform-ation and ideas in an organisation. They can also be used to confirm verbal messages.

CASE **S**TUDY

Responding to staff opinions

In 1995, European Passenger Services carried out a survey to find out how their staff felt about working for the organisation. After reading through the results, the Managing Director reported the results to staff:

'You have now seen the key results of the survey. I confirm my commitment to taking the issues further.

'I can promise you that EPS senior management will:

- *take your views seriously*

- *treat your views with respect*

- *draw up action plans*

- *address our weaknesses and build on our strengths*

- *continue the work of the Project Groups*

- *make sure positive change is brought about*

'I have no doubt that together we can bring about change.'

TASK

1   What do you think were the purposes of the staff opinion survey?

2   What do you think were the purposes of reporting the results to staff?

3   How does the two-way communi-cation process help managers to make the organisation more successful?

Memos

One of the most often used forms of internal communication is the **memorandum**, or **memo** for short. The word comes from the Latin meaning 'a thing to be remembered'. Today memos are used to pass on information, instructions and enquiries and are like letters sent within the company.

The organisation's name does not normally appear on a memo, and there is no need to start with 'Dear Sir', or finish 'Yours faithfully', as with a letter.

Memos are often sent to several people at the same time, although they are also sent to individuals.

Most large organisations have pre-printed memo pads for their employees. Memos should be concise and to the point.

Reports

A **report** is a written communication from someone who has collected and studied some facts or issues. It is usually sent to someone who has asked for it for a particular purpose. The report will often form the basis for a decision that needs to be taken.

Typical examples of situations in which reports would be sent include:

◆ to supply information for legal purposes, perhaps as a result of an accident

◆ to supply information to be given to shareholders

◆ to present the results of some research and to recommend action

◆ to weigh up the possible results of changing a policy

Reports should be well written, concise and to the point. They should not contain anything the reader does not need to know. They should be clear and arranged in a logical order. A suggested form of presentation for a written report is:

1 Title page

2 List of contents

3 Terms of reference

4 Procedure

5 Findings

6 Conclusion

7 Recommendations

8 Signature

```
MEMO

To: Heads of Department
From: The Principal
Date: 25.6.97

Fire Drill

Please make sure that all staff
and students are familiar with
the fire drill which is set out
in the college handbook. A copy
of the drill must be displayed
in every room in the college in
a prominent place.
```

A typical memo

TASK

1   Make out a memo from the principal of a college or school to members of staff, to make sure that they complete class registers in an appropriate way.

2   Make out a memo from the sales manager of a company asking sales representatives to provide details of the sales they have made during the first three months of the year.

The **terms of reference** explain why the report is being written, by stating the group or persons for whom it is being prepared. For example:

'This report is being written in response to a request from the owner of the Regal cinema for our business group to carry out some market research to see if there is a demand for a second screen at the cinema.'

The **procedure** section describes how the report has been put together. What letters have been sent? Who has been interviewed? What else has been done?

The **findings** indicate what has been discovered as a result of the investigations which have been carried out.

The **conclusions** contain a summary of the findings. For example:

'There appears to be a strong opportunity for a new cinema screen. Seventy per cent of those interviewed stated that they would visit the cinema more often…'

Recommendations may be included where appropriate. For example, you may be trying to look at ways of solving a problem through your studies. If so, you may want to suggest some form of action as a result of your report.

Agendas and minutes

An **agenda** is a written outline of the issues to be discussed at a meeting. It is set out under a number of headings, and must contain the date, time and place of the meeting. It should be sent in advance to all the people who will attend the meeting so that they have the chance to prepare their contributions.

Minutes are a written record of a meeting. Sometimes they may be placed on a noticeboard so that more people can read them. Minutes should be clear, concise and accurate.

Notices and house publications

Notices are written displays placed in obvious places in order to give out information. They can be used to set out instructions, advertise future events, set out policies and so on. They can be a useful way of motivating staff. Notices should be designed and presented so as to attract people's attention.

House magazines, journals, and company newspapers can be used to share information inside an organisation. They are particularly important in large organisations for communicating information to employees.

HEALTH & SAFETY COMMITTEE
Meeting to be held on
Thursday 21st March 1996
at 10.30 am in the Committee Room

AGENDA

1 Apologies for absence

2 Minutes of last meeting

3 Visit by Environmental Health Officer

4 Fire Drill

5 Report on Health & Safety at the Warehouse

6 Any other business

7 Date of next meeting

A typical agenda

A company magazine

2 Verbal communications

Verbal communication involves direct word-of-mouth contact. Much of the time it involves face-to-face exchanges with the aim of giving messages, providing advice, personal discussion, instructions and guidance.

Face-to-face contact enables communicators to get to know each other. It also allows for instant feedback. However, the main disadvantage is that there are no permanent records. It can also lead to confusion when messages are not clear.

Body language is an important part of face-to-face communication *(right)*. It is important to take an honest and open posture when dealing with other people.

Meetings

Nearly all employees at all levels in an organisation will spend some time at meetings. This is particularly true of managers and administrative staff. Meetings are held to discuss issues and problems, to come up with new ideas and to develop plans.

In a meeting you are able to draw on the specialist skills of a group of people, all of whom will be able to make a useful contribution.

A notice of a meeting will be accompanied by an **agenda** setting out the order of the meeting.

Some meetings will be **informal** discussions between groups of people. Other meetings will be more organised or **formal**.

A **chairperson** has certain duties and powers in a meeting. He or she makes sure that there are enough people at the meeting for decisions to be made. The word **quorum** means the minimum number of people needed before business can be carried out in a meeting.

The chair has the task of making sure that the meeting concentrates on the tasks in hand, and seeking the views of those who are involved. The chair makes sure that votes are taken properly, and corrects anyone who wastes time or disrupts the meeting.

At the start of the meeting, the secretary will say which people have given apologies for not being able to attend, and will read out the minutes of the previous meeting. Members are asked to approve the minutes from the previous meeting as being correct.

Body language is an important part of everyday communication

What sort of messages do you think Ron Rust is giving in his body language in the situations below?

The chair then works through the minutes of the meeting in the order that they have been set out in the agenda.

The final item is called **Any other business (A.O.B.).** This allows people at the meeting to bring up minor matters for discussion. It should not be allowed to go on for too long.

Committees

Committees are groups of people who come together regularly to take part in decision-making. Most large organisations have committees for dealing with particular aspects of work, e.g. a Health and Safety Committee, a Sports and Recreation Committee, etc.

Teams

Many modern organisations involve a number of self-managing teams, or project teams. Instead of having a 'top-down' communication system within an organisation, decision-making can be put in the hands of these teams. Verbal communication is very important in these teams. Employees need to have excellent communication and interpersonal skills.

Quality circles

Quality circles are small groups of employees who meet regularly to discuss work problems. They are made up of managers, supervisors and employees, all sharing ideas in a democratic way. The aim is to increase communications, motivation and efficiency.

3 Visual communications

Visual communication is often the best way of getting a message across. If people can see what is expected of them, or how something works, they are more likely to remember it. Visual communication techniques are being used more and more within organisations. Examples are the use of overhead projectors, television and multimedia. For instance, medical specialists are able to view a patient's injuries from hundreds or thousands of miles away by means of television screens and Virtual Reality systems.

Modern companies like Shell UK use visual communications at their annual general meetings. These might include a video showing highlights of the year's performance, or a slide presentation using computer-generated graphics.

CASE STUDY

Communications at EPS

European Passenger Services recognise that communication is crucial in giving employees a sense of ownership and achieving business success. At EPS there are several initiatives to encourage people to come forward with ideas to change methods of working.

* **Team briefing.** Regular team briefings are held to facilitate two-way communication.

* **Local forums.** These provide an opportunity for senior managers to meet with employees to present and discuss business issues.

* *In Brief* is a weekly bulletin containing information on current events affecting EPS. A copy goes to each member of the company.

* *EPS Express* is a regular staff magazine for EPS. It carries news and features, and reflects the company's activities from the viewpoint of its staff.

TASK

1 Which of the above communications are mainly (i) written; (ii) verbal?

2 What is the main purpose of each of these communications?

Similar techniques are now being used for training and development within organisations. CD-ROM and CD-I have also had a great impact on communication, as has the development of Virtual Reality.

4 Information technology

Information technology has revolutionised communications both within and between organisations. Today many employees are networked together, and are able to share vast information systems. Increasingly, large numbers of employees are able to work from home and many people work with shared information systems such as the Worldwide Web. We will look in detail at information technology communications in Chapter 55.

MATCH IT!

Can you help Frankie and Cleo to match the following terms and definitions?

Internal communication	An outline of the results of an investigation
	Communications that take place within an organisation
External communication	A written study of a topic or issue
Memo	The minimum number of people required for a business meeting
Report	A group of people in an organisation given responsibility to deal with specific issues
Terms of reference	An organised and highly structured meeting
Agenda	A written account of the main points covered in a meeting
Recommendations	A common way of communicating information in short written notes circulated to selected people within an organisation
Procedure	
Minutes	Communication between an organisation and outsiders
Formal meeting	The programme of what will be discussed in a meeting
Informal meeting	Suggestions made as a result of carrying out an investigation and producing a report
Quorum	An unstructured meeting between a number of people in the workplace
Committee	An explanation of the reasons for carrying out a report
Findings	Steps and methods involved in producing a report

54 Communication Outside a Business

Purposes of external communications

External communication is concerned with how an organisation communicates with and is viewed by people and organisations outside the business.

There are a number of purposes of external communications (*see diagram below*):

1 **Providing information.** For example, railway and bus companies provide their customers with access to timetables, businesses provide annual reports for shareholders, etc.

2 **Giving instructions.** For example, telling suppliers where to deliver goods or telling customers to use products in a certain way.

3 **Confirming arrangements.** This may include confirming meetings or conferences or perhaps details of transactions.

4 **Improving customer service.** Good communication can help to reduce errors, provide customers with plenty of feedback and deal more efficiently with enquiries.

5 **Public relations.** Good communication can help to project a more positive image and overcome prejudices which people may have against the company.

'My business provides a valuable environmental service! I reckon local people see me as a sort of successful business entrepreneur.'

'Funny, I'm sure I've seen letters of complaint about Ron's business in the local paper…'

Below: The purposes of external communications

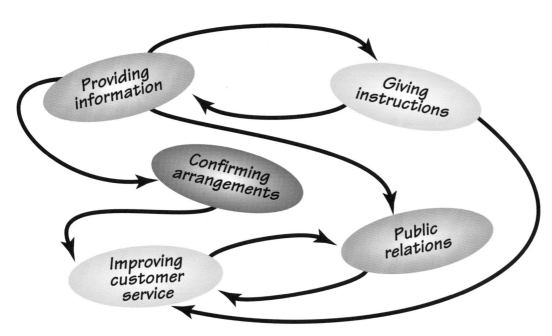

Providing information

Giving instructions

Confirming arrangements

Public relations

Improving customer service

Methods of external communication

There are a number of different methods of external communication:

The business letter

The business letter is probably the most widely used form of external communication. To write an effective letter you need to prepare properly. It may be necessary to investigate the background first by searching through previous correspondence.

A letter may be written to:

◆ Seek information

◆ Place or confirm an order

◆ Deal with a problem

◆ Obtain quotations

◆ Quote a price, etc

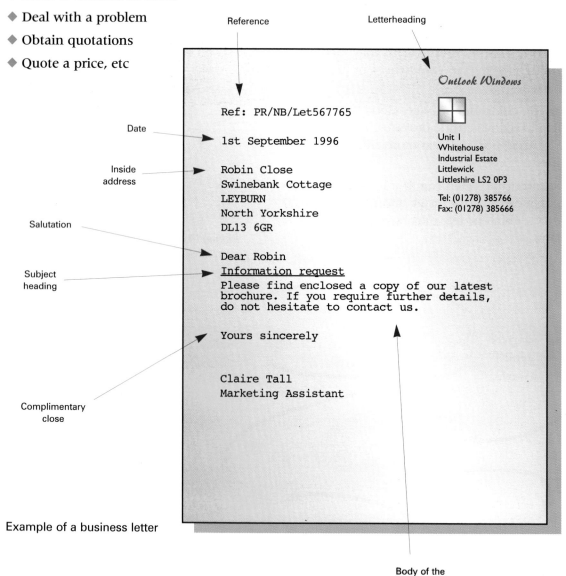

Reference

Letterheading

Outlook Windows

Ref: PR/NB/Let567765

Date

1st September 1996

Unit 1
Whitehouse
Industrial Estate
Littlewick
Littleshire LS2 0P3

Inside
address

Robin Close
Swinebank Cottage
LEYBURN
North Yorkshire
DL13 6GR

Tel: (01278) 385766
Fax: (01278) 385666

Salutation

Dear Robin

Subject
heading

Information request
Please find enclosed a copy of our latest
brochure. If you require further details,
do not hesitate to contact us.

Yours sincerely

Claire Tall
Marketing Assistant

Complimentary
close

Body of the
letter

Example of a business letter

CHAPTER 54

CASE STUDY

EPS external communications

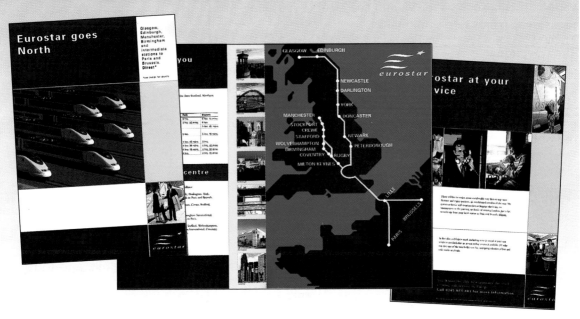

The layout, style and appearance of a business letter will vary from one organisation to another. A typical business letter will have the following features *(see example on opposite page)*:

- Heading or letterhead
- Reference (so that enquiries can be traced)
- Date
- Inside address
- Salutation (e.g. 'Dear Sir')
- Subject heading
- Body of the letter
- Complimentary close (e.g. 'Yours faithfully' or 'Yours sincerely')

Customer newsletters
These can be a useful way of communicating product or service changes and developments to different groups of customers *(see Case Study above)*.

Customer newsletters may contain information about staff, new services such as the opening of new branches, or about developments within an industry.

 TASK

1   What do you think is the purpose of the above magazine?

2   What sort of images does it portray?

3   Why is it important for European Passenger Services to develop a strong positive image with groups of people outside the organisation?

Advertisements

Advertisements are a form of external communication which we are all familiar with. They can be found in various media such as television, the local or national press, magazines or on billboards.

The telephone

The way employees deal with enquiries on the telephone can often have a big influence on the way customers feel about a company. Politeness and efficiency are vital when dealing with telephone enquiries from members of the public.

TASK

Collect a series of business letters which have been sent either to you or to a member of your family.

Compare them to the letter on page 204.

MATCH IT!

Can you help Frankie and Cleo to match the following terms and definitions?

Salutation	Stationery printed with a company's details and logo
Public relations	Formal greeting in a letter such as 'Dear Sir'
Letterhead	Formal ending to a letter such as 'Yours sincerely'
Complimentary close	Communications aimed at projecting a positive image of a company or institution

55 The Role of Information Technology

The information revolution

In recent years, office functions have been transformed by the use of computers and the spread of information technology.

Modern information technology means that today employees:

- have access to more information than before.
- can undertake a wider variety of tasks
- are more efficient
- can use data in different ways
- can present data in many different forms

'I enjoy using computers. They help to make you feel in complete control of your business.'

IT in the office

In a modern office, information is usually processed by means of a **computer system**. This will usually contain the following key elements:

- **Input devices.** These allow information to be fed into the system. Keyboards and scanners are examples of input devices.

- **Storage devices.** These store information and data so that it can be accessed when needed. A computer hard disk or CD-ROM drive is a storage device.

- **Software/programs.** These allow the data or information to be processed or manipulated *(see examples below).*

- **Output devices.** These produce the processed data in the form required by the user. A printer is an example of an output device.

Software for business

There are many different types of program to help business people to communicate with each other. Some you will already be familiar with.

Word processing

Word processors enable text to be keyed in, stored, altered easily and printed out.

Desktop publishing

Desktop publishing (DTP) programs make it possible to produce pages of combined text and graphics to a very high standard. DTP is used to produce reports, newsletters, training materials – even books.

Spreadsheets

A spreadsheet is a table of numbers which can be organised and analysed on a computer. A **spreadsheet program** is used when making forecasts and doing calculations – the advantage being that the computer does all the work for you!

Spreadsheets are particularly useful for financial forecasting and 'what if' modelling. For instance, a business may forecast all the money that will come in and go out over a twelve-month period. The figures can then be adjusted to show the effect, for example, of reducing a heating bill by a certain amount each month. The computer automatically recalculates the columns to change the heating figures, total cost figures and cashflow for each month.

Below: Three generations of information processing…

The age of the quill pen

The age of the mechanical typewriter

A modern office with computers and telecommunications equipment

CASE STUDY

Users of IT

The figures below show how IT is used by various socio-economic groups. Look at the figures and then, working in groups, discuss their significance and report back to the whole class.

	AB%	C1%	C2%	DE%
Personal computers	59	40	37	19
Mobile phones	47	18	18	13
Pager/bleeper	6	15	13	9
Home computer game	24	20	22	24
Modem	26	13	15	3
Internet	14	11	3	4

Databases

A database is like an electronic filing system which can be used by, for example, a bank or a building society to store information about its customers' accounts.

A church may keep a database of members of its congregation, or a football club may keep details of tickets sold for matches.

Under the Data Protection Act, companies wishing to store any personal information on a computer system must register with the government-appointed Data Processing Officer.

Graphics packages
In recent years there have been a number of developments in the type and range of graphics packages. These enable data to be translated into a graphical form such as charts, pictures and graphs. Presentation graphics can also be used for overhead transparencies (OHTs) or high-resolution colour slides.

Project planning
Project planning packages may be used for planning a complex project with a series of interrelated activities.

Expert systems
These are programs consisting of a set of rules based on the knowledge of experts. These rules can be used to help users to find answers to problems that the program works on when it is given information.

COURSEWORK ACTIVITIES

Find out about the use of information technology in your school or college office.

Present a report to show how this technology is used.

The Internet

The Internet, or Worldwide Web, is currently transforming global communications. It is a global 'network of networks' which can be accessed from a personal computer by means of a modem or telephone link. It enables users from anywhere in the world to communicate and share information quickly and easily.

Many believe that the Internet will revolutionise the business world in the next decade. However, controlling access to information on the Internet is a serious problem for governments and politicians.

MATCH IT!

Can you help Frankie and Cleo to match the following terms and definitions?

Expert systems	Global network of computers linked by modems
Database	Means by which processed data is produced in the form required by the user – e.g. a printer
Internet	Use of computer software to create pages combining text, graphics and images
Spreadsheet	Means by which raw data is fed into a computer system – e.g. a keyboard
Input device	Computer software used for input and manipulation of text
Graphics package	Program widely used by businesses for financial forecasting and 'what if' modelling
Desktop publishing	Computer programs which predict outcomes based on pre-determined rules and knowledge
Output device	Computer program used for storing and analysing data
Word processor	Software enabling data to be presented in the form of graphics and charts

7 56 Human Needs at Work

Job satisfaction

Many people spend a considerable part of their lives at work. So it is not surprising that they expect to be rewarded and satisfied with the job they do.

To some people, work is a great pleasure, giving them a sense of personal fulfilment, but for others it is just a necessary way to make a living.

'What do you think? Should work be a pleasure, or simply a way of making money to buy pleasure?'

Motivation

Motivation is what causes people to act or do something in a positive way. By understanding why people behave in the way they do, managers can make work more fulfilling for people, and thus **motivate** them. A well-motivated workforce will work harder and contribute more to the success of a business.

We all have different motives for the things that we do. For example, some people strive to be successful and powerful. Others strive for money. Others just want to be liked or to help other people. What drives us depends on our personality, our background and other important factors.

Satisfying needs

A lot of research has gone into finding out what motivates people at work. One of the leading theories is that of **Abraham Maslow.**

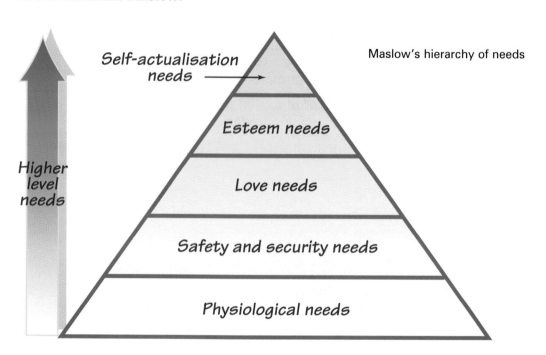

Maslow's hierarchy of needs

Self-actualisation needs
Esteem needs
Love needs
Safety and security needs
Physiological needs

Higher level needs

From his research Maslow drew up what he called a **hierarchy of needs**, with basic needs at the bottom and higher needs at the top *(see diagram on opposite page)*.

Maslow claimed that people must satisfy their lower-level needs before moving on to a higher level.

1 Physiological needs

Physiological needs are for basics such as food, shelter and clothing. These basic needs must be met in order to keep the body functioning. Some sections of our society such as people sleeping under railway arches in London are not even satisfying these basic needs.

At work, the basic level of need is for employees to receive payment for their work. The workplace also needs to be safe from accidents and danger.

2 Safety and security needs

In order to be safe from danger, people need to be able to work in a clean and orderly workspace. The job itself needs to be secure, and employees should have the right to take part in pension and sick-pay schemes.

Today, many jobs are under threat – so again, there are many people for whom this need is not being met.

3 Love needs

Love needs arise because we all need to be able to give and receive love. This involves building up good relationships and a feeling of belonging.

In the workplace these needs can be satisfied by the companionship of fellow employees, the pleasure of working in a group or team and company social activities.

4 Esteem needs

Esteem needs are based on our desire for self-respect and the respect of others. Employees have a need to be recognised as individuals, to have a job title or some form of status or prestige, and to have their efforts noticed.

5 Self-actualisation needs

Self-actualisation is about our need to develop our skills and creativity and achieve our full potential as individuals.

In order to meet these needs at work, we need to have the chance to progress and develop through training, and to use our creative talents and abilities to the full.

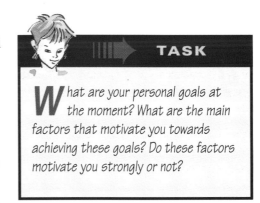

TASK

What are your personal goals at the moment? What are the main factors that motivate you towards achieving these goals? Do these factors motivate you strongly or not?

Everyone has a basic need for food and shelter

TASK

How do each of the following individuals fit against Maslow's hierarchy of needs?

1 Joseph (right) is a talented violinist who has dedicated his life to music. He plays first violin in one of the top orchestras in the UK. Frequently he plays solo pieces, and is always being allowed to develop new ideas. However, there is some uncertainty about the future funding of the orchestra.

2 Maria (left) is a children's book illustrator. Her work is nationally recognised and she always has a string of projects on the go at the same time. She is able to pick and choose the work she does, and can work on her own ideas.

3 Ben (right) left school with no formal qualifications. He expected to get a job as an electrician in the factory where his father worked. However, the factory closed and he now has little prospect of getting a job. He has barely enough food to live on and has recently been made homeless.

4 Stephanie (left) works as a nursery nurse. The pay is not very good but she has enough to make ends meet. She loves working with children and the work gives her tremendous satisfaction. However, she sometimes finds it frustrating that there is little opportunity to develop her managerial skills. Sometimes she also feels a bit undervalued.

Human Resource Management

In modern businesses we use the term **Human Resource Management** to describe the way in which people should be looked after at work.

The idea of Human Resource Management contrasts with the way in which people were treated in the early part of the twentieth century, when employers like Henry Ford used an approach based on what was known as **Scientific Management**.

Case Study

Finding the motivation

A senior manager in a company was surprised at the performance of an employee who had only been in the post for three years.

The employee had the right qualities for the job, as well as the skills, but was not doing as well as expected. He was running a department with 30 highly skilled people working under him. His role was to lead and motivate the team in order to get things done. Despite a generous salary, health insurance, company car and pension scheme, his heart just did not seem to be in the job. Instead of taking pride in running the department, he busied himself in technical work.

After talking with this employee, the senior manager found that the role was no longer challenging enough for him. He had been chosen on the basis of his technical ability and management potential. But what management failed to realise was that he also needed to be constantly involved in projects that required skill and imagination.

This case is not uncommon. Attitudes to work often depend on how much chance individuals have to express their talents and skills. Although the individual in this case was being well paid, he was not being **motivated.** The solution in this case was to move him to a job at a similar level which enabled him to use his skills to the full.

Scientific Management involved treating employees as if they were a resource no different from a machine. Employers worked out the best way of using their human 'machines' to get the most output from them. They reduced the movements that workers needed to make to a minimum and made them repeat the same movement over and over again.

Of course, if they worked hard and productively, they were well paid. But this approach did not meet the higher needs of employees.

Human Resource Management involves humanising work. It involves finding out how to motivate people by treating them as human beings with their own dreams and aspirations.

This often means organising people in teams, encouraging them to solve problems, make decisions and set their own targets.

Human Resource Management also requires organisations to communicate their objectives to people at work. In return employees are encouraged to communicate their hopes and dreams to managers in personal interviews called **appraisals** *(see page 239).*

Human Resource Management is the best way of meeting people's needs at work.

TASK

1   Explain why material rewards are not the only things that people look for in a job.

2   What are the things that would make a job satisfying for you?

3   What do you understand by the term 'motivation'?

MATCH IT! Can you help Frankie and Cleo to match the following terms and definitions?

Esteem needs	An employee's need to feel that there is affection in the workplace
Basic needs	The need for a minimum level of food, shelter and clothing
Love needs	Approach aimed at maximising output by regarding employees as 'human machines'
Self-actualisation	
Hierarchy of needs	The need for job security and orderly, clean and safe working conditions
	Levels of needs ranked into order
Safety and security needs	The process of developing personal creativity and achieving self-fulfilment
Scientific Management	The need for self-respect and the respect of others
Human Resource Management	Treating people as people, in order to enable them to achieve fulfilment and satisfaction and at the same time maximise their contribution to the company

57 Roles Within the Workplace

Who does what in an organisation?

Some organisations are very small while others are very large. On the whole, the larger an organisation, the more complicated its organisational structure.

Large organisations often have several 'layers' of command (see Chapter 20). Some people spend a lot of time making important decisions while others are mainly involved in carrying out routine tasks.

This chapter examines 'who does what' in an organisation. It looks at three different layers of responsibility: managers, supervisors and operatives.

'How are responsibilities shared in organisations?'

1 Management

Managers have the job of managing the other resources in the workplace, including other people. It is the manager's job to develop systems for 'organising the organisation'.

Strategic-level managers

Top-level decisions concerning the organisation are made by **strategic managers**. These include what range of products to concentrate on, what markets to sell in, what new investments to make, and so on.

'What do strategic-level managers do?'

Middle managers

Middle managers organise and control the resources of an organisation within the guidelines set out from above. Middle managers often have considerable scope for using their own judgement and for bringing in new ideas after consultation with senior management. Examples of middle management decisions include setting and controlling a departmental budget, organising a salesforce, and changing the price of some products.

Junior/supervisory management

Junior/supervisory managers are usually concerned with short-term and routine decisions.

These generally involve areas that are predictable and straightforward. Examples include managing stock, arranging the delivery of goods, organising hours worked by staff, etc.

Unfortunately, because the title 'manager' has a certain status, companies often advertise jobs for 'junior' or 'trainee' managers in the hope of attracting people who will work hard for relatively low pay. If you apply for this kind of job, be sure to check that it really does offer opportunities for promotion.

'That is our new junior supermarket cleaning manager.'

2 Supervisors

Supervisors are often the backbone of an organisation. These are people who know how things should be done at ground level. They work with middle and junior managers to put plans into practice.

Below are some of the typical duties of a supervisor:

◆ Set daily schedules

◆ Oversee work being carried out

◆ Identify and sort out operational problems

◆ Introduce new staff to work tasks

◆ Give advice and guidance

◆ Keep check on levels of stock

◆ Apply expert knowledge of production

◆ Liaise with management

Supervisors know the capabilities of all the resources (machines, people and materials) because they work alongside them every day.

Supervision is a skilled and demanding job. The supervisor is like a sergeant major in the army giving orders to the ground troops. He or she will be first in line to deal with day-to-day problems as and when they occur.

'The best supervisors are the ones that bark! Their job is to be ruthless and to rule the people under them with a rod of iron!'

Do you agree with Ron?

TASK

Which of the following decisions or activities in a supermarket chain would you expect to be carried out by (i) strategic (ii) middle, and (iii) junior managers?

• The decision to move nationally into more organic products

• The decision in a supermarket branch to change the procedure for opening the store in the morning

• The decision to bring in a new system of electronic stock control which will cover the whole supermarket chain

• The decision to open up three new stores per year until the year 2010

• The decision to discount a series of items in a store which are nearing their sell-by date

• Scheduling the hours which staff will work in a given week

• Opening up new tills when existing tills become overloaded

• Designing a training programme for new staff in a particular supermarket

• Making sure that safety notices are put up after spillages

Organisations therefore look for people with good qualifications to become supervisors. They are likely to have mathematical and communication skills as well as a good knowledge of the technology of their industry. Supervisors may have 'risen through the ranks' of their organisation by hard work and the ability to cope with responsibility, so they need to upgrade their skills periodically through training courses.

3 Operatives

Whilst operational activities may be routine, they need to be done with great care and precision. There are many different types of operatives.

In a supermarket there are shelf-fillers and checkout staff; in a textile company there are cutters, stitchers and packers. Operatives need to feel that they are valued, and there should be opportunities for them to learn new skills, so that they can move on to higher-grade work.

TASK

*I*nterview three people – one at management, one at supervisory and one at operational level. Compare the qualifications, knowledge and skills required by each.

MATCH IT!

Can you help Frankie and Cleo to match the following terms and definitions?

Operative	A 'thick of the action' employee entrusted to make sure that operations are carried out properly
Middle manager	Person responsible for making the top-level decisions in an organisation
Strategic manager	Person responsible for carrying out the routine activities of an organisation
Junior manager	A trainee manager often responsible for fairly routine tasks
Supervisor	Person responsible for managing an organisation at departmental level

7 58 Wages and Salaries

Methods of payment

Staff workers – usually office workers – are paid an annual salary. This is divided into twelve equal parts and normally paid directly into the employee's bank account each month by credit transfer.

The amount paid each month does not usually vary a great deal because staff workers do not tend to receive overtime or piece-rate payments.

Non-staff employees such as machine operatives are paid weekly **wages.** Usually employees receiving wages will be asked to work for a week in advance before they are paid.

Calculating pay

The sum paid for a normal working week is referred to as a **basic wage** or **salary.** Many employees receive extra benefits on top of their basic wage, either in money or some other form.

Not all employees receive a wage or salary. For example, salespeople may be paid on a **commission** basis, i.e. according to their success in selling the firm's products. The main ways of calculating pay are described below.

Flat rate

This is a set rate of pay, based on a set number of hours – for example, £120 for a 20-hour week. This is easy to calculate and administer, but it does not give the employee any incentive to work harder.

Time rate

Under this scheme, the worker receives a set rate per hour. Any hours worked above a set number are paid at an **overtime** rate.

Piece rate

This system is sometimes used in the textile and electronics industries, among others. Payment is made for each item produced which meets a given quality standard.

The advantage of such a scheme is that it encourages effort. However, it is not suitable for jobs which require time and care. Also, the output of many jobs in service industries is impossible to measure accurately. For example, how could you measure the output of a teacher, bus driver or doctor?

'I wonder what the difference is between a wage and a salary...'

COURSEWORK ACTIVITIES

Study the job advertisements in a national newspaper. Make a list of the non-money benefits offered with different jobs.

TASK

Peter works in an office and is paid £500 per month.

Emma makes sandwiches and earns £80. She is paid weekly.

Does Peter or Emma earn a salary?

Bonus

A bonus is paid as an additional encouragement to employees. It can be paid out of additional profits earned by the company as a result of the employee's effort and hard work. Bonuses may also be used as an incentive to workers around Christmas or at times when they might be inclined to slacken effort.

Commission

This is a payment made as a percentage of the sales a salesperson has made.

Attendance records

In order to make up pay packets, it is necessary to keep a fair record of how much work is being done. Today, most large employers pay their employees' wages by bank **multiple giro**.

With a multiple giro system, the firm's payroll department has a record of the bank and bank account number of each of its employees. A wages clerk then simply fills in a multiple giro form authorising the firm's bank to make payments to its employees' bank accounts. Large firms can now make out giro payments by computer.

There are several ways in which a record can be kept of attendance at work:

Clock-cards

Large firms will often have a **clocking** system so that the employee 'clocks on and off'. Each employee picks up his or her card on arriving at work and punches it into the clocking device. Employees may have to clock off and on again when they take a lunch break and then off again when they finish work. In modern firms this is done through an electronic swipe card.

Using computerised systems, wages can be automatically calculated at the end of the week.

Time books

Smaller firms may keep a **time book**. Employees simply sign in and out of the book.

Time-sheets

This method is often used for employees who do not always work at the same place each day, e.g. contract workers such as painters and decorators, film crews, road builders, etc. The sheet is filled in each day and is signed by the supervisor to prove accuracy.

	Average salary		
Clerical	1991 £	1994 £	1995 £
Clerical staff	8,463	9,301	8,439
Accounts staff	10,491	9,613	8,384
Secretarial staff	9,418	9,750	9,661
Juniors	5,694	4,504	5,048
Telephonists/receptionists	7,507	9,321	8,048

	Average hourly rate		
Manufacturing	1991 £	1994 £	1995 £
Sewing machinists	–	3.48	3.82
Assemblers	3.88	4.23	5.01
Labourers	4.11	4.82	4.14
Drivers	4.50	4.47	4.67
Cleaners	–	3.81	3.11
Warehousemen	–	4.03	4.28

	Average salary		
Professional/technical	1991 £	1994 £	1995 £
Graduate trainees	9,876	11,300	10,750
Legal staff	15,941	19,302	19,178
Computer staff	14,545	16,410	16,515
Engineers	14,649	15,413	15,148
Managers	18,471	18,238	21,395

Comparative earnings by sector in Nottinghamshire, 1991-1995

Flexitime

Flexible working time (FWT) is increasingly used in the modern workplace. At 'peak' times all members of staff will be at work. Outside these 'core' hours, there is more flexibility and staff have a certain amount of choice about when they work, provided they work a minimum number of hours.

The advantages of flexitime are:

1 It gives employees more control over when they work. Employees may enjoy this type of freedom. It also makes it easier for them to fit in private engagements such as hair and dental appointments and to take their children to and from school.

2 At least for the basic core time, all the workforce are operating together.

Shift work

In many industries it is important to have machinery working all the time in order to make the most efficient and profitable use of resources. This is true of industries such as textiles, chemicals, steel, coal-mining, food processing and many others.

There are a number of ways of doing this. In some textile businesses, for example, there are distinct day and night shifts. In the North Sea oil industry, production workers may work on a rig for two weeks and then take a two-week break. In the chemical industry, employees sometimes work the day shift for one week, followed by a week on the night shift – and so on.

Employees will be paid higher rewards to make up for having to work unsocial hours.

Gross and net pay

Gross pay is the total amount of money earned by an employee before any deductions have been taken off. It includes the basic pay, plus any additional payments such as bonuses and overtime.

Net pay is the total amount of money received by an employee after deductions – i.e. an employee's take-home pay:

Net pay = Gross pay – deductions.

The difference can be shown by examining a typical pay slip – see the example in the Case Study on the opposite page.

'Flexitime sounds barmy to me. It is a shirker's charter! The best workers are those that work to a company's hours, not pick and choose their own!'

Is Ron right that the best workers do not need flexibility?

CASE STUDY

A typical pay slip

The pay slip below belongs to Milorad Rajic who works in the accounts department of Tasty Sweets PLC. Let us look at the pay slip one column at a time.

Column 1	Column 2	Column 3	Column 4
PAY ADVICE	**NAME**	**Ref No** (Quote on any query)	*27 Nov 96*
(1) TASTY SWEET PLC	(5) M Rajic	27 2687 2017	
Basic Pay/Additions	**Deductions**	**Pay Cumulatives**	**Your net pay has been credited to your account as stated below:**
(2) Basic pay 1052.25	(6) Tax Code: 0450H 209.96	This year	(17)
(3) Overtime 40.50	(7) Nat. Insurance 78.41		Bank Nat. Westminster
	(8) Superannuation 63.13		Sorting code 06 17 25
	(9) Union 4.00		Account Number 76256905
	(10) Nat. Insurance no YT82034B		
	(11) Date of payment 28 Nov 96		
	(12) Income Tax Year 96/97		MR M RAJIC
	(13) Pay period 08		
	(14) Enter 'X' if final pay period in tax year ☐		
(4) **TOTAL PAY ADDITIONS £1092.75**	(15) **TOTAL DEDUCTIONS £355.50**	(16) **NET PAY £737.25**	

Column 1

1. The name of the company
2. The employee's basic month's pay
3. Milorad has worked some overtime.
4. If we add (2) and (3), we get Milorad's gross pay.

Column 2

5. The employee's name
6. Milorad is a married man with a mortgage. He is entitled to some tax-free pay as an allowance each month. He pays income tax on any earnings above this allowance each month.
7. As well as income tax, employees have to pay a compulsory National Insurance contribution. This money goes towards providing benefits like pensions and unemployment benefit.
8. Milorad also contributed £63.13 towards his company's pension scheme.

Column 2 (Contd.)

9. This is Milorad's trade union membership subscription
10. This is Milorad's national insurance number
11. The date on which money will be transferred to Milorad's bank account by giro payment.
12. The tax year runs from 1st April 1996 to 31st March 1997
13. The pay period is for the eighth month, i.e. November.
14. An 'X' would appear in this box in March.
15. This is the total value of deductions.

Column 3

16. Net pay, i.e. gross pay minus deductions.

Column 4

17. This statement shows that the money is being paid by multiple giro into Milorad's bank account.

In addition to the above details, the pay slip would typically show the overall amount of gross pay, tax, superannuation and national insurance paid in the financial year up to that date.

Statutory deductions from pay

Income tax

This is paid through the **pay-as-you-earn system (PAYE)**. People of working age are sent a tax form to fill in. They have to state the name of their employer, and their earnings from this source. Any extra earnings will also need to be recorded on the tax form, e.g. interest and dividends from investments. People whose work involves expenses can make claims for these to be allowed against tax so that they do not pay so much.

The amount of income tax a person pays depends on their income and tax **allowances**. These will depend on their marital status, the size of their mortgage, whether they have dependent relatives at home, etc. Each employee is given a **tax code** by the Inland Revenue. By looking at the 'free-pay' table issued by the Inland Revenue, the wages department knows how much to deduct.

Self-assessment

In 1996 a new system of **self-assessment** of tax was introduced in the UK. This means that everyone has to work out how much tax they should be paying by adding up their income and expenses. Leaflets explaining self-assessment are available from your local tax office.

'Do you think it is a good idea for people to assess their own tax payments?'

Changing job

When an employee leaves his or her job, the employer completes a form **P45.** The P45 must then be given to the new employer, who can then continue tax deductions without complications.

At the end of the tax year, an employee receives a form **P60,** which is a summary of their gross and net pay during the year. It must be kept safely because they may need it in order to apply for a mortgage, or claim sickness or unemployment benefit in the coming year. These benefits are **earnings-related**.

A person taking up work for the first time will probably not have a tax code or P45. To begin with, they are normally taxed on an emergency code. If they are over-taxed they will be entitled to a **rebate**.

National insurance contributions

These are paid to the government jointly by the employer and the employee. Contributions from national insurance go into the National Insurance Fund, the National Health Service and the Redundancy Fund. These contributions pay for sickness and unemployment benefit, old age pensions and the National Health Service. The employer's contribution makes up the greater part of the overall contribution. Contributions are not made by the unemployed or when an employee is claiming sickness benefit, provided a doctor's certificate is obtained.

'I think it is outrageous that the unemployed don't have to pay National Insurance!'

Do you agree with Ron?

Voluntary deductions from pay

1 Superannuation/private pension schemes
   Many employees nowadays choose to pay money into a private pension scheme to supplement their state pensions. For some employees this is a condition of employment. The pension paid depends on how much the employee contributes to the fund.

2 Savings
   Some employees contract to pay a certain amount each month into a fund such as the government's **Save-As-You-Earn (SAYE)** scheme. By saving regular sums, the employee is entitled to a lump sum with interest after a given period of time.

3 Trade union contributions
   These can also be paid directly from wages.

4 Private medical scheme contributions
   An increasing number of people contract to make payments into private medical schemes.

Other voluntary contributions include contributions to the company social club and donations to charity.

Statutory sick pay (SSP)

The government has now made businesses largely responsible for paying sick pay to employees. This is called **statutory sick pay (SSP)**. These payments are made if a worker is sick on normal working days.

Computerisation of wages

Today much routine payroll work is done by computers. This includes the calculation of wages, the printing of pay slips and the production of payment instructions to the bank. Computers are able to handle a lot of work quickly and accurately. As with any other computer work, it is essential to take a back-up copy.

Fringe benefits

Many jobs include a wide range of **perks** or benefits which do not appear directly in the pay packet. Railway employees and their families, for example, may be allowed free rail travel. Managerial jobs often include perks such as subsidised company cars and phone bills. Other fringe benefits include subsidised canteen facilities, free training courses, or the right to buy the firm's products at discount prices.

 MATCH IT!

Can you help Frankie and Cleo to match the following terms and definitions?

Terms	Definitions
Fringe benefits	A system whereby a firm can pay a list of individual wages directly into employees' bank accounts
Net pay	Perks which do not appear directly in the pay packet
Gross pay	Contributions paid to the government by employers and employees to pay for National Health Service and Redundancy Fund
Overtime	Hours worked on top of the standard working week
Multiple giro	A summary of tax paid by an employee at the end of the tax year
National insurance	Earnings which are non-taxable
Income tax	Money earned from work activity
Income	Form setting out income tax paid, completed by employer when employee changes job
P45	Money received back by an employee who has paid too much tax
P60	The amount deducted from income to pay for a pension
Allowances	Tax and other contributions whose amount varies according to the size of income earned
Tax rebate	Income before deductions
Superannuation	Income after deductions
Earnings-related	Tax paid to the government on income, the rate varying with size of income

59 The Employment Contract

What is a contract?

A contract is an agreement between people or organisations to deliver goods or services, or to do something on jointly agreed terms.

When a new employee is taken on, he or she must be given a written contract of employment within 13 weeks of starting work.

What does a contract of employment cover?

Under the Contract of Employment Act, 1972, the contract must include the following:

◆ Job title

◆ Date the job starts

◆ Hours of work

◆ Rate and method of pay

◆ Holiday arrangements

◆ Period of notice that must be given when employment is terminated

◆ Pension scheme arrangements

◆ Rights concerning trade unions

◆ Details of the organisation's disciplinary procedures

This is a lot of information, but it is important for employees to know exactly what rights and entitlements they have at work, and what is expected of them.

The contract date

The contract exists in law before it has been written out. As soon as a person agrees to work for an employer and the employer agrees to pay wages, then a contract exists, even though the terms and conditions do not have to be written down for 13 weeks.

The written statement is not a contract of employment in itself. Once the employer makes an offer of employment to an individual and this is accepted, a contract is in existence. The details of the contract are known as the **terms and conditions**, and these must be set out in writing within the specified time of 13 weeks.

The contract of employment is not very exciting to look at. It is a legal document so it includes lots of legal terms. The Case Study on the next page shows what the first part of the contract looks like.

COURSEWORK ACTIVITIES

Study the contract of employment of someone you know. Identify each of the features listed on the left on their contract of employment.

Remember that an employer must give all employees working for sixteen or more hours per week written details of their main terms of service.

'When does the contract become binding?'

TASK

*R*oger has been working for a local business for the last five months.

What should he have received within 13 weeks of starting the job?

CASE **S**TUDY

A typical contract of employment

Contract of employment for restaurant employees

This document sets out the terms and conditions for kitchen staff at JOLLY RESTAURANTS. It is drawn up in accordance with the Employment Protection Act, 1978, and the Contract of Employment Act, 1972.

Employee: Sally Davies

Address.   314 The Laurels, Grantham, NG31 9HL

Job title   Kitchen porter

This contract takes effect as at: 8.00.a.m.

Your employment with JOLLY RESTAURANTS starts on:

1st January, 1997.

1. Pay

Your rate of pay and overtime has been established nationally by the Trade Union and the Hotel Employers' Association. A copy of this agreement is available for reference from the personnel manager.

Your current rate of pay is £4.40 per hour for a 36-hour working week, and is paid in arrears normally on a Friday.

Each payment will be accompanied by an itemised pay statement. In addition to the above rate of pay, the company operates a bonus scheme depending on the number of customers using the restaurants. A copy of this scheme is available from the personnel manager for reference.

1

  TASK

1   How clear do you find the above introduction to a contract of employment?

2   Why is it set out so precisely?

3   What details have been included so far in the contract which must be there by law? (Note that employers must provide an itemised pay statement!)

CHAPTER 59

Dismissal

Over the years, the rules for dismissing employees have become more and more complicated. The heart of the matter lies in the difference between what the courts regard to be 'fair' and 'unfair' dismissal.

Fair dismissal can take place when an employee can be shown to be guilty of:

◆ Wilful destruction of company property

◆ Sexual or racial harassment

◆ Continuous bad timekeeping

◆ A negative attitude at work

◆ Inability to do the job

◆ Sleeping on the job

In some cases employees would normally receive written warnings and suspensions before dismissal. **Unfair dismissal** would almost certainly be deemed to have occurred in any of the following circumstances:

◆ **Pregnancy:** An employee can be sacked only if she is unable to do her job properly as a result of being pregnant (e.g. stacking shelves).

◆ **Race:** A worker cannot be sacked on grounds of race.

◆ **Homosexuality:** A person should not be sacked on grounds of their sexual orientation unless it can be proved that his or her standard of work is affected.

◆ **Union membership:** An employer cannot sack a worker for belonging to a trade union.

◆ **Criminal record:** If an employer does not find out about an employee's criminal record until some time after employment starts, they cannot sack them unless they were convicted of a 'relevant' crime (e.g. a cashier who has a record of stealing petty cash).

  TASK

*L*ook at the following examples. What do you think the legal position would be in each case (i.e. would it be fair or unfair dismissal)?

1 A taxi firm dismisses one of their drivers after a tabloid newspaper identifies him as a homosexual. The taxi firm argues that this will lose them business.

2 An employee is caught on the firm's security cameras writing graffiti about the chairman on a wall in front of the company headquarters.

3 A senior manager of a company is reported to the managing director for persistently pinching the bottom of one of the junior employees and making lewd comments.

4 An employee of the firm persistently sets out to recruit other members of a company to a trade union during breaks and lunch hours.

5 A new employee of a firm reports an existing employee for being involved in an assault charge 20 years ago.

'I often take people on to see what they're like. However, if they don't come up to scratch during the first thirteen weeks I get rid of them!'

Is Ron keeping within the letter of the law?

MATCH IT!

Can you help Frankie and Cleo to match the following terms and definitions?

Contract	Arrangements for dealing with employees who fail to obey company requirements and rules
Unfair dismissal	Situation in which an employee loses his or her job because they have not met the fair and legal requirements expected of them
Fair dismissal	An agreement between people or organisations
Disciplinary procedures	Period of time required to inform an employee that their job is finishing, or for an employee to inform their employer that they are leaving
Period of notice	Agreement between an employer and an employee covering terms and conditions of work
Contract of employment	Situation in which an employee is served notice for unacceptable and illegal reasons

60 Personnel

What do we mean by 'personnel'?

The word 'personnel' means the people employed in an organisation or a service. Within an organisation, the personnel department interviews, appoints, keeps records of employees, and carries out other tasks shown below.

The important responsibilities of a personnel department

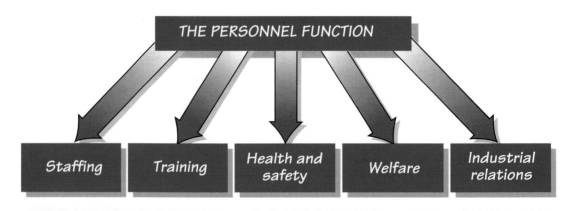

THE PERSONNEL FUNCTION

Staffing · Training · Health and safety · Welfare · Industrial relations

Managing human resources

Today, organisations depend on the individual qualities of people more than ever before. Human Resource Management is therefore very important. Good human relations at work is one of the best ways of adding value to output.

Personnel management is a specialist area concerned with all aspects of developing interpersonal relationships within a firm. This includes recruitment and selection, dismissal, training, discipline, pensions, wage negotiations and other matters.

The employment procession

One way to remember what personnel work involves is to think about what is called the **employment procession**.

This involves looking after the needs of employees from the time they are chosen to work in an organisation to the time they retire.

The employment procession starts with the **recruitment** process – finding new recruits and choosing who to take on. New staff then need to be helped to 'fit in', so they go through a period of **induction.**

During their employment they will need to be **trained** to upgrade their skills and knowledge. Then, when the need arises, they can be **transferred** to other jobs or areas.

When they finish working for the organisation they need to have their jobs **terminated** in a satisfactory way. This includes making sure that pension and other matters are dealt with according to the law.

Other personnel functions

The personnel department is also responsible for:

◆ Health and safety

◆ Equal opportunities

◆ Pay bargaining

◆ Appraisals

◆ Discipline

◆ Payment systems

TASK

*R*ead the Case Study on the following page, then answer the questions below:

1 How many stages are there in the employment procession?

2 If Tommy started work at 16 and retired at 63, how many years did he spend at work?

The employment procession

We can see the employment procession more clearly by looking at the cartoon strip below which shows stages in the working life of Frankie's grandad, Tommy.

1 Recruitment

On leaving school at 16, Tommy went for an interview at a local engineering works along with 100 other boys. He was lucky to be one of 20 taken on as an apprentice.

2 Induction

For his first month at work, Tommy sat alongside a more experienced worker, Frank, who taught him how to work a lathe, and generally 'showed him the ropes'.

3 Training

Tommy worked four days a week learning his work 'on the job'. He also went to the local technical college for one day a week – learning 'off the job'.

4 Transfer

Later on, Tommy became a skilled engineer. He was transferred to another section of the company as a foreman in a plant producing racing cars.

5 Termination

In 1995 Tommy took early retirement at the age of 63. In return for his loyalty, he was presented with a two-week holiday in Bermuda, a gold watch, and a miniature replica of the first racing car he produced.

All of the above stages in Tommy's career path had been planned and prepared for him in discussion with the personnel department of his company.

Can you help Frankie and Cleo to match the following terms and definitions?

Personnel	Health, happiness, and prosperity in general
Staffing	Making sure that an organisation has the right people to do the jobs required
Recruitment	To enrol or obtain new members for an organisation
Transfer	To choose the best members for an organisation
Termination	Planning, organising and co-ordinating the use of people in the workplace
Selection	Arranging for an employee's retirement from work
Industrial relations	Moving employees from one job or section in an organisation to another
Personnel management	The process of bringing a person to a required standard or proficiency
Induction	Relations between employers and employees in an organisation
Welfare	The people employed in an organisation or service
Training	Helping new employees to fit into the patterns of working life

7 *61* **Recruitment and Selection**

The purpose of recruitment

From the personnel department's point of view, the purpose of recruitment is to buy in and keep the best people to work for the organisation.

The first step in the process is to set out clearly what the particular job involves.

'How do firms recruit new people?'

Job analysis

Before advertising a job, the personnel department need to think clearly about what the duties and responsibilities of the job-holder will be. Once they have analysed what they are looking for, they can make out a **job description**.

A job description is a written statement setting out how a particular employee is to fit into an organisation. For example, the job of a trainee manager in a supermarket could be described under the following headings:

◆ Title of post

◆ The main purposes of the job

◆ Supervisory/management responsibilities

◆ The sort of decisions he or she will need to make

◆ Responsibility for assets, materials, etc.

A job/personnel specification

A **job** or **personnel specification** is more than a simple description of the job. It describes the mental and physical requirements of the job-holder. The layout of a personnel specification may look something like this:

Personnel specification for a shop assistant		
Attributes	Essential	Desirable
Physical	-	To be healthy, and able to lift packages, and stack shelves
Qualifications	Maths,English	NVQ Intermediate equivalent GCSEs (A-C)
Experience	-	Previous experience of working as a shop assistant
Etc.		

Having drawn up a job/personnel specification, the personnel department can use it to:

◆ Make sure that a job advertisement covers the qualities that a new job-holder will need to have

◆ Enable interviewers to check that candidates for a job have the right qualities

◆ Check from time to time that people who have been appointed to a job are doing what is required of them

The recruitment process

Organisations can recruit **internally** or **externally**, i.e. they can choose people from inside the organisation or widen the field to outsiders.

Advantages of internal recruitment are:

1 There is less risk involved, because the employer already knows the person who will be filling the vacancy.

2 It saves the cost of press advertising and is therefore cheaper.

3 It saves on induction costs.

4 The opportunity for promotion in the organisation encourages people to work hard.

Disadvantages of internal recruitment are:

1 No new ideas are brought into the organisation from outside.

2 There is no 'buzz' that follows when a new person joins the organisation.

3 Appointing from within the organisation may cause jealousy and resentment among other staff, who may feel they have been 'passed over' for promotion.

'I have heard that organisations often appoint people "from the inside". What are the advantages and disadvantages of this?'

COURSEWORK ACTIVITIES

Study the job description of someone you know who is currently working. If you are working part-time, you may like to use your own job description.

Set out a brief report for other students showing how each section of the job description works in practice. How accurately does it describe the tasks and responsibilities which the job-holder actually performs?

EMPLOYMENT SERVICE

Serving People through Jobcentres

Above: The government Employment Service provides help for firms and job-seekers.

External recruitment

There are a number of ways of recruiting externally.

1 Placing a newspaper advertisement
   On the right is an example of the type of job advertisement you may see in your local newspaper.

2 Advertising in a Jobcentre
   Jobcentres can be found in most towns. They are run by the Employment Service which is part of the Department for Education and Employment. They are used by job-seekers and employers.

   Jobcentres display details of vacancies on cards in their window (*see example, right*). Job-seekers can apply for jobs locally and further afield. They can also get information about training opportunities which will help them get back into work.

3 Commercial employment/recruitment agencies

   There are many commercial employment agencies that help businesses to recruit staff. Fields in which these agencies often specialise are professional, secretarial, high technology, nursing and casual work.

Selection

Selection is all about choosing the best person to do a job. Methods vary according to how the job has been advertised, and the experience, skills and expertise required.

Methods of application

Sometimes employers will ask candidates to apply by letter. A good letter of application will tell them whether the candidate is worthy of an interview (*see opposite page*).

In other cases candidates will be asked to fill in a printed **application form**. This enables them to set out information about themselves in a standardised way, which helps firms to choose candidates for interview later on.

Book-keeper
Required Central Leeds
Janet Davis Advertising Agency, starting salary £6,000 p.a.

We are looking for a book-keeper who has experience of handling the purchase ledger and other account books and is familiar with operations leading to a trial balance.

The successful applicant will be entitled to Luncheon Vouchers and transport to work expenses.

Please apply in writing to Mrs S. Grose Personnel Manager, The J. Davis Advertising Agency, Prince St., Leeds LSU 9BJ

(*Please state names and addresses of 2 referees.*)

A job advertisement in the local press

EMPLOYMENT
Man or Woman

JOB	Full-time sales assistant
DISTRICT	Central Northampton
WAGE	£4 per hour. Annual staff bonus. Fringe benefits
HOURS	40-hour wk. 6-day flexible work pattern
DURATION	Permanent
DETAILS	Ladies fashion dept. Age 25–45. Experience essential.
JOB NO.	15

Ask for COR: 12345

A vacancy advertised in a government Jobcentre

Nina Mistry
20 Belton Lane
Grantham
Lincolnshire
NG31 9HL

10th September 1997

Dear Ms Stevens

I am writing to apply for the position of Design Engineer
which I saw advertised in the Grantham Jobcentre (COR: 7547).

My last job was in a small electronics company who were
involved in making electronic equipment for refrigeration.
The company, Whitegoods International, made energy-saving
motor controllers enabling reductions in the cost of refrigeration in an environmentally-friendly way. I worked for the
company for three years, and this enabled me to build up an
extensive understanding of refrigeration equipment. I enjoyed
working for the company but am now looking for a post with
more responsibility.

As you can see from my CV, I am 25 years of age and my
qualifications are of a high standard in both electronics and
programming. Recently I have learnt to use a variety of
programming languages to a good level of competence.

I hope my application is of interest to you and I look
forward to hearing from you in the near future.

Yours sincerely,

Nina Mistry

Nina Mistry

Above: A typical letter of application

The interview

The interview is the most common method of selection.
This is a face-to-face meeting between the candidate
and the employer to find out whether the applicant will
be suitable for the job, and vice versa. Sometimes an
organisation will ask for **references** before interviewing.
However, often they will interview first and then make a
job offer, 'subject to suitable references'.

|||||> **TASK**

Working in groups of four (two pairs), complete the following tasks:

1 Pair A should prepare a job advertisement for a hotel porter in a firm called Jolly Hotels. Meanwhile Pair B should prepare an advertisement for a receptionist at Jolly Hotels. Make up details where necessary.

2 Each pair sends a letter of application for the job advertised by the other pair.

3 Each pair writes to the other pair inviting them for interview.

4 Interviews are held with all four candidates. If possible, make a video.

5 Analyse the performance of both interviewers and candidates. Then make a list of interviewing techniques for interviewers, as well as a list of interviewing techniques for applicants.

 MATCH IT!

Can you help Frankie and Cleo to match the following terms and definitions?

Job analysis	A commercial organisation which helps firms to fill job vacancies
Job description	The key requirements looked for in an applicant for a job
Essential qualities	Where a firm recruits from people already working within the organisation
External recruitment	Studying the requirements for a job before creating a job description
Job/personnel specification	Written statement of how a particular job will fit into an organisation
Internal recruitment	A government-run service to help firms and job-seekers to fill vacancies
Desirable qualities	Choosing new employees from outside an organisation
Employment agency	A detailed list of the mental and physical requirements of a job-holder
Employment Service	A list of requirements of a job-holder which may be desirable but which are not essential

62 Training and Development

What is training?

Training involves guiding or teaching someone to do something by providing them with a planned programme of exercises and activities. Training develops the skills and knowledge of employees to help them to do their jobs better, and prepares them for more demanding jobs in the future.

Training should be a rewarding process. If employees can do their jobs well, they will feel confident in their abilities and enjoy their work more. This leads to greater job satisfaction.

'What are the advantages to a firm of training its people? After all, it is costly.'

Training costs money

A business needs well-trained employees if it is to be competitive. But training costs money. Special instructors may have to be employed; courses need to be paid for and will require materials, equipment, space and time.

A business therefore has to decide how much money it wants to spend on training, what sort of training should be given, and to whom.

How and when is the training to be carried out?

Who gets trained?

How much should be spent on training?

What sort of training?

Training issues for the employer

Training – a two-way process

Training helps those being trained *and* the organisation they work for. Training can therefore be one of the most effective ways for an organisation to add value.

- ◆ **Benefits to individuals** include greater skills, more knowledge, confidence, better career prospects, etc.

- ◆ **Benefits to the organisation** include more productive employees, better-quality work, more job satisfaction leading to lower absenteeism and staff turnover, greater ability to use the latest technology, etc.

CASE STUDY

Training opportunities in a biscuit factory

The following is a short extract from an employee's handbook in a biscuit factory:

'This company values training and development for all our employees, in order to widen your experience and help you to gain promotion.

'Your most important contact is your line supervisor or manager (the person directly above you). This person will help you to deal with any immediate problems.

'In your first six months there will be opportunities to discuss your training needs with your immediate superior. The training needs of all employees are constantly examined. Together with your supervisor, line leader and training instructors, we will teach you the skills you require, including the importance of safety at work.

'The company also encourages you to continue with education courses in your spare time. If you choose an appropriate course we will refund your tuition and exam fees.'

Types of training

There are a number of different types of training:

1 Induction

Induction training is given to new employees. Its aim is to familiarise them with the organisation and its rules. It can also be used to show the new employee particular job skills. For example, as part of the induction process, a supermarket cashier may be trained how to use electronic scanning equipment and follow other checkout procedures.

2 Upgrading skills

Work changes all the time. This is particularly true in organisations which rely on new technology. It is therefore essential for businesses to **upgrade** the skills of their employees. For example, in the UK today many employees still lack important information technology skills.

3 Retraining

As time moves on, some jobs change or disappear. As a result the employees who previously did these jobs may need to **retrain** to do something else.

4 Multi-skilling

Multi-skilling is the process of training employees to do a number of different tasks. Today's employees need to have different skills and be able to turn their hand to a variety of tasks. We also call this **flexibility**. Work flexibility can be developed through training.

TASK

1   Why does the company in the Case Study above train its employees?

2   Who benefits from training?

3   Give one example of on-the-job training and one example of off-the-job training.

CHAPTER 62

Training methods

Training methods can be split into two main types:

◆ On-the-job training

◆ Off-the-job training

On-the-job training

On-the-job training involves learning new skills through experience at work. A new employee may observe a more experienced worker and copy the methods they use. This is a cheap and often an effective method of training.

Off-the-job training

This involves taking employees away from their jobs to be trained. It can be done within a company, or employees may be sent outside to courses run by educational and training groups.

Appraisal

Many organisations today run **appraisal schemes**. The scheme usually requires individual job-holders to collect and record, in a set way, their impressions of the people working under them. They can then assess strengths and weaknesses in the employees' performance and identify suitable training and development to meet their needs.

Appraisal also helps the employee by allowing them to identify and work towards their chosen career path.

'Appraisal is a good idea. It helps managers to find out who's causing problems in an organisation! It is a good way of getting rid of bad workers!'

Do you think that Ron understands the real purpose of appraisal?

COURSEWORK ACTIVITIES

Interview somebody who has recently had an appraisal interview. What was the format of the interview? What sort of questions were they asked?

How useful did they find the appraisal process?

The appraisal interview

Appraisal interviews are held at regular intervals – say, once a year. The **appraisor** (the superior who carries out the appraisal) will usually ask the **appraisee** (the employee being appraised) to fill in a questionnaire before the interview. This form then becomes a basis for discussion. Typical questions will include:

◆ What were your most important targets/achievements this year?

◆ How successful were you in meeting those targets?

◆ What do you feel are your current strengths?

◆ What do you feel are your current weaknesses?

MATCH IT!

Can you help Frankie and Cleo to match the following terms and definitions?

Appraisal	Training for new employees
Appraisor	Training people to do something different to what they were originally trained for
Induction	Training carried out in the workplace
Retraining	Training people to do a variety of different tasks
Multi-skilling	Ability of employees to switch easily from one operation to another
Upgrading skills	The person carrying out an appraisal interview
Staff training	Monitoring an employee's performance in order to identify strengths, weaknesses and areas for future training
Flexibility	Training away from the place of work
Training schemes	Bringing employee capabilities more into line with modern developments, e.g. in new technology
Off-the-job training	The process of enabling individual employees to improve their knowledge, skills and hence their prospects for promotion
On-the-job training	Organised programmes to improve specific groups' abilities in a particular field, e.g. apprenticeships

63 Health and Safety

Accidents in the workplace

Over 500 people die each year as a result of accident or injury in the workplace. Several hundred thousand lose time at work through injury or illness.

These statistics immediately show the importance of health and safety – and why organisations need to take health and safety very seriously.

'Why is health and safety at work such an important issue?'

A written safety policy

In law, if an organisation employs five or more people, it must have a written **safety policy**. This must set out:

◆ Who is responsible for workplace health and safety

◆ The arrangements that have been made for health and safety

This policy must also be communicated to everyone in the workplace. All employees should be given the training and information they need in order to work safely. There should be regular safety inspections, and large organisations should also have an active health and safety committee.

CASE STUDY

Safety in the modern workplace

One of the major retailing organisations in this country has set out the responsibilities of management for health and safety as being:

• *The provision as far as is reasonably practicable, of safe plant and safe systems of work*

• *Arrangements for ensuring, so far as is practicable, safety in the use, handling, storage and transport of substances*

• *The provision of such information, instruction, training and supervision as is necessary to fulfil the responsibilities for health and safety*

• *The provision, as far as is reasonably practicable, of a workplace and environment which is safe and without risks to health*

• *The reporting of accidents, injuries, reportable illnesses and dangerous occurrences as required by the law.*

Providing protective clothing for workers is an important management responsibility

TASK

Can you help Frankie and Cleo to list all the unsafe working practices shown in the picture?

Employee responsibilities

But safety in the workplace is not *just* a management responsibility. It is also up to employees to take steps to ensure their own – and other people's – health and safety. In particular, employees must:

◆ **Comply** with company arrangements and procedures for securing a safe workplace

◆ **Report** incidents to management that have led, or may lead, to injury

◆ **Co-operate** in the investigation of accidents in order to prevent them happening again

CHAPTER 63

Health and safety laws

There are many laws today governing health and safety. Not only must safety officers in firms be aware of general laws governing safety in the workplace. There are also special health and safety codes for particular industries – for example, coal-mining, the explosives industry and textiles. Many industries also establish their own safety regulations, often in conjunction with trade unions.

The main laws covering health and safety are:

The Factories Act, 1961

This applies to most businesses that use machinery, including a wide range of premises, such as garages, printing works, building sites and engineering workshops. The Act covers toilet and washing facilities, ventilation and heating, fenced screens and guards on machinery and fire escapes.

The Offices, Shops and Railways Premises Act, 1963

This is particularly important for offices and shops. It covers areas such as temperature, ventilation, toilet and washing facilities, lighting and floorspace.

The Health and Safety at Work Act, 1974

This Act places a responsibility on both employers and employees to maintain safe conditions at work. According to the Act, the employer has a duty to ensure, 'as far as is reasonably practical, the health, safety and welfare at work of all employees.'

The employee's duty is to take reasonable care to ensure both his/her own safety and the safety of others who may be affected by what he or she does or does not do.

Employers who do not abide by these rules can be punished in a court of law.

To enforce the Act, the Health and Safety Executive was established, consisting of representatives of employers, employees and local authorities.

Reporting of Injuries, Diseases and Dangerous Occurrences Regulations, 1985 ('RIDDOR')

These regulations require that any injuries resulting from accidents at work where the employee is unable to work for three or more days must be reported to the authorities within seven days.

Listed diseases must be reported, and accidents involving work equipment.

COURSEWORK ACTIVITIES

Ask if you can borrow a copy of the safety policy for your school or college. Make a list of the major points of interest that you find in this policy and discuss them with other students.

'I can't be bothered with all these laws. At the end of the day it's up to my workers to operate in a safe fashion. The responsibility is basically theirs if something happens. They're the ones that'll be taken to court!'

Is Ron right?

Control of Substances Hazardous to Health Regulations, 1988 ('COSHH')
This states that employers must identify work tasks which are likely to be harmful and take steps to minimise the risks. Workers dealing with hazardous substances must be given detailed information and training.

Noise at Work Regulations, 1989
Employers must reduce the risk of hearing damage to employees to the lowest practical level, for example, by providing ear protectors when noise reaches a certain level.

Can you help Frankie and Cleo to match the following terms and definitions?

Factories Act, 1961	Act requiring that injuries, diseases and accidents must be reported within seven days
COSHH, 1988	Regulations covering the use of potentially harmful substances
RIDDOR, 1985	Act requiring employers to take measures to prevent hearing damage caused by noise
Safety policy	Requirement that all organisations employing more than five people must set out in writing how they will protect employees in the workplace
Health and Safety at Work Act, 1974	Act setting out requirements for businesses that use machinery
Noise at Work Regulations, 1989	Act governing temperature and sanitary facilities in offices and shops
Office, Shops and Railway Premises Act	Act setting out responsibility of both employers and employees to create safe working conditions

64 Equal Opportunities

What do we mean by equal opportunities?

Equal opportunities exist in the workplace when individuals have identical rights and opportunities regardless of gender, racial group, age, physical characteristics, sexual orientation or other features.

Many business organisations now realise that it is actually in their own interests to provide equal opportunities *(see Case Study below)*. After all, it is only by offering equal opportunities that they can gain most benefit from all the different people that make up our society.

'Does the fact that there are now more women at work than men mean that we have equal opportunities?'

CASE **S**TUDY

Equal opportunities at Shell and Sainsbury's

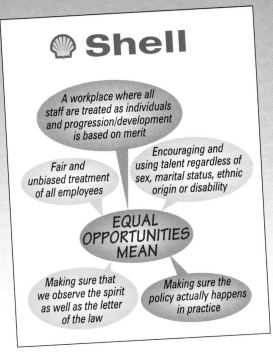

Shell

A workplace where all staff are treated as individuals and progression/development is based on merit

Fair and unbiased treatment of all employees

Encouraging and using talent regardless of sex, marital status, ethnic origin or disability

EQUAL OPPORTUNITIES MEAN

Making sure that we observe the spirit as well as the letter of the law

Making sure the policy actually happens in practice

SAINSBURY'S

Our policy is designed:

• To ensure that no employee receives less favourable treatment on the grounds of sex, race, colour, ethnic origin, religion, disability or marital status.

• To ensure fair and equal access to training, career development and promotion through a well established appraisal scheme.

• To promote a positive environment that enables the organisation to tap the widest possible sources of talent.

  TASK

1. What similarities can you see in the two companies' attitudes?

2. How do the two organisations stand to benefit from having such clear equal opportunities policies?

3. Is there anything you would add or change in the statements made by these two organisations?

The Sex Discrimination Act, 1975

This Act sets out to make sure that both sexes are treated equally in the workplace. It makes it illegal for employers to discriminate in the following key areas:

◆ Selection procedures

◆ Terms on which employment is offered

◆ Opportunities for training and development

◆ Fringe benefits

◆ Choice of who will be made redundant

Unlawful discrimination means giving less favourable treatment to someone because of their sex or because they are married or single.

Under the Act, discrimination can be either **direct** or **indirect.** Direct sex discrimination means treating someone less favourably than a person of the opposite sex would be treated in the same circumstances. For example, if only men are made managers, and sex is the criterion for appointment, this counts as direct discrimination.

Direct **marriage discrimination** means treating a married person less favourably than an unmarried person of the same sex.

For example, a policy not to recruit married people for a job that involved being away from home would be classed as discrimination.

Indirect sex discrimination is less easy to pinpoint. It means making a requirement which on the face of it applies equally to both men and women, but which in practice can be met by a much smaller proportion of one sex than the other – for example, when an organisation restricts certain grades of work to males.

The Sex Discrimination Act, 1985, also covers **victimisation.** Victimisation means treating someone less favourably than others because – 'in good faith' – they have made allegations about discrimination or unfair treatment.

The Race Relations Act, 1976

In the same way as the Sex Discrimination Act sets out to ensure that both sexes are treated equally in the workplace, the **Race Relations Act** sets out to protect members of ethnic minorities from discrimination and unfair treatment.

'Can discrimination at work ever be legal?'

CHAPTER 64

The Equal Pay Act,1970

This states that employers must pay equal amounts to men and women if they are doing the same work, or work which rates as being equivalent, or if they are doing work of equal value.

Under the Act, anyone making a claim for equal pay must be able to compare themselves with a person of the opposite sex doing the same work.

Disabled workers

The Disabled Persons (Employment) Acts, 1944 and 1958, state that employers of more than 20 people must employ a given quota of disabled people. The present quota is 3% of the workforce. However, in practice few firms have been prosecuted for falling short of this target.

  TASK

What forms of discrimination or victimisation are being employed in the following examples of job advertisements and working practices? Choose from:

a) Victimisation

b) Direct sex discrimination

c) Indirect sex discrimination

d) Direct marriage discrimination

e) Indirect marriage discrimination

f) Direct race discrimination

g) Indirect race discrimination

'NO WOMEN'

'Applicants must be over 2 metres tall'

'Bar staff must wear short skirts.'

'No hair coverings can be worn.'

'Applicants must be below the age of 30.'

'Male applicants only'

'Applicants must be single.'

A line worker is sacked because she claims that the supervisor is continually harassing her.

Line workers are not allowed to stop work at any time during scheduled working hours.

'All employees to be clean-shaven'

A man is refused a job as a sales assistant in a women's clothing shop because it was argued that he would be unable to go into the fitting room.

 MATCH IT! Can you help Frankie and Cleo to match the following terms and definitions?

Terms	Definitions
Victimisation	Giving less favourable treatment to someone because of their sex, race, or because they are married or single
Disabled Persons Act(s)	Making a requirement which appears to be fair to men and women, but which in practice favours one group
Marriage discrimination	Treating a married person less favourably than an unmarried person of the same sex
Indirect sex discrimination	Treating someone less favourably after they have honestly complained of discrimination
Unlawful discrimination	Law requiring employers to reward employees equally for doing the same work
Equal opportunities	Law setting out that it is unlawful to discriminate on grounds including 'colour, race, nationality or ethnic or national origins'
Race Relations Act, 1976	Giving individuals identical rights, regardless of gender, racial group, age, physical characteristics, etc.
Sex Discrimination Act, 1975	Legal requirement for firms employing more than 20 people to employ a minimum of 3% of disabled people
Equal Pay Act, 1970	Law outlawing any form of discrimination in the treatment of men or women in the workplace

65 Job Satisfaction

Why is job satisfaction important?

Work is a very important part of life. Ask someone what they 'do' and typically they will say 'I'm a plumber/nurse/teacher', rather than 'I enjoy gardening', or 'I play the piano' – which may be what they enjoy doing in their leisure time. Most people have strong feelings and attitudes about their work. That is why job satisfaction is so important.

'Does job satisfaction depend on the individual concerned?'

Requirements of a satisfying job

People look for many different ingredients in a job. These include:

◆ A good rate of pay

◆ Possibilities of promotion

◆ Long holidays

◆ Job security

◆ Friendship with workmates

◆ A degree of independence

◆ Responsibility

◆ Fringe benefits

◆ Convenient working hours

◆ Status

The order in which these ingredients are arranged will be different for every individual. Pay is a major consideration, but it is not necessarily the main factor.

 |||| ➡ **TASK**

Read the Case Study below then answer the following questions:

1 Why do you think that job satisfaction might be low in a production-line job?

2 What sort of compensation might an employer have to offer in order to make up for low job satisfaction?

3 How might it be possible to increase job satisfaction for production-line workers?

CASE STUDY

Job satisfaction (1)

The following is an extract from an interview with a worker on the production line in a canning factory:

'I find work here really boring. The pay is good but it has to be because the work is tedious. I just try to think about what I'm going to do at the weekend or how I'm going to spend my money. I feel that I'm stuck with this job because there's nothing else going and all the time I'm counting up the money against the hours. The problem is that we have to repeat the same task time after time and we don't get the chance to put something of our own personality into the work. I'd like to be a footballer, but I'd never make the grade.'

Influences on job satisfaction

There are a number of influences on job satisfaction including:

◆ The individual concerned

◆ The job

◆ The employing organisation

◆ The rewards

◆ The working environment

The individual

Everyone takes to work different attitudes and desires. Some people are mainly interested in money, so they may not care what sort of work they do providing the pay is high. Other employees may hate being bored, so they will choose a job which they see as being interesting – for example, one that gives them personal freedom, challenges, and opportunities for promotion.

The job

The work itself has a big influence on job satisfaction. For example, boring and repetitive work may suit someone who 'doesn't want to think', but would be soul-destroying for a creative person. Jobs which involve greater freedom and responsibility will motivate people who enjoy challenge and variety.

CASE STUDY

Job satisfaction (2)

Below is an extract from a book about women who have lost their jobs. The example deals with the case of a textile factory:

'[The firm] *rarely had to recruit labour on the open market. Once employed, their people tended to draw in members of their own family. When people said that the factory was like "family", there was some measure of truth in that, as well as indicating their attachment to the factory.*

"I enjoyed every minute, because all my friends were on that section. We used to have a right laugh and joke and I miss them all now. We could chat when we were working, that's what I liked."

Female worker

From *Redundant Women* by Angela Coyle,
The Women's Press, 1984

  TASK

1   What elements of job satisfaction are expressed in the extract in the Case Study?

2   Why did the firm find it easy to recruit labour?

3   Would you expect wages to be high or low in the firm? Why?

CHAPTER 65

TASK

1 Make a list of six jobs that you would only be prepared to do if you were paid a lot of money. Then make a list of six jobs that you would be prepared to do for very little money. What are the main differences between the two lists?

2 Make a list of what you consider to be the main five ingredients of a good job. Compare your list with those of another student. Note the differences.

'The only factor you need to consider in job satisfaction is the reward. Give them a rate of pay equal to your nearest rival, and a small bonus at Christmas and just before the summer break and you'll have a contented workforce. Nothing else matters!'

Do you agree with Ron?

The employing organisation

Some businesses try to involve their employees in decision-making, for example by encouraging them to work together as a team. The **Quality Circle** is a Japanese idea in which teams of workers meet regularly to discuss ideas for improving the work situation.

Other employing organisations treat employees more like pieces of machinery. Again, this can be very frustrating for creative people.

The rewards

Because money and benefits are **prime motivators** at work, employers need to think about how they can create an attractive package of rewards. **Incentives** for work may include:

◆ Bonuses and commissions

◆ Company pensions

◆ Help with school fees

◆ Company cars

◆ Mobile phones and help with phone bills

◆ Profit-sharing schemes

◆ Luncheon vouchers

◆ Discounts on company goods and services

The working environment

The environment in which an employee works is very important. There is a big difference between working in a brightly lit, well furnished office, with curtains, telephone and your own personal computer, and sharing a cramped, sparsely furnished attic office with no facilities. Working conditions are very important in helping to make people feel good about their work.

COURSEWORK ACTIVITIES

Compare the jobs of two people working in similar positions in different organisations, e.g. checkout operators in two rival supermarkets. Compare the work they do in terms of:

• The individual

• The job

• The employing organisation

• The rewards

• The working environment

How satisfied are the two people? What are the most important factors leading to different levels of satisfaction?

MATCH IT! Can you help Frankie and Cleo to match the following terms and definitions?

Job satisfaction	A group of employees working together as a team to improve quality and solve work problems
Quality Circle	Pleasure, satisfaction and sense of achievement derived from working
Incentives	Money and other key benefits offered to employees in return for work
Prime motivators	Benefits additional to wages or salary which can increase employee motivation

66 Trade Unions

What is a trade union?

A trade union is an association of employees formed to protect and promote the interests of its members, and to achieve other jointly agreed aims.

What do trade unions do?

The diagram on the facing page shows some of the aims of trade unions. You can see that a union's main aim is to secure the best possible conditions of work for its members. Unions know that the decisions a firm makes will affect the livelihood of workers and their families. They therefore try to influence some of the decisions made by owners and managers of businesses.

Trade unions are formed, financed and run by their members in their own interests. Several have existed for over 100 years.

In British law, a union must be 'independent' – that is, it must not rely on an employer for funds, facilities or organisation. It must show that it can provide adequate services to its members and (if necessary) sustain itself during a dispute.

'I wonder if I should join a trade union?'

'Then you couldn't work for me!'

The aims of trade unions

Shorter working hours

Better working conditions

Health and safety

Benefits for members

TRADE UNION AIMS

Better pay

Influence over decisions at work

Equal opportunities

Training

The main actors in industrial relations

The term **industrial relations** refers to the communications that take place between employers and trade unions. Let us look at the main actors on both sides:

Industrial relations: the union side

The union president
The **president** or **general secretary** of a union is elected nationally to represent the whole membership in dealing with employers, government and other unions.

The full-time official
Union officials are appointed and paid by the union. They will cover a number of firms in a particular area, and keep in close contact with union headquarters.

The shop steward
Often factories are split up into areas called **shops**, e.g. the cutting shop, the sewing shop, etc. In the past, each shop would elect at least one **shop steward** to represent them in the workplace. The work was part-time and hardly ever paid.

The convenor
Originally the **convenor** was the shop steward who called or 'convened' union meetings in a large workplace. Today the term simply means the senior shop steward. It is an important post and most convenors hold the job for long periods of time.

COURSEWORK ACTIVITIES

Follow reports of trade union activities over a four-week period in the national and local press. Collect stories which show how the trade unions' activities match with each of the aims shown in the diagram above.

Bill Morris, General Secretary of the Transport and General Workers Union

A day in the life of a shop steward

Sylvia Holt is a machine operator on production lines making metal packaging at Huntley, Boorne and Stevens. She has been with the company for 20 years. She is also a shop steward for the GMB.

7.15 am   Clock in for work.

7.30 am   Start work on line.

8.55 am   A worker complains that her bonus has been underpaid. She explains to me what job she was doing and how many trays she has done. I explain the situation to the supervisor who then takes it further.

9.05 am   I return to my job.

9.20 am   Supervisor returns, informing me that the worker is owed £1.05.

9.45 am   Tea break – I inform the worker of the amount she is owed.

10.00 am   Tea break over – start back on line.

11.05 am   Another worker comes to me. He has caught his trousers on a broken wooden box. I take him down to the personnel department to report the accident. He is given the option of buying a new pair, with the firm paying a percentage, or getting them repaired at the firm's expense. I then go back to the shop floor and investigate whether the

broken box can be repaired or needs to be thrown away.

12.20 pm   Lunch break.

12.50 pm   Lunch break over – start back on line.

14.00 pm   A worker tells me he has been working alongside two other men for over a week and that they have been offered one hour's overtime a night, but he has not been offered any. I tell the worker to go back to his job and that I will go and see the supervisor. I explain the situation to the supervisor and I am told that the worker is only helping out in the department. I then state that if he is good enough to work on the line in the daytime with them, helping out, it is only fair that he should be offered overtime as well. The supervisor agrees and the one hour overtime is given. I then inform the worker of his overtime.

14.20 pm   I return to my work.

16.30 pm   Clock out – day is over.

  TASK

1   What do the letters GMB stand for? What type of employees does the union represent?

2   Does Sylvia work full-time for the union?

3   What is the leading shop steward in a large workplace called?

4   How many hours did Sylvia work? How much of this time was spent in her work as a shop steward?

5   Does the company pay Sylvia for her union work? How does the company benefit from Sylvia's union work? How important is it to the company to have shop stewards?

6   Who does Sylvia represent? How does this group benefit from her work?

7   Who does Sylvia negotiate with?

8   Do you think that Sylvia is powerful in the workplace? Explain your answer.

Industrial relations: the management side

The board of directors
This is a committee chosen by the shareholders to represent their interests.

The managing director
This is the senior director with responsibility for the day-to-day running of the business.

The personnel manager
This is the manager responsible for the recruitment, training, welfare and safety of employees. The personnel manager will be at the 'sharp end' of day-to-day dealings with the unions.

The charge hand
This is a working supervisor responsible for a particular group of employees in an organisation.

Union organisation

The way a union is structured varies considerably, but a typical form is shown below.

Groups of members form a **branch.** They choose branch officials to represent them. The branches also choose representatives to represent them at a regional committee. Regional groups then choose representatives to go to an **annual conference.** The annual conference makes decisions relating to the industry and chooses a full-time body of officials known as the **national executive.** The top official in the union is the **president** or **general secretary.**

A typical union structure

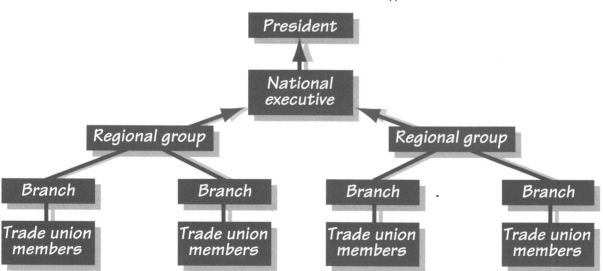

Official and unofficial action

Official action is action which has been approved by the union's headquarters. **Unofficial** action takes place when members carry out actions not approved by the union. An example of this might be when local stewards call out workers in a lightning strike.

In the UK most industrial action is unofficial and short-lived. Union funds cannot be used for unofficial action, because it is not approved by union officials. Unofficial action will generally take place if local union members feel the national union is out of touch with their feelings or if they want to act quickly without notifying the union HQ.

Types of trade union

There are four main types of trade union:

1 Craft unions

2 Industrial unions

3 General unions

4 White-collar unions

However, many unions do not fit easily into these groups. Often they have characteristics common to more than one group.

Craft unions

The earliest type of union in this country was the **craft union**. Craft unions were made up of highly skilled craft workers in a particular trade. Often these groups were mutual benefit societies before the welfare state came into being. Subscriptions could be quite high, and in return the union would provide sick pay, unemployment pay, a pension and other benefits.

These unions are less important in the UK today and their membership is relatively small (one or two have under ten members).

Industrial unions

Industrial unionism is common in many European countries, notably Germany. The economy is divided up into industrial sectors and workers in each sector belong to the industrial union for that sector.

The advantage of an industrial union is that it caters for all employees in an industry, whatever their job. Negotiating with employers is greatly simplified, and all employees are united in their efforts.

Craft unions
Musicians Union
Pattern Weavers Society
Associated Metalworkers Union

Industrial unions
National Union of Mineworkers
National Union of Railwaymen

General unions
Transport and General Workers Union
General, Municipal, Boilermakers and Allied Trades Union

White-collar unions
National Union of Teachers
Banking, Insurance and Finance Union

Examples of the four main groups of union

General unions

These are some of the largest unions in the UK today. They recruit workers from several industries. They include semi-skilled and unskilled workers. A particular advantage of this form of union is that it gives strength to workers who would have little power on their own. These unions can be well funded and organised.

White-collar unions

White-collar workers are non-manual workers such as civil servants, bank workers and teachers, as opposed to **blue-collar** workers who do manual work. White-collar unions have been the most rapidly expanding groups in the 1980s and 1990s. This has coincided with the growth of the tertiary sector of the economy.

 **MATCH IT!** Can you help Frankie and Cleo to match the following terms and definitions?

Terms	Definitions
Trade union	A manual worker in an organisation
Craft union	The leading shop steward in a plant
General union	A union made up of all employees working in the same industrial sector
Shop steward	The union representative of an area of workers in an organisation
Convenor	Trade union activity which is approved by the union head office
Official action	A working supervisor responsible for a given section of employees
Industrial union	An association of highly skilled craft workers
White-collar union	An association of employees formed to improve working conditions and rewards
White-collar worker	A union of office and administrative or professional employees
Blue-collar worker	Union activities which are spontaneous and do not have the backing of the union head office
Charge hand	A union made up of people from a broad cross-section of jobs in several industries
Unofficial action	An employee engaged mainly in non-manual work

7 67 Employers' Associations

Protecting common interests

Just as employees have formed trade unions in order to protect their common interests, so employers have formed and joined their own groups.

Examples are the **Confederation of British Industry (CBI)** and the **National Farmers Union (NFU)**. These and other associations have two main functions:

1 To represent employers in dealings with trade unions

2 To give help and advice to employers on a wide range of issues, such as training, calculating tax, etc.

In some industries an employers' association will bargain with a trade union to set a minimum wage for a given period of time. Individual employers will then negotiate additional payments with shop stewards at company, plant or workplace level.

Most employers' associations carry out the greater part of their work at local rather than national level – for example, through regional conferences, joint training sessions, etc.

The Confederation of British Industry (CBI)

The CBI was set up to provide a national organisation to represent the views and interests of employers. It acts as a mouthpiece for employers to present their opinions to trade unions, government, the media and other interested parties.

The CBI collects and publishes information on many things. Its *Industrial Trends* survey, published quarterly, gives up-to-date information on the state of business. It also produces a magazine, *CBI News*, giving employers up-to-the-minute information on a wide range of business issues.

The CBI has a permanent staff who collect statistics, process information, publish articles, and deal with queries from industrialists and the media. It is led by a **director general**, whose views are listened to with respect by government and many other groups.

Professional associations

A **professional association** is a special organisation to look after the interests of people who work in a particular professional field such as law, medicine or accountancy. There are many types of professional

'I don't belong to any employers' association. There's nothing I can learn from other people in my industry. Anyway, we're competitors and I'm not going to share any of my secrets with them.'
Do you think that Ron is right?

TASK

Why might an employer want to join the CBI?

associations, reflecting the wide number of professions. Many were established under the Companies Acts or by the granting of a Royal Charter. Their functions include:

◆ Acting as examiners and upholders of standards and providing study facilities and guides (for example, people wanting to be bankers have to sit exams organised by The Chartered Institute of Bankers).

◆ Controlling entry into the professions

◆ Keeping up high standards of **professional conduct** in order to protect the public. (For example, the British Medical Association sets professional standards of conduct for doctors.)

◆ Providing members with up-to-date information about their profession and reporting on new developments in their field, e.g. conferences on medical breakthroughs.

As more people have joined the professions in recent years, the importance of these bodies has grown.

COURSEWORK ACTIVITIES

Find out who the current director general of the CBI is. Then look for reports about him/her in a national newspaper for a two-week period. Find out the sort of work that he or she is doing.

Alternatively, use the director general's name as a keyword for a search in a national newspaper archive on CD-ROM.

 **MATCH IT!** Can you help Frankie and Cleo to match the following terms and definitions?

Profession	Grant from the crown to set up a legally recognised body
CBI	Survey carried out by the CBI giving information on the state of business in the UK
Royal Charter	Established standards of behaviour within a line of business or activity
Employers' Association	Business or occupation requiring special training and with nationally recognised conditions of entry
Professional Association	National organisation representing the interests of employers
Professional conduct	Body serving the common interests of a group of employers in a particular trade or field
Industrial Trends	Body offering exclusive membership to suitably qualified people within a particular profession

7 68 Collective Bargaining

What is collective bargaining?

Collective bargaining means negotiation between a trade union and an employer, or an employers' association, over the income and working conditions of employees.

To **negotiate** means to talk with others in order to reach an agreement.

Industrial relations

As we saw in Chapter 66, **industrial relations** refers to the communication which takes place between representatives of employees and employers.

Much of industrial relations involves employees and employers working together. Indeed, part of the aim of the European Union's social policy today is to create a system of shared responsibility of employers and employees for working practices, conditions and other areas of working life. This policy of shared responsibility is called **co-determination**.

However, employers and employees do not always agree and this can lead to arguments and disputes.

Day-to-day industrial relations

On a day-to-day basis, the main process of industrial relations bargaining takes place between managers, supervisors and employee representatives. Normally representatives of the groups meet regularly – say, once a week.

At this meeting will be staff, shop stewards, personnel managers and other interested managers. Discussions will be about such things as:

◆ Pay
◆ Bonuses
◆ The work environment
◆ Disputes
◆ Work schedules
◆ Grievances
◆ Health and safety
◆ Hours of work
◆ Production targets

INDUSTRIAL RELATIONS

Employers

Disagreements / Agreements

Employees

Communication between employers and workforce

TASK

Make a list of things that employers and employees generally agree about. Then make a list of the things that they sometimes disagree about.

Why do you think these disagreements arise?

CHAPTER 68

CASE STUDY

The story of an industrial dispute

Frankie's Aunty Amber is a shop steward at a local food-processing plant. Recently the workers there were upset to discover that people in other factories were getting bigger pay increases than them.

Amber and the other shop stewards called a meeting of employees in the factory. The feeling of the meeting was that they should put in for a 20% pay rise.

However, when they put this request to their employers at their weekly meeting, the personnel manager said that because the company had only been making a small profit, they could only offer 5%.

When the shop stewards told the employees about the management offer, they were furious and said that they ought to go on strike straight away, and that they wouldn't accept anything less than 15%.

Eventually the managers offered a compromise. They suggested 8%, explaining that they faced various difficulties and might have to reduce the workforce.

Eventually the two sides agreed on 9.5%, on the understanding that no employee would be made redundant for the next twelve months.

 |||⏵ **TASK**

1 What factors do you think are most likely to determine the size of a pay demand made by employees?

2 What factors do you think are most likely to determine the management offer?

3 What factors do you think will determine whether the settlement is nearer to employees' demands or management's offer?

Major industrial relations issues

As well as local bargaining about smaller-scale industrial relations issues, larger issues may be discussed on an industry-wide scale. Wages for government employees, for example, are normally established via an annual pay award. The parties involved are normally the central executive of the relevant union, and employers' representatives.

Union industrial action

Picketing at a factory gate

In the event of an industrial dispute, unions can put pressure on employers in a number of ways.

1 Picketing

Primary picketing is lawful. This involves members of a union who are on strike standing outside a firm's entrance and trying to persuade other workers not to cross the picket line.

Secondary picketing is not lawful and occurs when workers from one firm try to persuade workers at a firm not involved with the strike not to go to work. Secondary picketing takes place when union members try to spread the impact of their action.

2 Withdrawal of goodwill

This is when workers become obstructive over issues on which they normally co-operate, such as overtime *(see below)*.

3 Go-slow

During a go-slow, workers deliberately reduce their work-rate.

4 Work-to-rule

During a work-to-rule, workers reduce their productivity by strictly applying the rules governing their particular job. For instance, railway workers may check that every carriage door is firmly closed at each station before allowing the train to depart.

5 Ban on overtime

During an overtime ban, workers refuse to work more than the hours laid down in their contract of employment.

6 Official strike

Workers cease work (with the authority of the union).

7 Unofficial strike

Workers cease work (without the approval of the union).

8 Sit-in

The workers occupy their workplace. If a factory has been threatened with closure, the workers may operate a work-in, i.e. refuse to stop working.

9 Blacking

This occurs when members of a firm refuse to handle particular materials or pieces of machinery.

10 The closed shop

In the past, unions could put pressure on management to operate a closed-shop policy whereby all workers in a plant or factory had to belong to the same union.

Sometimes employers encouraged this, because they found it easier to negotiate with one union than several.

11 Demarcation disputes

Sometimes unions have disputes with each other about 'who does what' at work. Unions are sometimes very protective about the work their members do.

Forms of employer action

Although unions have certain powers, employers can also put pressure on employees in various ways.

The most obvious is to threaten to stop privileges such as the payment of bonuses. They can also threaten to close down plants or parts of the business which make a loss. They may say that a pay rise would make the firm uncompetitive. If there are no other jobs in the area, the union will be in a weak bargaining position.

Other weapons that employers can use are:

◆ **The sack.** The employers cease to employ certain workers.

◆ **Suspension.** Workers can be laid off without pay. This could be done to encourage fresh thinking about the dispute, or as a form of punishment.

◆ **Lockouts.** Sometimes employers will physically prevent workers from entering their premises.

MATCH IT! Can you help Frankie and Cleo to match the following terms and definitions?

Terms	Definitions
Negotiation	A strike that is approved by the head office of a trade union
Picketing	Refusing to handle certain products, materials, equipment, etc., as part of an industrial dispute
Work-to-rule	Slowing the rate of work by sticking meticulously to the rules set down for the job
Official strike	Situation in which employees are physically prevented from entering a firm's premises
Blacking	Laying workers off without pay
Closed shop	A disagreement over 'who does what'
Industrial relations	Communications between the representatives of employers and employees
Collective bargaining	Employees are given their cards and their work contracts are ended
Demarcation dispute	Negotiations over pay and conditions between a trade union and relevant employers
Sack	Situation in which employment in a particular firm or workplace is restricted to trade union members
Lockout	Talking to others with the common aim of reaching an agreement
Suspension	Attempt by union members to dissuade others from working during an industrial dispute

69 Conciliation and Arbitration

Resolving disputes and grievances

The word 'conciliation' means helping the sides in a dispute to reach an agreement. The term is also used in industrial relations in situations where a third party helps employers and trade unions to settle their differences.

Arbitration means the hearing and resolving of a dispute, especially an industrial one, by an impartial referee selected or agreed upon by both sides.

The Advisory Conciliation and Arbitration Service (ACAS)

The Advisory, Conciliation and Arbitration Service (ACAS) was set up in the 1970s to act as a 'third party' in industrial disputes. It can do this in a number of ways:

ACAS – resolving industrial disputes

◆ **Conciliation** is the process by which an independent outsider, such as an ACAS official, acts as a channel of communication between an employer and a union. The conciliator will usually meet the parties separately before trying to bring them together at the negotiating table.

◆ **Mediation** is a stronger process whereby an independent outsider proposes the basis for a settlement. However, the parties involved do not have to accept it.

◆ **Arbitration** involves both parties agreeing in advance to accept the recommendations of an independent body like ACAS.

Below: The role of ACAS

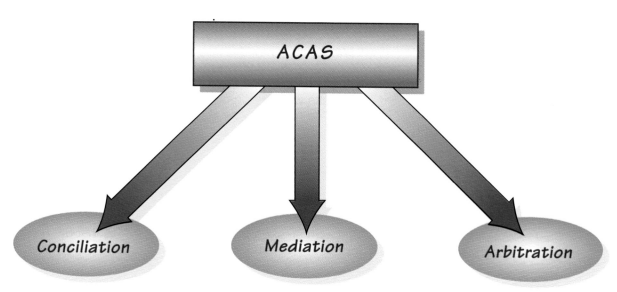

The work of ACAS

The greater part of the work of ACAS involves individual grievances. Every year ACAS has to deal with over 50,000 cases of individual arbitration. Individual disputes involve a variety of grievances, including unfair dismissal and sex discrimination cases.

If the dispute cannot be settled by any of the means described on page 265, then the case is heard before an **industrial tribunal**. This is a panel made up of experts who will seek to resolve the dispute.

As part of its work, ACAS sets out **codes of practice** which provide guidelines for employers and employees. For example, it has published a code of practice on dismissal. Parties to a dispute can simply refer to these codes of practice, rather than going through the lengthy process of ACAS arbitration.

ACAS has a legal obligation to try to resolve individual grievances before they reach industrial tribunals. Most individual cases will be resolved either through conciliation or because the complaint is dropped. Nine out of ten disputes involving ACAS are settled before industrial action is taken.

The rest of ACAS's resources are used for advisory work involving both unions and employers, including surveys, projects, training activities and advisory visits.

TASK

*R*ead the Case Study below then answer the following questions:

1 Why is it necessary sometimes to call in a third party to resolve a disagreement?

2 What was the role of ACAS in the dispute below?

3 What do you think of the solution that was arrived at? Why do you think all the parties would be happy with this arrangement?

CASE STUDY

Working on Christmas day

Dave Jenkins runs a large plumbing firm, employing a number of plumbers on a contract basis. In 1995 he insisted that these plumbers made themselves available on a rota to handle emergencies over the Christmas period. However, the contractors were not prepared to do this. Dave therefore threatened to replace them with others who were prepared to work over this period, and to reduce bonuses owing to them.

After a time, both sides realised that the dispute was getting out of hand. They agreed to bring in a mediator from ACAS. The mediator listened to both sides of the argument and came up with some suggestions. She then arranged for both parties to sit down together, and they quickly agreed to the following terms:

• The existing group of plumbers were to keep their contracts.

• They were also to keep the bonuses that they had already earned.

• Contractors were not to be forced to work over Christmas. However, those contractors who wished to work (and enough did) would earn an extra Christmas bonus. Those that did not work over Christmas were to cover for the others in the period immediately after Christmas.

CHAPTER 69

Towards co-operation

As we move towards the millennium, there are signs of increased co-operation between employers and employees in many (though not all) workplaces. The new style of management based on human relations increasingly stresses the importance of including employees in decision-making processes. In return, employees are expected to take on wider responsibility for their own actions. For example, multi-skilling involves employees being prepared to do many different jobs, rather than concentrating on a single job skill.

At the same time, many employers have introduced single-union deals. This means that rather than bargaining with many individual trade unions in the same workplace, they recognise and bargain with a single union representing all the workforce.

'You wouldn't catch me adopting a "new style of management." Allowing your employees to make decisions and to act responsibly is going soft! You have to tell people what to do or they'll take advantage of you!'

Do you agree with Ron?

 Can you help Frankie and Cleo to match the following terms and definitions?

Conciliation	A generally agreed framework for actions and behaviour
Arbitration	An independent body which seeks to resolve disputes and grievances in the workplace
ACAS	Process by which an independent outsider acts as a channel of communication between two sides in a dispute
Mediation	
Co-operation	Agreement by an employer to recognise and negotiate with one union representing all the workforce
Single union deal	Process by which an independent outsider suggests the basis for a settlement
Code of practice	Process by which both parties in a dispute agree to accept the recommendations of an independent third party
	Practice of employers and employees working together to create harmonious industrial relations

8 70 Innovation and Change

Understanding innovation

In order to get ahead and stay ahead, businesses need to have a positive attitude to change and innovation.

There is a difference between innovation and invention. An **invention** occurs when a new product or technology is created. For example, one of the most famous inventions was the steam engine.

Innovation is producing new solutions to problems. It should involve the whole organisation and occur at every stage of business activity.

'What is the difference between invention and innovation?'

The 'checkout nightmare'

For example, the 'checkout nightmare' at our supermarkets today is a problem that is crying out for innovation. Shoppers go around a supermarket, loading their groceries into a shopping trolley. They then take all the shopping out of the trolley and on to a revolving belt so that barcodes can be checked and a price list made out. The goods then go back into the trolley and are wheeled out to a waiting car, where they are unloaded all over again.

What a waste of time and effort!

Currently, new innovations are being developed so that shoppers can scan their own shopping. In time, no doubt there will be many other innovations to make shopping more comfortable and less stressful.

TASK

Study the illustration below. It shows a number of innovations since the 1950s. Can you place them in a rough chronological order?

CHAPTER 70

Innovative steps

Innovation should be seen as a staircase to progress. In nearly every field, innovation is going on all the time.

Often it happens in small steps. For example, a motor car manufacturer with a range of models will gradually add new features such as side-impact bars, airbags, power-steering, etc. Each successful innovation will be included in all the future models produced by the company.

But sometimes businesses seem to take a great leap forward – often following some new invention or technological breakthrough.

For example, for years tabloid newspapers kept adding new features to the way they presented the news. Then suddenly the *Today* newspaper pioneered the use of computer technology and colour printing. Very soon all the other newspapers were following suit.

In practice, a great deal of what appears to be innovation comes from borrowing ideas, imitating what other organisations are already doing, or from firms bringing in people from outside with new ideas.

One thing is certain. If you do not change in today's business environment, you will not simply stay still – you will go backwards! When everyone else is pushing ahead with new ideas, you need to take positive steps to innovate too, or you will soon be left behind.

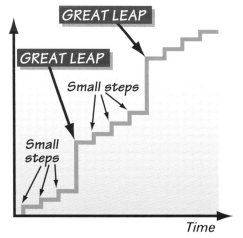

The staircase to progress

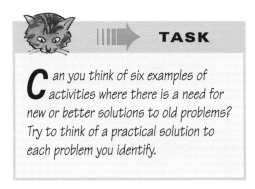

TASK

Can you think of six examples of activities where there is a need for new or better solutions to old problems? Try to think of a practical solution to each problem you identify.

MATCH IT!

Can you help Frankie and Cleo to match the following terms and definitions?

Invention	A major breakthrough bringing with it substantial development in production, organisation, etc.
Small step	A minor innovation or development
Great leap	The process of creating new solutions to problems
Innovation	Creation of a new product, device or technology

8 *71* Controlling Business Activity

What are the factors that limit business activity?

Businesses today are not free agents. There are many different factors which limit their activity.

'Which are more important – internal or external constraints on business activity?'

Internal constraints

Within a business there are likely to be a number of **internal constraints**. These include:

1 Objectives of internal stakeholders
   Businesses must take account of the wishes of internal stakeholders such as shareholders, managers, and employees.

2 The availability of resources
   The availability of resources is a key constraint on business activity. Without adequate finance, for example, a business will not be able to afford the machinery it needs to produce high-quality products.

3 The management and organisation of the business
   There is no point in having the best resources in the world if you cannot manage them effectively. Successful management involves combining resources in an effective way.

The 'three C's'

The success of a business depends on the 'three C's' – costs, competition and customers.

◆ **Costs** can be kept down by efficient management. However, costs of materials, fuel, and components will often be outside the firm's control.

◆ The **competition** must always be considered. A firm's competitors will always be trying to get one step ahead in the marketplace.

◆ Finally, **customers' needs and wants** are the biggest constraint on business activity. No organisation can succeed unless it is able to meet the needs of its customers.

The external environment

The **external environment** in which businesses operate is constantly changing. This process of change has a great impact on what businesses can and cannot do.

The diagram on the opposite page shows how some of these changes can have an impact on business organisations.

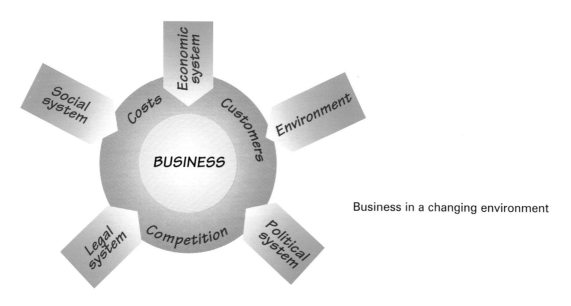

Business in a changing environment

Legal controls on business activities

One of the most important controls on business activity is the law. Some of our laws have developed slowly through common practice, gradually turning into what we call **common law**. It is often impossible to find out when these laws first came into being.

One example is the right of people to walk on a particular village green, or along a country pathway. Often, people have had these rights since time immemorial.

Other laws are new laws passed by Parliament. Laws created by Parliament are called **statute law**.

Competition laws

Some of the most important legal controls on businesses are the laws governing competition.

1 The Fair Trading Act, 1973

A **monopoly** is when one powerful firm dominates a market. **Mergers** occur when firms join together. The **Fair Trading Act** is concerned with mergers of large firms, or with firms that dominate a market.

> The Fair Trading Act, 1973, deals with monopolies and mergers.

Under the Act, a monopoly is defined as a situation where one company supplies or buys 25% or more of all goods or services of a particular type in the whole country, or in a particular geographical area.

The **Director General of Fair Trading** keeps a strict eye on monopolies. If necessary, he can ask the **Monopolies Commission** to investigate worrying cases.

CASE STUDY

Sunday trading

Sunday trading at a busy supermarket

As time goes on, social attitudes change. A hundred years ago, many people would have been horrified at the thought of Sunday trading. Today things are different, and Sunday trading is an accepted part of modern life.

In the early 1990s, it was against the law to trade openly on a Sunday. Some local councils tried to prosecute traders who broke the law. However, many of these prosecutions failed to hold up when taken to higher courts.

Many people felt that traders were able to escape prosecution partly because the government lacked the will to enforce the law more strictly.

Today many people find that their only chance to get to the shops is on a Sunday. Perhaps they are busy on other days of the week. At the same time there are many people who are prepared to work on a Sunday. Supermarket chains are naturally keen to increase their sales and profits by opening seven days a week.

Not everybody has welcomed Sunday trading, however. There has been some opposition from residents living near busy shopping areas – particularly supermarkets. They argue that supermarkets are noisy and cause congestion and pollution. Some have formed pressure groups to try to restrict the activities of supermarkets as a result of Sunday opening.

  TASK

1   Try to identify the social, legal, political, economic and environmental issues raised in the Case Study.

2   What effects do you think that Sunday opening has had on a supermarket's costs, customers and competition?

2 The Competition Act, 1980

The Competition Act states that an 'anti-competitive practice' is any practice that 'has, is intended to have, or is likely to have' the effect of restricting or preventing competition.

> The Competition Act, 1980, deals with anti-competitive practices.

3 The Restrictive Trade Practices Act, 1976

Much of the buying and selling which takes place between businesses is based on agreements. Some of these agreements are useful, but some are undesirable because they restrict competition.

> The Restrictive Trade Practices Act, 1976, prevents agreements between firms which restrict competition and are against the public interest.

The Restrictive Trade Practices Act requires firms to register certain types of trading agreements which they have with other firms. These agreements will cover areas such as:

◆ Restrictions on prices or charges

◆ Conditions under which business is carried out

◆ People with whom business takes place

◆ The quantity of goods to be produced, etc.

4 The Resale Prices Act, 1976

In the past manufacturers tried to fix the price which retailers charged for their products in the shops. Today this is illegal.

> The Resale Prices Act, 1976, deals with attempts by firms to impose minimum prices at which their goods can be sold in the shops.

EU competition laws

The European Union has its own competition regulations. In a number of cases these go beyond national laws.

For example, Article 85 of the Treaty of Rome forbids agreements which may be harmful to trade between the 15 member states. It particularly forbids agreements which are aimed at limiting competition within the Union. This includes any attempt at price-fixing, market-sharing or restriction of production or technical development.

Such agreements are automatically disallowed unless specifically exempted by the European Commission.

Environmental controls

Another important control on business activity is the growing volume of **environmental law**.

Increasingly governments worldwide are developing laws and regulations which force organisations to think about the effect of their actions on the environment.

A glass cartel

A **cartel** is a group of individual firms that make agreements together which restrict competition.

In February 1988, following complaints by a glass purchaser in the West Midlands, the Office of Fair Trading (OFT) discovered a network of glass supply cartels across the country. The Director General chose a team of three investigators to look into the industry. The team interviewed glass buyers and issued legal notices to companies suspected of operating cartels, ordering them to give details of their agreements.

Among these agreements was one which showed that managers from Pilkington had secretly met with other glass suppliers to agree on common price increases. Pilkington admitted to meeting several times with five other glass suppliers between 1978 and 1982.

Their purpose was to agree the same percentage increase to each company's prices and to certain other items normally charged as extras, such as the drilling of holes in double-glazing units.

This document was one of a catalogue of admissions from seven UK glass suppliers. It referred to 12 different cartels and named a total of 60 different companies.

'Can you find a more recent example of anti-competitive practice by a cartel? Try searching a CD-ROM using the word "cartel".'

The Environmental Protection Act, 1990

This Act created two new systems for regulating industrial pollution. **Integrated Pollution Control (IPC)** applies to many industrial processes with the largest pollution potential. IPC regulates all releases to land, water and air and is enforced by an **Inspectorate of Pollution.** The second system is enforced by local authorities. It covers 27,000 complex processes and controls emissions to air.

Under both systems, operators have to employ the 'best available techniques not entailing excessive cost', to minimise releases of the most harmful substances.

The Inspectorate sets out to make sure that businesses achieve the least environmentally damaging solution overall. This is called the 'best practicable environmental option', or **BPEO**.

As time goes on, no doubt our ideas of what is 'best' and 'practical' will change. Technology is advancing rapidly all the time. What was 'best' only a few years ago is thought unacceptable now, and improved technology will allow a new 'best' to be achieved.

TASK

1 Why do you think that agreements like the one described above are undesirable?

2 How do consumers, and other producers stand to lose from such agreements?

3 Why is it important for the Director General of Fair Trading to force firms to register agreements that they may have with other businesses?

MATCH IT! Can you help Frankie and Cleo to match the following terms and definitions?

Terms	Definitions
Common law	The Best Possible Environmental Option at a given time
Statute law	Government body with responsibility for enforcing the law relating to fair trading
Merger	Body of rights and laws that have been established by long years of use
Monopoly	Person or group working within an organisation with a vested interest in its success and profitability
Office of Fair Trading	Legislation preventing suppliers from fixing prices at which retailers can sell their goods
Monopolies Commission	The joining together of two commercial organisations
Resale Prices Act, 1976	Agreements that limit the opportunities to carry out trade in a free and fair way
Fair Trading Act, 1973	Legislation passed and approved by Parliament
BPEO	Domination of all or part of a market by a single powerful firm against the public interest
Social environment	Body responsible for investigating cases where firms dominate a particular market against the public interest
External environment	Influences outside a business which affect the way in which it operates
Internal stakeholder	Legislation dealing with monopolies and mergers
Restrictive practices	The ideas, attitudes and behaviour patterns of groups in society

8 72 Competition

A global marketplace

Competition is a key element of the changing business environment at global, national and local level. Organisations *must* be competitive in order to survive.

International competition

Internationalisation refers to the way in which companies expand their operations overseas in order to exploit new markets.

Globalisation refers to the way a company sets out to operate in exactly the same way throughout the globe – using the same packaging, the same products, the same adverts, etc., in every country in which it operates.

Today many companies find that their home market is no longer rich in opportunity. Companies are forced to operate on a more international scale because of increased competition at home and because there are often opportunities to grow faster in other regions of the world.

'What is the difference between internationalisation and globalisation?'

New markets, new competition

A dramatic change in the world today is that billions of new consumers are breaking through new thresholds in spending power. People who in the past bought locally-produced goods are now purchasing global brands such as Ford, Honda, Apple, Mars, Canon and many others.

By using just-in-time stock control, robots, information technology, and all the latest methods in a highly competitive way, the giant businesses of the Pacific Rim pose a serious threat to the UK. However, at the same time, the huge new markets opening up in countries such as India and China present a tremendous opportunity for UK firms.

In order to survive, UK businesses need to continually improve what they do, while at the same time innovating and developing new products. The business world of the 21st century will be a very competitive one.

Being competitive

Being competitive involves taking a long hard look at everything an organisation does, as well as at how rival firms operate. Firms not only need to look at what the competition is doing now, but also at what they are likely to do in the near future.

CHAPTER 72

EPS: developing a competitive edge

'The aims of European Passenger Services today are to:

* Offer high quality European journeys
* Be first choice in our main markets
* Anticipate the needs of our customers
* Operate safely, reliably and profitably
* Be efficient and flexible
* Look always for improvement
* Respect and use each other's talents
* Take pride in our company
* Be fair and professional in all our dealings

A strong emphasis is placed on the customer experience. The customer experience is seen as giving a competitive edge and is made up of:

Quality
Conforming to requirements, providing the customers with a service to agreed specification and cost

Customer care
Consistently meeting the emotional needs and expectations of the customers to make them feel special and make life easy for them.

Service excellence
A business-driven strategy that builds on quality and customer care and adds value to the customer experience, making it measurably better than the competition.'

TASK

1   Which of the aims of EPS do you see as being concerned with:

   (a) the product; (b) the human resource; (c) the customer; (d) safety, and (e) beating the competition?

2   Explain in your own words how EPS sets out to gain a competitive edge.

3   Describe what sorts of practical activities EPS will engage in to ensure (a) quality; (b) customer care, and (c) service excellence.

To be competitive an organisation needs to make sure that it:

◆ Provides quality products that meet customer requirements

◆ Values its people – the most important resource of any organisation

◆ Uses modern technology, including information technology, to its full potential

◆ Ploughs back funds into new investment, research and product development

◆ Experiments with new ideas and sets out to lead rather than follow the field

◆ Makes sure that it has outstanding customer and community relationships as well as respecting the environment

◆ Takes into consideration the requirements of all its stakeholders

 **MATCH IT!** Can you help Frankie and Cleo to match the following terms and definitions?

Internationalisation	Products that are recognised instantly worldwide
Globalisation	Markets consisting of millions or billions of consumers
Customer care	Meeting the requirements of buyers before, during and after sales are made
Quality	Conforming to the highest standards demanded by customers
Global marketing	Providing the same product, packaging, advertising, etc., in a standard way throughout the world
Huge markets	Spreading an organisation's operations into many countries
Global brands	Developing a superb reputation for service to customers
Competitive edge	The advantages that an organisation has over its rivals
Service excellence	Using the same or a similar marketing mix throughout the world

73 Economic and Demographic Change

The wider business environment

Economic and demographic changes are changes which take place in the wider environment that surrounds businesses.

'Could these changes in the wider business environment affect me?'

Changes in the economy

In a period of **recession** there is a marked reduction in the level of output and a considerable waste of resources. The illustration below shows the impact of recession. **National output** is the total value of all goods and services produced in an economy.

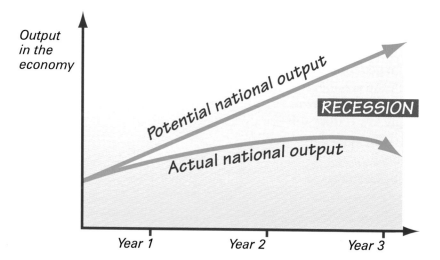

Left: How recession wastes resources and output

The trade cycle

The twentieth century has seen regular cycles of **booms** and **slumps** in economic activity.

In a **boom:**

◆ Output rises

◆ Firms take on more employees

◆ Wages and prices rise

◆ Prosperity rises

◆ Businesses boom

In a **slump:**

◆ Output falls

◆ Firms lay off workers

◆ Wages and prices fall

◆ Prosperity falls

◆ Businesses do badly (some cease trading)

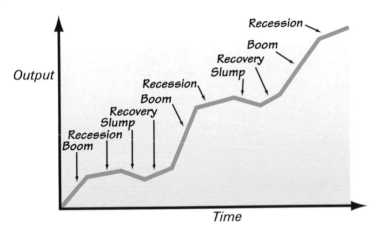

Output

Time

Recession

Boom

Recovery

Slump

Recession

Boom

Recovery

Slump

Recession

Boom

Recovery

Slump

Recession

Boom

The 'boom-bust' cycle

Because countries are interdependent, the trade cycle tends to be a worldwide experience. Countries go into periods of slump together, and they pull out together.

One of the most important functions of governments is to try to manage the trade cycle. When the economy starts to pick up, the government needs to slow down growth so that it does not peak too quickly. It does this by raising taxes and interest rates so that people have less money to spend.

In a period of slump the government lowers taxes and interest rates to 'pep up' the economy.

Changes in demographics

Demographic changes are changes in the overall population or in parts of the total population. For example, we might say that the population of a country is increasing, or we could look at a smaller section of the population and say that the number of old age pensioners is increasing – and so on. Both of these changes could have a major impact on business activity.

There are a number of aspects of demographics which are particularly relevant to business students.

'What is an "ageing population" and why is this a problem?'

World population changes

Changes in population are very important on a global scale. Different parts of the world experience different rates of population growth. These changes are of particular importance when considering changes in demand for products and resources, the likely impact of population increases on the global environment and many other issues.

The illustration on the facing page shows estimated changes in population in different parts of the world up to the year 2025.

The growth of the world population by 2025

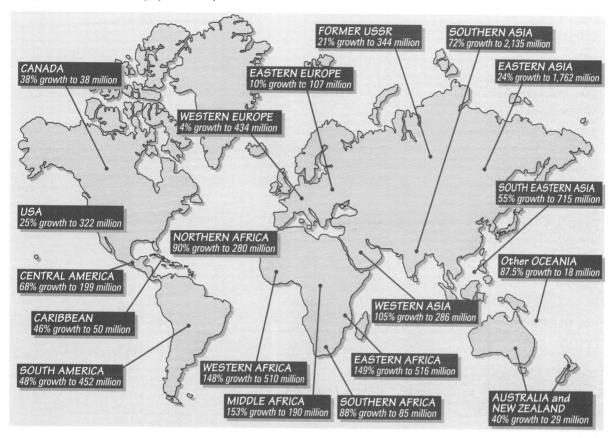

  TASK

1   Which areas are experiencing the fastest rates of population growth?

2   Which areas are experiencing the slowest rates of population growth?

3   How can these changes be seen as (a) an opportunity and (b) a threat to UK business?

An ageing population

One of the most significant demographic changes today is the ageing of the population. This has many implications for business. On the one hand it means that there is a bigger demand for the products that older people buy. On the other, it means that there are fewer people available to work, and that those people who are in work have to support a larger and larger **dependent population**.

The dependent population is the number of people who depend on those with jobs.

CASE STUDY

Germany's ageing population

In Germany today the proportion of over-60's is 20%. By the year 2030 it will be over a third. In a recent report, *The Elderly of the Future*, the government revealed that in 35 years' time, assuming a pensionable age of 60, there will be just 100 people working to sustain benefits for 80 pensioners.

Germany is not alone in contemplating such dramatic changes. Throughout the Western world, a similar demographic trend is forcing governments to re-think whether they can afford to give such generous pensions to people. In Germany, however, this demographic squeeze is particularly harsh. In the post-war baby boom its population grew faster than in most other countries, and then fell away steeply.

The illustration shows how the age structure of Germany's population is changing as we move into the next century.

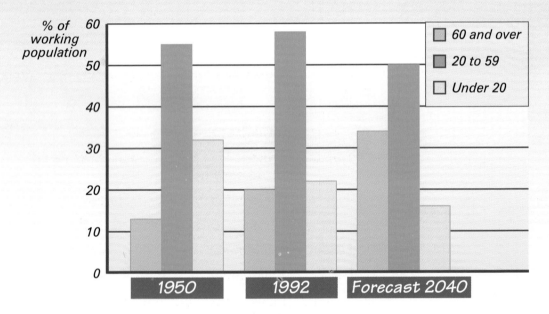

Germany's ageing problem

  TASK

1   What major changes can you see in the age structure of Germany's population?

2   What sorts of difficulties might this present for:

    (a) Germany's government; (b) German business; (c) the German people generally?

3   What opportunities does it present for business?

A Europe-wide problem

The International Labour Organisation has warned that spending by the government on pensions and healthcare for the elderly will become the largest budget item for most industrialised countries during the next ten years. By 2055 in Europe, there may be 1 dependent to every 1.5 members of the working population.

The ageing of the population is one of the most important demographic changes facing businesses today. Clearly there are plenty of opportunities for businesses to cater for this growing group of consumers. As the number of older people increases, it becomes increasingly worthwhile to target products at this group, many of whom have savings and spare cash to spend on holidays and leisure, luxury goods, etc.

The dependency ratio

 MATCH IT! Can you help Frankie and Cleo to match the following terms and definitions?

Demography	Period in which economic output falls
Trade cycle	Period in which increases in output in the economy start to slow down
Slump	Pattern of rise and fall in economic output
Boom	Changes in the wider economic environment of business
Recession	The structure and make-up of the population
	The proportion of non-workers to workers in an economy
Dependency ratio	Period in which prices, output, and employment are all rising steadily
Economic change	

8 74 The Costs of Business Activity

The price of progress

When a new supermarket opens up in your area, are you better off as a result?

On the positive side, you may be able to get a part-time job there. You may also find you have a wider range of goods to choose from than before. But what if the supermarket is right next door to your house? Suppose you have to put up with all the extra noise of cars parking and trolleys being stacked?

Counting the cost of business decisions

All communities are made up of individuals and groups who have different views about whether a particular decision is 'good' or 'bad'. This is because the decision affects each of them in a different way.

To get a clearer picture of net benefits, we therefore need to look at the **social benefits** and the **social costs** of business activity.

'So what is the difference between private costs and benefits, and social costs and benefits?'

◆ Private benefits

These are all the benefits to an individual or group resulting from a particular activity, e.g. the dividends that shareholders get from the profitable growth of their firm.

◆ Private costs

These are all the costs to an individual or group resulting from a particular activity, e.g. the cost to an individual of buying a new toothbrush, and the cost to a firm of the raw materials, labour and other inputs needed to make the toothbrush.

◆ Social benefits

These are the private benefits, plus all the good effects for other members of the community, resulting from a particular activity.

For example, if I set up as a florist I will (hopefully) receive money from my sales. This is a private benefit to me, but because I am a member of society, the money is also a social benefit.

Other social benefits will include the pleasure that customers receive from buying my flowers, the enjoyment of passersby whose day is brightened up, the wage that my assistant receives, the tax that the local council receives, the rent that my landlord earns, and so on.

Social benefit, private gain – or both?

CHAPTER 74

◆ Social costs

Social costs are the private costs, plus all the bad effects for other members of the community, e.g. the extra traffic congestion caused by vehicles pulling up outside my shop, the clearing up of confetti that I sell as a sideline, and so on.

The benefits of business activity

Industry brings together resources to produce wealth. In doing so it produces the following major benefits:

1 **It provides employment.** Millions of people are employed in industry and commerce.

2 **It creates wealth.** Shareholders receive profits, landlords receive rent, lenders receive interest, workers receive wages, etc.

3 **It creates products.** Value is added at each stage of production to create a more valuable end-product.

4 **It raises living standards.** By creating wealth, industry makes it possible for people to enjoy better living standards and more leisure time.

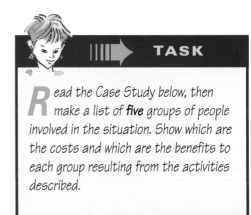

TASK

*R*ead the Case Study below, then make a list of **five** groups of people involved in the situation. Show which are the costs and which are the benefits to each group resulting from the activities described.

C ASE S TUDY

The Centreville Rock Festival

Every year there is a rock festival just outside Centreville. Typically, 6,000 young rock fans converge on the park to spend three days in the sun listening to loud music and meeting up with friends. The event is organised by a millionaire 'rock entrepreneur' Justine Villeneuve. Justine runs several rock enterprises and has her own record company. The Centreville festival is always a sell-out and the rewards to Justine are considerable.

However, not everyone is happy with the festival. Local farmers say that crops are trampled and broken bottles are a danger to livestock. Cattle-owners have even reported that their cows give a reduced milk yield. Other local residents have mixed feelings. Many young people and their parents support the festival as a valuable source of entertainment. Others are strongly opposed to it, describing it as 'three days of filth, noise and declining values'. All police leave is cancelled during the festival and the bill for policing the festival is shared equally between the town of Centreville and Justine Villeneuve.

The costs of business activity

Much of this book has been about the benefits of business activity. But business also brings with it costs. When a firm produces something, it has to bear in mind a number of internal costs, e.g.:

1 Production costs

2 Marketing costs

3 Financial costs

4 Administration costs

5 Distribution costs

However, in addition to these are the external (social) costs which go beyond the trading account of the firm. These costs are sometimes known as **externalities** or **spillover costs**.

External costs = Social costs – Private costs

Industrial pollution

The most obvious social cost of business activity is **pollution**. This can take a number of forms:

Water pollution

It has been standard practice for a long time for industry to locate by canals, rivers and seas. Industries such as paper mills, chemical plants and breweries not only use water in their manufacturing process, but also pour out their waste into rivers and the sea.

TASK

*I*magine that the eyesores shown below exist in a town near you.

How could each of the eyesores above be redeveloped or put to new use? Make a list of four suggestions for each, and produce a detailed scheme for one of them.

Perhaps the most notorious example of this type of activity is the disposal of waste products from the nuclear fuels industry. Water itself can be treated in purification and filtration plants, but it is difficult to break down the effects of industrial chemicals, which can cause widespread and lasting damage to pond and animal life.

Air pollution

The dangers of air pollution were dramatically illustrated by several events in the 1980s. First, there was the leak of poisonous gas from the Union Carbide plant at Bhopal in India. More than 2,000 people died and at least 10 times as many suffered from breathing and eye complaints.

Perhaps even more dramatic was the nuclear disaster at Chernobyl in 1986. Wide tracts of land were declared unfit for farming for years afterwards, threatening the future of whole economies. The livestock of Welsh hill farmers were banned from sale because of the heavy contamination.

Thirdly, emissions from UK factory chimneys and power stations have been recognised as major sources of 'acid rain'. This has been shown to result in the pollution of forests and lakes in Scandinavia and Germany.

Disaster at Chernobyl – the deserted city of Pripyat with the nuclear reactor on the horizon

Dereliction

If we consider the decision to build a new mine, or to drill for oil or natural gas, we can see that this might destroy areas of natural beauty for ever. But often when a business pulls out of an area, the effects can be worse: not only do jobs disappear, but the community is left with derelict land which is unpleasant to look at and contains dangerous chemicals and other hazards.

Traffic congestion

The speed of business development has put great pressure on our road networks. The M25 orbital road around London was opened in 1986. But by the time it was fully operational, it was already inadequate for the volume of traffic using it. It has been described as the longest traffic jam in Europe.

In the late 1990s we have come to question whether road building actually eases congestion. The feeling today is that improving or widening a road simply adds to the volume of traffic using it.

'Having a scrap metal business means that you have to make a noise. People nearby often complain. But if I hear that the local council are coming round to check on me I simply keep the noise down and act the innocent. There's nothing they can do about it!'

Is Ron right?

Long-term waste

British Nuclear Fuels PLC reprocesses nuclear waste at its plant at Sellafield.

Highly radioactive spent nuclear fuel is transported by road or rail in nuclear-waste 'flasks'. The waste is then either dumped in the sea or buried in stores underground. Although defenders of the nuclear industry claim the process is safe, critics argue that it simply stores up problems for the future.

Noise

Concorde is British Airways' flagship passenger service. But it is also a considerable nuisance for people who happen to live close to its take-off points. Noise from road and rail traffic can also be a nuisance to householders.

In the UK, noise nuisance is controlled through by-laws enforced by local authorities. People can be prosecuted for continually making a noise.

The activities of businesses and construction firms are controlled, and certain areas may be designated by the local authority as Noise Abatement Zones.

Food additives

Today consumers often demand interesting presentation of products and value for money. Artificial colouring and flavourings and synthetic ingredients are used to make food and drinks more attractive and cheaper to produce. However, medical experts have pointed out that additives can have dangerous spillover effects, notably hyperactivity in children.

Insufficient testing of products

In the rush to become market leaders, firms may be tempted to put their new products on the market before they have been thoroughly tested.

A well known example of this was the production by the Distillers Company of a drug used by women to reduce the effects of morning sickness in pregnancy. The spillover cost was the terrible side-effect of Thalidomide, which caused babies to be born with limbs missing.

Cost-benefit analysis

Society benefits if resources are used well. Businesses and governments should weigh up the costs and benefits of any development, both in terms of private and social effects. This is called **cost-benefit analysis**.

'How then can you weigh up the costs and benefits of business activity?'

Food additives: an acceptable price to pay for cheap, attractive products?

Can you help Frankie and Cleo to match the following terms and definitions?

Private cost	Contamination of land, air, water or other natural resources, e.g. with harmful substances
External cost	The private cost of a business activity, plus the cost to society at large
Dereliction	The difference between benefits and costs
Pollution	Conscious or wilful neglect
Net benefit	Benefits to an individual or group from a particular activity
Spillover effect	The negative effect of an activity on society at large
	The positive benefit of an activity for society at large
External benefit	Technique for weighing up all the costs and benefits of an activity or project
Cost-benefit analysis	The cost of an activity to the individual or group responsible for it
Private benefit	

75 Pressure Groups

What is a pressure group?

A pressure group is a group of people who try to influence those who make laws, form public opinion, or take important decisions.

It may be just a few people, such as a group of parents demanding a public enquiry into a local hospital. Or it may be a large organisation like the environmental pressure group, Greenpeace.

Business and pressure groups

Businesses have many stakeholders, all of whom exert different pressures on the organisation.

Internally, the business needs to make a profit for shareholders, and shareholders need to be satisfied with the way the business is being run. Externally, the business will have even more pressures to contend with.

'What sorts of people form pressure groups?'

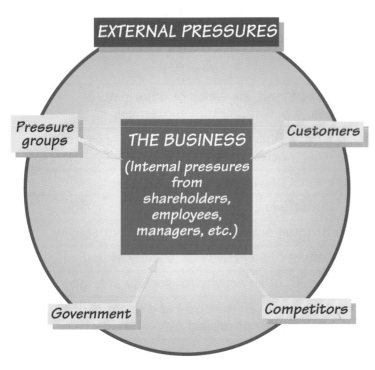

Left: Pressures on a business

1 Perhaps the biggest pressure is to sell its products. Consumers will not buy products they do not want.

2 The business must also face pressure from its competitors. Competition often acts as a spur to an organisation to perform better.

3 The government also exerts pressure on business to meet standards and comply with legislation.

4 In addition, there is the influence placed on businesses by organised pressure groups.

Types of pressure group

The two main types of pressure groups are:

◆ **Protection groups.** These are groups which are set up to fight on a specific issue, such as a dangerous road or a controversial tree-felling scheme.

◆ **Promotional groups.** These are more formal groups which fight campaigns on a wide range of issues. Some are large-scale and highly organised. Examples are Greenpeace and Friends of the Earth.

Such groups have clearly defined long-term objectives. Their sustained pressure on various authorities helps to create new ways of thinking. Groups like Friends of the Earth and Greenpeace have had a tremendous impact in changing the ways in which organisations operate.

Below: Protection and promotion-type pressure groups

For example, many supermarkets have moved towards 'green' and organic lines in recent times. Once a fringe concern, green issues are now an everyday part of mainstream political and business activity.

Pressure groups use a range of measures which vary from attention-grabbing stunts (e.g. climbing up Nelson's Column with a banner) to high-profile media advertising campaigns.

Consumer pressure groups

A well known and powerful consumer pressure group is the **Consumers' Association**. This is funded by subscriptions from members who buy the consumer magazine *Which?* The Consumers' Association uses its funds to test and report on a wide variety of products. It also produces books on consumer-related matters.

Nationalised industries have consumer councils, such as the Post Office Users' National Council (POUNC). The government has also set up consumer councils to watch over the privatised utilities.

Consumer boycotts

Sometimes pressure groups will run campaigns in order to stop consumers from buying certain products. These are known as **consumer boycotts**.

Throughout the 1970s and 1980s anti-apartheid campaigners put pressure on customers to stop using Barclays Bank. This sort of pressure finally influenced Barclays in 1986 to sell off its South African branches. Today, however, with the development of 'the rainbow nation' in South Africa, Barclays have moved back.

Local lobbying

Often local residents will form pressure groups in order to force a business to change its practices. Reasons may include:

1 Traffic danger

2 Emission of fumes and pollution

3 Safety hazards such as tips, pits, etc.

If letters to the press and protest meetings fail to get results, the group may try to put pressure on local and central government to influence the activities of the firm. Wise firms will try to avoid alienating local residents in case it brings them bad publicity.

Greenpeace protesters on board the Shell oil rig, Brent Spar

COURSEWORK ACTIVITIES

Take a look at the activities of a particular pressure group in your area.

Find out what their objectives are, when the group was set up, how it is funded, how you become a member, what members do, how the group operates, etc.

'I've been featured on "Watchdog" three times! Any publicity is good publicity, that's what I say!'

Do you agree with Ron?

Methods of persuasion

Some groups seek to influence opinion-formers through a form of personal contact known as **lobbying.**

Others use powerful advertising and promotion to get their message across. Trade unions use this method of persuasion quite often. Groups like teachers, miners and printworkers have all used national advertising to try to win support from the public and political parties. Picketing and industrial action are another way for a union to put pressure on an employer.

The employers' organisation, the CBI, and the unions' organisation, the TUC, also exert influence at national level through statements to the press and media. Other promotional pressure groups, such as the campaign for lead-free petrol and the anti-smoking lobby, use similar techniques.

Sometimes groups use less peaceful methods to impress their views on the public. Demonstrations, protest marches and sit-ins often lead to publicity on television or in the press.

TASK

R ead the Case Study below then answer the following questions:

1   What does the Case Study tell you about the potential influence of pressure groups?

2   Do you think that McDonalds have handled the case in a sensible way? How else might they have handled it?

3   How do you think the campaign will affect the way McDonalds operates?

4   What do you see as being the main value of pressure groups?

CASE STUDY

The McLibel case

In December 1995, the McDonalds libel trial became the longest civil case in British history.

McDonalds sued two environmentalists from North London to stop a stream of allegations against the international burger chain. Helen Steel, 30, and David Morris, 41, had claimed the company sold food which was linked to heart diseases and cancer, cut down rainforests, abused its workforce and corrupted children with its advertising. The allegations were contained in a leaflet called *What's wrong with McDonalds.*

One and a half million leaflets have been handed out since the start of the trial, and reports of the story in the media have given the two campaigners worldwide coverage.

McDonalds claimed they were forced into taking legal action in order to answer the allegations being made against them. During the trial a number of high-ranking McDonalds executives were forced to testify, and resources worldwide were used to counter media stories.

The legal bill for McDonalds is estimated to be more than £2m. The defendants have been financed by dole cheques and donations from well-wishers. A support campaign for the two produced regular trial summaries on the Internet which have been read by computer-users all over the world.

Business response to pressure groups

There are a number of ways businesses can respond to pressure groups.

1 Ignore them. Businesses may argue that consumers can choose whether to buy the product or not. In the meantime they can make sure that their products meet all the necessary legal requirements.

2 Run a counter campaign to win public support. This is the policy adopted by British Nuclear Fuels PLC. 'Come to Sellafield. Look around the place. See for yourself how safe it is' – loosely paraphrased, this is the message of a multi-million pound advertising campaign which British Nuclear Fuels has used for several years *(right)*.

3 Take advice from consumers and compromise in order to win back public support.

> BRITISH NUCLEAR FUELS PLC
>
> *request the pleasure of your company to view their Sellafield Exhibition Centre.*
>
> *Open from 10am-4pm every day of the week from Easter to the end of October, or from 10am – 4pm Monday to Friday, November to March*
>
> ---
>
> *Exhibition Centre, British Nuclear Fuels PLC, Sellafield, Cumbria.*
>
> *(Off the A595 at Calderbridge between Millom and Whitehaven)*

 Can you help Frankie and Cleo to match the following terms and definitions?

TUC	Body representing the interests of trade unions as a group
Lobbying	Organisation representing the interests of consumers, financed by subscriptions to *Which?* magazine
Pressure group	Group of people seeking to influence the public and specific organisations
Protection group	Attempting to put pressure on opinion-formers by means of personal contact
Promotional group	Group whose aim is to raise awareness of, and win support for, a particular cause
Consumers' Association	Group set up to defend members' interests or to fight on a specific issue

8 76 Ethical Activities

What is meant by ethics?

An ethic is a moral principle or set of moral values held by an individual or a group.

Ethical behaviour is behaviour which is considered to be correct and moral.

Business ethics

Ethics are the values and principles which influence how individuals, groups and society behave. Business ethics are therefore the values and principles which operate in the world of business.

In business, it is possible to carry out many practices which are not strictly ethical, and yet stay within the letter of the law. However, many successful companies are based on strict ethical principles, and most people would argue that businesses ought to keep within some form of moral framework.

Ethical decisions

Whether business owners and managers recognise it or not, all business decisions have an ethical dimension.

For example, here are some of the ethical questions that a business might have to face:

◆ Should products which might damage the health of consumers be withdrawn from the market?

◆ Should the firm make sure that its business activities do not damage the environment?

◆ Should money be spent on wheelchair access to workplaces and retail outlets?

◆ Should the firm reject a bribe given to secure an overseas contract?

◆ Should part-time staff be offered the same rights as full-time staff?

◆ Should a workplace crêche be provided for working parents?

A firm that answers 'Yes' to these questions might be described as operating in an ethical way.

In contrast, a firm that pays a 17-year-old employee £1.47 for working in a shop, or one that imports cosmetics ingredients from the Amazon region of South America, paying only a pittance to the local people, could be considered to be behaving in an **unethical** way.

'You kids have got to realise that business isn't a game. There's no room for ethics in business. The ethical businesses are the first ones to go bankrupt!'

Do you agree with Ron? Can you think of any businesses with an ethical basis?

CHAPTER 76

CASE STUDY

Whale hunting

The illustrations below show the stages in hunting for whales in a modern whaling fleet.

1 The hunt

The quarry is the 10-metre-long whale. The factory ship is about the size of a cross-channel ferry and is accompanied by 'catcher ships' with harpoons.

2 The attack

The harpoon holds a powerful grenade and a large hook. The grenade blasts a hole in the whale's side. The hook is used to pull the animal to the side of the ship.

3 The kill

Electrodes are fired into the body of the whale. A strong electric charge immobilises the whale. Death may take up to 25 minutes.

4 The sale

The factory ship strips the whale in 35 minutes. During a whaling season as many as 330 whales may be caught by a fleet. This produces more than 3 million pounds of meat sold at £130 per lb.

TASK

Do you consider the modern whale-hunting techniques that you see illustrated in these pictures to be ethical? Explain your arguments.

Internal and external responsibilities of a business

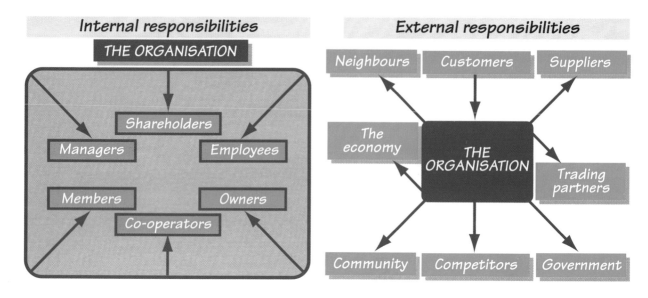

Social responsibility

A firm which behaves ethically towards the local community and society as a whole can be described as being **socially responsible**.

What then makes an ethical business?

Different individuals and groups will have different views about what makes an ethical business. The diagram below illustrates some of the characteristics of a 'good business'.

> **TASK**
>
> **M**ake a list of what you consider to be the twelve most important characteristics of an ethical business.
>
> Think about areas such as its relationship with its employees, the environment, the community, its obligation to pay taxes, etc.
>
> Write each characteristic in the form of a statement, i.e.:
>
> "An ethical business is one which ...."

Characteristics of an ethical business

Can you help Frankie and Cleo to match the following terms and definitions?

Ethics	Obligations towards the wider community, rather than just a few individuals
Morals	People within an organisation with a concern for how it is run and organised, and for its values
Social responsibilities	The distinction in human behaviour between good and bad, right and wrong
Internal stakeholders	The values and principles which govern the world of business
Business ethics	People who are not members of an organisation but who have an interest in how it is run and organised and its values
External stakeholders	Moral values or principles held by an individual or group

77 The International Environment

Understanding world trade

Business activity in the UK takes place against a wider background of world trade. Many UK businesses are owned by foreign companies. Similarly, many UK businesses have operations overseas.

Increasingly, UK firms are buying and selling their products internationally. They are also facing greater competition than ever before from foreign firms.

Imports and exports

For centuries, the UK has gained enormously from international trade. We buy goods and services from other countries, and in return we sell them goods and services produced here.

'What are imports and exports?'

◆ An **import** involves the purchase of products or services from overseas by a UK citizen or business.

◆ An **export** is a sale by a UK citizen or business to a member of another country.

Visibles and invisibles

All the tangible goods (things that we can touch and see) that we trade are called **visible** items. Services that cannot be seen or touched are called **invisibles**.

'What are visibles and invisibles?'

Countries trade in order to benefit from each other's resources and skills. For example, in the UK we are very good at producing whisky (mainly because of our climate), Land Rovers (because of our engineering skill) and insurance (because of our years of experience). We are not so good at producing rice (because of our climate), motorbikes (other countries can do it better) and snow tyres (because of our lack of experience).

International trade allows countries to gain from specialisation. The UK, for example, is able to concentrate on producing its most saleable goods and services, such as banking, insurance, whisky and bio-technology. By trading these items on world markets, we are able to buy things which we would find it less easy to produce, such as pineapples, washing machines, and motorbikes.

Other reasons why we trade include the following:

1 Some items, such as scarce minerals, are impossible to obtain naturally in the UK

2 To foster good relations with other countries

3 To earn foreign currency

4 Because we cannot fully supply our own market in many items

TASK

Which of the items shown below are visibles (goods) and which are invisibles (services)?

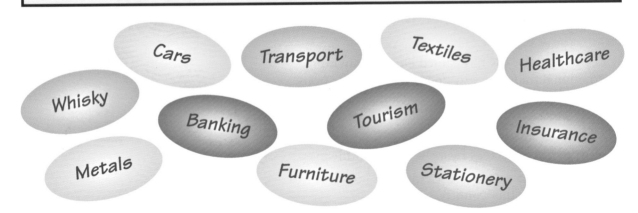

Cars Transport Textiles Healthcare Whisky Banking Tourism Insurance Metals Furniture Stationery

Why do countries trade?

To answer this question, let us consider the following case.

Once there were two islands separated by a sea that was too dangerous to cross.

On the first island, which was very flat, wheat could be grown in plenty, but the waters around the island contained few fish.

The second island was very hilly and only a little wheat could be grown. However, around this second island, fish were plentiful.

One day an explorer found a sea passage to the south of the two islands that was not too dangerous to cross.

Let us suppose that before the trade route was discovered, half of the people in each island spent their time farming, and the other half spent their time fishing.

In a year, the amount of wheat and fish that could be produced was:

	Wheat	Fish
Hilly island	20 baskets	100 baskets
Flat island	100 baskets	20 baskets

  TASK

*R*ead the Case Study above, then answer the following questions:

1 How do you think the people of these two islands could benefit from the opening up of the sea passage?

2 Can you think of any problems that could be caused by the opening up of trade between the two islands?

3 Supposing that all the people on the flat island just grew wheat, and the people of the hilly island just fished. Can you show how the people on the two islands could be better off than before?

4 Why might this not always be true?

The balance of payments

Exports bring money into the UK, whereas imports lead to an outflow of money.

The UK has always done well on her invisible trading account. This is because we have developed a worldwide reputation for commercial services.

Some of our major invisible earnings come from the following:

1 Selling insurance policies

2 Offering banking services to foreign nationals

3 Carrying goods for foreign companies by sea and air

4 Attracting tourists and providing hotel and leisure facilities for them

5 Earning money on investments overseas in the form of interest and dividends

On the news every month we hear that the UK has made a **surplus** on invisible trade, showing that we have sold more invisible services than we have bought. The figures for a particular month might be, for example:

'Why has the UK's visible balance been so poor in recent times?'

Invisible exports	£100 billion
Invisible imports	£80 billion
Invisible surplus	£20 billion

At the same time, the UK frequently makes a loss on her visible trade. In the 1990s the UK has run a very high loss on its visible account. For the first time since the industrial revolution, we have started to import more manufactured goods than we sell.

♦ The **visible trade balance** is the money from the sale of visible goods minus the money paid for the purchase of visible goods.

♦ The current trading account of the balance of payments is made up of the **visible and invisible balances**, as shown in the table below:

Visibles		Invisibles		Totals	
Visible exports	500	Invisible exports	400	Total exports	900
Visible imports	650	Invisible imports	200	Total imports	850
Visible balance	−150	Invisible balance	+200	Current balance	+50

Balance of payments problems

While it is normal today for the UK's visible balance to run at a loss, this is greatly helped by the surplus on our invisible account. There are no easy ways of solving our balance of payments problem. Because we are a member of an international community, any actions we take at home will affect other countries and their actions will likewise affect us. The following are ways of improving the balance of payments:

Improving competitiveness

If we produce more up-to-date products than other countries, produce goods more cheaply, offer better after-sales service and meet our deadlines, then we will sell more of our products.

Raising import tariffs

If we tax foreign imports, they will be more expensive to home buyers, who will switch to buying more home-produced goods. However, the danger is that other countries will retaliate, and tariff barriers will go up around the world. This will reduce world trade and in the end everyone will lose out.

Imposing import quotas

Sometimes the UK will limit the quantities of foreign goods entering the country, such as suits from Eastern Europe. This can be done by a voluntary agreement between trading countries, or by law. Once again, this can lead to retaliation. It can also be avoided by foreign companies setting up factories in this country.

Government subsidies

The government can give financial help to UK companies to make it easier for them to sell their products at lower prices. However, again this often leads to retaliation and the breakdown of trading.

Exchange controls

In most countries the government-controlled central bank manages a central pool of foreign currency. If the government wants to cut imports, it will instruct the bank to limit the supply of foreign currency.

Usually this will mean that the central bank will only supply currency to important users. For example, importers of important raw materials will find it easy to get hold of foreign currency, whereas people wanting to holiday abroad may find that they can only take a limited amount of foreign money out of the country.

Promoting home-produced goods

The government might run a campaign encouraging citizens to buy their own, home-produced products. This has been done in the UK from time to time, and is sometimes done by other countries too, as is illustrated by the photograph from Pakistan *(right)*.

Other forms of trade restrictions

International trade exposes UK businesses to foreign competition. This can be a major problem if UK businesses are competing with subsidised imports or with dumped products.

Dumping occurs when a firm sells goods at lower prices overseas than in its home market. It is an illegal practice.

Promoting home-produced goods in Pakistan

The importance of the European Union

Today there can be no doubt that UK trade is closely linked to its partners in the European Union. In fact, over 60% of our exports go to EU countries.

When UK firms sell their goods in the UK, they are selling to a market which contains at most 60 million people. But when the same firms extend their horizons to the Single European Market, the opportunities are far greater, with 80 million people in Germany, 56 million in France, etc., all able to buy their products.

The European Union therefore presents a huge market. If a company can produce goods for a mass market, there are many economies of scale to be gained.

'Why should businesses develop trade links in the European Union?'

The Single European Market

In 1992 the Single European Market came into being. This means that today goods can move freely between countries without being taxed each time they cross international borders.

People, too, can move freely from one country to another and work where they like. Professionals such as doctors can also work to commonly agreed professional standards.

The Single European Market means that technical standards are gradually becoming the same in all member countries. It allows money to flow freely from one country to another for investment purposes. Common standards have also been set up in areas such as consumer and environmental protection.

Demand side
Millions of potential customers

SINGLE EUROPEAN MARKET

Supply side
Opportunities to lower unit costs through mass production

The advantages of the Single European Market

What next?

The next step is the move towards a common currency called the **Euro**.

The Euro will be used throughout the European Union. The advantage of the single currency is that it will no longer be necessary to change money when moving from one country to another. Businesses will welcome this change because it will lead to stable rates of exchange.

'Having a single European currency is a disaster. The new currency would be the German Mark. There's absolutely nothing in it for British business!'

Do you agree with Ron?

Can you help Frankie and Cleo to match the following terms and definitions?

Import	A limit on the number of goods that can come into a country
Export	A payment made by the government to the producer or seller of an item
Visible	A good or service that enters a country with payment for it leaving the country
Invisible	A restriction on foreign currency allowances to people who import goods
Tariff	The new European Union-wide currency
Euro	A group of 15 countries with close economic and political ties, of which the UK is one
European Union	A tangible good
Exchange control	A tax on imports or exports
Invisible surplus	A situation in which the value of invisible exports is greater than the value of invisible imports
Current balance	The difference between the value of all exports and all imports
Quota	A good or service which leaves a country, bringing revenue into that country
Subsidy	A service which cannot be seen or touched

8 78 The Future of Business

What will businesses be like in the future?

In the future, businesses will need to be able to respond quickly to change.

Twenty years ago, most large business organisations had a pyramid structure. People at the top made the big decisions. These flowed down to middle managers, who then passed their instructions down to operatives.

These 'command and control' organisations are no longer desirable. They are slow and clumsy.

Today we have new **dynamic organisations** in which there are far more decision-making points. If we look at how big corporations are working, we can see that each operating company is broken down into a loose network of business units. The parts of these organisations only link up when they need to exchange information and work together on shared projects. The name of the game is flexibility.

The importance of interdependence

Today more than ever, interdependence lies at the heart of business relationships. Business has been transformed by new technology. The development of information technology means that the lowest-level operative in an organisation can now have access to almost as much information as a top-level manager. Information technology makes it possible to process vast quantities of work at great speed.

Information is one of the greatest assets of an organisation. By sharing information efficiently, it can build a strong competitive advantage over its rivals.

But it is not just interdependence within a business that is important. Companies need to build excellent links with customers. The successful business of today and the future is the one that is able to identify, anticipate and meet customer needs.

Excellent links with suppliers are vital too. Businesses need to have quality raw materials and semi-finished products delivered 'just in time' to be made into final products.

The challenge of new markets

Today many companies are moving into new markets. Large companies need to see the world as their marketplace. By doing so, they are able to spread their

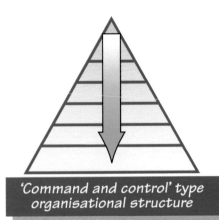

'Command and control' type organisational structure

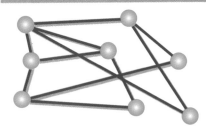

Dynamic organisational structure with many decision-making points

Changing business structures

'That must mean that any student completing a Business Studies course will benefit enormously from having good IT skills!'

Shell moves into new markets

The map below shows Shell's recent moves (1995) into new markets.

These markets serve roughly half the world's consumers and involve the employment by the company of one billion extra workers.

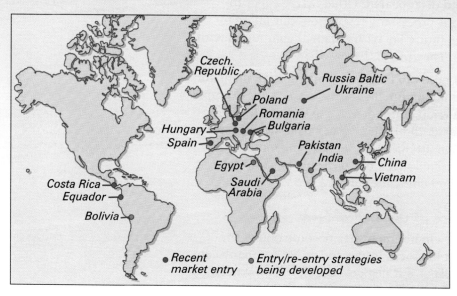

Czech. Republic

Poland
Romania
Bulgaria

Russia Baltic
Ukraine

Hungary
Spain

Egypt
Saudi
Arabia

Pakistan
India

China
Vietnam

Costa Rica
Equador

Bolivia

 Recent
market entry

 Entry/re-entry strategies
being developed

costs over a larger output. The costs of international communications and transport have been greatly reduced. Also, rather than transporting goods to other countries, companies are preferring to set up their own manufacturing plant there, either by building from scratch or setting up a joint venture.

The importance of new technologies

New technology has transformed our lives and will continue to do so in the future. Long-established technologies offer considerable scope for improvement. For example, the use of unleaded petrol has made the internal combustion engine much more environment-friendly, removing 90% of harmful emissions such as carbon monoxide.

In spite of its phenomenal developments in recent years, information technology still has immense potential. We quickly become frustrated with current technology, yet five years ago we would have been astounded at the speed of today's computers. Information technology will continue to astound us and to transform our lives.

TASK

1   Why do you think that Shell has been able to enter the markets shown on the map above?

2   Why is it important for a company like Shell to move into these markets?

3   What do you think will be the long-term impact on Shell's prosperity and growth, and on people living in the regions where Shell is developing production capacity?

Investing for the future

Business success involves a continual process of preparing for tomorrow. Businesses cannot rest on their past successes. They need to build for the future.

Many companies famous for producing typewriters failed to respond to the word-processing revolution of the 1980s – and disappeared. Others were eager to exploit the word-processing revolution, but failed to realise that the future lay with personal computers with a WP package. They too disappeared.

The emphasis needs to be on making effective plans for the future and taking intelligent risks. P&O, for example, realised that aircraft could deliver passengers to their destinations faster than their own cruise liners. Instead, they turned their attention to the ferry business, where journey times were longer, but passengers could take their own car and enjoy the fun of a sea voyage.

The importance of the environment

Concern for the environment has become one of the most important business issues today. No company can survive and prosper if it neglects the developing needs of the customer and the increasingly insistent needs of the environment.

In practice, the two sets of needs go together. Customers will not want to buy products and services from companies with a bad environmental record. In addition, government regulation and taxation will put greater financial burdens on companies who do not meet agreed environmental standards. The net result is that business policies will *have* to become environmentally efficient to survive.

Smaller businesses

Today there is more scope for small business than in the past. Because large organisations are 'downsizing' and streamlining, they need to buy in many of their 'non-core' requirements from outside. This is called **outsourcing.**

For example, in the past a large multinational company may have had its own photography department, perhaps employing a number of photographers with their own office.

Today these companies will buy in professional photography services from outside the organisation.

'If you ask me, the only reason to have an environmental policy is to avoid having to pay a fine or going to prison.'

Do you agree with Ron?

In the same way a big company will outsource design work, advertising work, training work, cleaning of offices and many other jobs, leaving it free to concentrate on its **core activities**.

At the same time, people have more leisure, and as incomes increase, they want to buy in a wide range of personal services. There are therefore plenty of opportunities for people to set up small businesses providing hairdressing, massage, gardening, cleaning, etc.

TASK

1 *What do you see as the main strengths of EPS's environmental policy, as set out below?*

2 *Draw up an environmental policy for an organisation you are familiar with, and present it to the rest of the class.*

CASE STUDY

Creating an environmental policy at EPS

European Passenger Services has set out the following environmental policy to take the company into the next century:

It is the objective of EPS, wherever possible, to promote and encourage policies and activities which benefit the environment in cost-effective ways and which win the confidence of our customers, our staff, the public and local and national authorities.

To achieve this objective, EPS is committed to:

1 Carry out our business in compliance with all relevant environmental laws and regulations.

2 In addition to legal compliance, to control and reduce adverse environmental effects caused by our activities and continually to improve our environmental performance by having regard to industry best practice.

3 Assess and take into account environmental issues arising from our activities, past, present and future and concentrate our management efforts on those issues which are identified as being significant.

4 Set clearly defined objectives and targets for our significant issues.

5 Apply programmes and practices to ensure the efficient use of energy, raw materials and natural resources.

6 Manage our waste efficiently through minimisation, recycling and re-use where practicable.

7 Openly and effectively communicate our policy to our staff, customers and the public.

8 Educate, train and motivate our employees to conduct their activities in an environmentally responsible manner through implementation of this policy.

9 Promote and encourage the adoption of this policy and/or principles by contractors acting on our behalf and encourage the adoption of its principles by our suppliers.

10 Carry out programmes of monitoring, audit and review to evaluate our performance and to check compliance against this policy.

11 Assign management responsibilities and provide sufficient resources and personnel to ensure successful implementation of this policy.

The Millennium

The onset of the **Millennium** will have a profound effect on business in this country. Psychologically, people will want to see widespread changes. The new century will offer new opportunities. There will be a great demand for change in and around the year 2000, embracing fashion, taste, popular culture and new products.

Today we cannot be sure what these changes will be. However, we can be sure that some people and firms will reap tremendous rewards from surfing this wave of change.

'I'm looking forward to the Millennium. It's going to be an exciting time in which people will hopefully adopt new and better values. Let's hope that they develop more caring and ethical approaches to business.'

Do you think that Frankie has grounds for optimism?

'You won't catch me surfing any waves of change!'

MATCH IT!

Can you help Frankie and Cleo to match the following terms and definitions?

Outsourcing	A period or cycle of one thousand years
Millennium	Activities which do not lie at the heart of a particular business
Non-core activities	The traditional 'command and control' top-down organisation
Environmental policy	Mobile, flexible and versatile business structures which use information technology to aid swift communications
Dynamic organisations	Buying in goods, services and materials from sources external to the organisation
Pyramid structure	Targets and plans directed towards helping an organisation achieve its environmental objectives

Index